Macclesfield at War

'WINGS for VICTORY'
MAY 8th to 15th

OUR AIM —

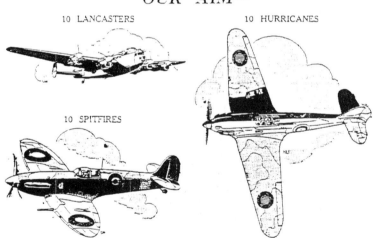

10 LANCASTERS

10 HURRICANES

10 SPITFIRES

Philip McGuinness

Acknowledgements

A large number of people from Macclesfield have given me information about the Second World War, mainly in response to a letter I wrote to the Macclesfield Advertiser and East Cheshire Gazette. I would like to thank the following particularly:

Mrs J. Barber.
Mrs Hilda Farr and her daughter, Mrs Jose Price.
Mrs Louanne Collins.
Mr Peter Higginbotham, especially for his authoritative knowledge of Macclesfield cinemas.
Mrs V. Kent.
Mr Paul Maybury.
Mr Ken Moss.
Mr Doug Pickford, for his generous help with photographs.
Mrs Jacqueline Potter.
Mr and Mrs Derek Way.
Mr Kevin Whittaker.
Mr Maurice Winnell.

I would also like to acknowledge:

David Broadhurst, *A History of Parkside Hospital*

Mr B. Hornsey for his booklet *Ninety Years of Cinema in Macclesfield* 1995.

John Lea, *Down the Cobbled Stones, Memories of a Cheshire Farmer*

Guy Morgan, *Red Roses Every Night*, 1958, an account of London cinemas under fire.

Bill Koranda, an American GI billeted in Macclesfield, through whom I was also able to contact the following US veterans of the Battle of the Bulge and subsequent battles, who had spent time in Macclesfield in late 1944 before being sent to Europe:

Colonel Carrol W. Bailey
Colonel Charles Connor
Rex O'Meara
Sanford Ziegler

In writing the account of Guy Gibson, I would like to acknowledge the book *Dambuster, Life of Guy Gibson V.C* by Susan Ottaway (Pen and Sword 1994)

CHURNET VALLEY BOOKS
6 Stanley Street, Leek, Staffordshire. ST13 5HG 01538 399033
thebookshopleek.co.uk
© Philip McGuinness and Churnet Valley Books 2002
ISBN 1 897949 84 7

CONTENTS

Acknowledgements

Missing at Sea

Third Officer Sherratt

A TIME-SERVING member of the Merchant Navy, John Roy Sherratt, elder son of Mr. and Mrs. J. E. Sherratt, of Belmont, Rainow Road, Hurdsfield, is reported missing. His parents received the sad news on Saturday morning, and it is believed he has been lost on Atlantic convoy work.

Twenty - one years of age, he had only recently passed his Third Officer's examination, and this was his first trip in that capacity. Always keen on the sea, he was apprenticed in the Merchant Navy on leaving the King's School nearly five years ago, and he had made excellent progress, as his position as Third Officer indicates.

Lost At Sea

MERCHANT SEAMAN MISSING

MR. and Mrs. G. Blench, of Moss House, Moss Lane, have received the following telegram, which tells its own tragic story about their fifth son: "Regret report R. G Blench disappeared at sea, Dec. 11th or 12th. Please inform next of kin."

The telegram was received on Friday by Mr. Carver, of Manor House, Prestbury, where Mr. Blench sen. is employed, and confirmed what they had already been given to understand unofficially, about their 18-years-old son, Raymond George.

The Central Station, now the site of the only Macclesfield Station, seen soon after the War.
It was at this station that the many evacuees arrived in 1939.

The platform of Hibel Road station, now demolished, decorated in 1948 for the visit of Princess Elizabeth. A desperately busy place in the War with the constant coming and going of servicemen and women.

CHAPTER 1
The Phoney War and Macclesfield
1 September 1939-10 May 1940

I was thirteen years old in September 1939. Like many of my Macclesfield contemporaries I was aware that something dreadful - a man called Hitler - was threatening the peace of Europe. At the time of Munich, the Munich 'peace' Conference of a year earlier, I had lain awake knowing that my father downstairs was listening to wireless bulletins in the hope of hearing the news that war would be averted.

The melancholy words of a song I have always associated with that worrying time drifted upwards from some BBC programme - *"Oh sailor man, come home again, sailor man, home again, across the sea."* The words had been set to the music of one of the beautiful but sombre airs used by Dvorak in the largo of his New World Symphony. To this day, whenever I hear that part of the symphony, I relive the troubled frightened foreboding of inevitable tragedy which I experienced at the end of September 1938. Chamberlain, the Prime Minister, flew back to Heston Aerodrome waving his deceitful peace of paper (though he himself had no intention to deceive), and I, together with my brothers and parents, breathed a sigh of relief. We knew vaguely that an area of Czechoslovakia called the Sudetenland had been occupied by Germany; and we were uneasy. But we felt able to push that unease into the back of our minds for the time being.

I sensed guiltily, however, that we were cheating ourselves. I felt within myself what I now recognise as being a cynicism over international events and statesmen which has never left me. The annexation of the rest of Czechoslovakia by Hitler in March 1939 was not a surprise. Nor were the evident preparations for war being made in Great Britain throughout the first half of 1939. We knew that what we saw in Macclesfield, especially the establishment of an Air Raid Precautions framework and then the digging of Air Raid Shelters in the parks, was happening over the whole country. We knew that war was on the way.

As the spring gave way to summer a new word was brought to our attention - 'evacuees'. We gathered that an enormous number of children from Manchester would come to Macclesfield in order to avoid the massive air raids which would be made on their city as on all Britain's cities immediately upon the declaration of war. We heard towards the end of August that the arrival of these children was planned for Thursday 31 August and Friday 1 September. We were very curious.

But nothing of note happened on the last day of August and our plans to besiege the railway stations of Macclesfield to welcome terrified children into our midst were dropped. I heard the wireless reports at breakfast time on Friday 1 September that Poland had just been viciously attacked by German military and air might, its fields overrun by tanks, its towns assaulted by bombs from the sky. My mother was disturbed but not surprised. I was somewhat taken aback when some mildly nasty things came out of her mouth as she tried to give her opinions about Hitler. I revelled in my maturity as I agreed with her, adding a few bellicose expressions of my own. We both took pleasure in our defiance of the dangers posed by Germany.

The sun shone. It was a lovely day. I decided to cast my cares aside and call on my friend, Raymond Roach, a short tubby little chap of my age, as brave as a lion. We opted to make our way to the Macclesfield Canal. There used to be an iron bridge in Macclesfield. It was situated at the end of a rough road called Laburnum Road which you reached (and still do) by going up Byrons Lane and turning left after about three hundred yards. The Iron Bridge was a most convenient way of crossing the Macclesfield Canal to reach the hills called the Hollins via a farm belonging to the Mitchell family. But often children would simply mount the first few steps of the bridge and then climb over the bridge wall on the left to reach a wide and pleasant stretch of the canal bank, an ideal play area of grass separated from the canal by banks of reeds.

This is where Raymond and I and a score of other children, still on holiday from school, went on that warm and radiant morning. We ourselves had no particular objective in view except to be there. But a few boys had come to fish for roach, gudgeon and perch with their sixpenny Woolworths fishing rods. Some children, both boys and girls, were playing with rubber balls or tennis balls, occasionally dashing to the water's edge to rescue one from the water. Here and there were other groups of children, particularly girls, who chatted excitedly and occasionally burst into song. The melody on most people's lips at this time was *"South of the border, down Mexico Way, that's where I fell in love when stars above came out to play; and now as I wander my heart seems to stray, South of the border, down Mexico Way."*

Other children were playing tag, the risk of falling into the canal adding zest to their frantic attempts to avoid being caught. Some older boys - and Raymond was quick to join them - decided to play on the bridge itself, which consisted of a wooden walkway slung some fifteen feet above the canal between two squat and sturdy stone pillars. Under the walkway was an iron frame which held it in place and on each of its sides was a strong iron trellis some four feet high. Both trellises were topped by a flat iron surface about six inches wide. It was this which attracted the boys. They vied with each other in mounting onto this iron surface and standing there.

It was, however, Raymond who pioneered there and then a new activity, 'iron-bridge walking'. Arms outstretched and body wobbling like an over-confident tight-rope walker, he hurried from one end to the other, shouting with bravado and casting occasional contemptuous glances at the dirty water below. His companions were hesitant, even climbing down from their stationary upright position to assess the situation, wondering if they dared follow the example of this bold exploit. But Raymond was already on his way back, still shouting defiantly. He did not climb down from the top of the trellis, he simply jumped down onto the bridge's walkway, ran down the steps, leapt over the wall and rejoined me on the canal bank. The children all around stared at him with wonder, pausing in their chatting or playing and looking with admiration at my friend. I was not slow to bask in the glory he obviously exuded as he now talked to me about mundane every day matters.

Occasionally a barge, drawn by a horse on the towpath opposite, would interrupt the young anglers, forcing them to lift their lines onto the bank. They consoled each other with reminders that the waving wake left by the barge surely contained characteristics and powers to lure fish into its orbit. All that they now needed to do was to cast their lines into the churned-up water. This ploy sometimes worked and, as they lifted their rod to see the wriggling silvery creature swinging at the end of their line, they whooped with pleasure. The

Evacuees leaving London and at their destination arriving with their gas masks.

Gas masks at all times.

whole scene was one of peace and enjoyment. The canal bank and the iron bridge represented an area of warm sunshine, pleasure and tranquillity. We played and were happy.

Some children came, some children went. The former brought stories of evacuees arriving at the Central Station (the site of which is now Macclesfield's only station). Some of us itched to make our way to Waters Green and see these new creatures for ourselves. To our minds the more important station in Macclesfield was the Hibel Road Station, a few hundred yards further north, and so we were a little puzzled by the sudden importance acquired by the Central Station at Waters Green. We hurried there and joined many other people. Scores of officials, many of them schoolteachers, watched by an eager crowd of bystanders, waited to welcome each train of new arrivals.

Most of the young evacuees had been turned out in their best clothes by their anxious parents. It was almost as if their offspring were going on holiday. The small boys wore stockings up to their knees, short trousers, blazers or jackets, a top coat which in nearly every case was a raincoat, and many wore their school cap. The girls had short socks, nearly always white and, over their dress, or over their blouse and skirt, they wore an overcoat, even in this warm September sunshine. Some of them also wore a round hat, perhaps decorated with a ribbon above the rim. Their lady schoolteachers all had hats on their head, whilst the male teachers were either bare-headed or wore the traditional trilby.

Over their shoulder all children had slung, mostly with string, the cardboard box containing their gas mask. Some carried bags, some small cases, some satchels. They all sported prominently their identity tag. Anxiety showed in varying degrees of intensity on their faces. Some held hands, some clung to each other, some tried to confront their predicament in a brisk and business-like way. Some were unnaturally cheerful and noisy and bold. But all witnesses of their arrival could detect the shock and bewilderment they were experiencing as they tried to come to terms with their sudden departure from their homes and finding themselves in a strange place.

Even the older Grammar School boys and girls were a little unsure as they contemplated the centre of what seemed to them a very small town. They could see market stalls in Waters Green and, way above them, the prominent St Michael's Church on the summit of the town. It was all so strange. Most children were too subdued to question the military way in which they were marshalled in groups and directed to various vehicles, including buses, in order to be distributed to different dispersal points around the town. Some tiny faces showed the signs of weeping. Not a few children tried to quell their burgeoning tears with quick little smiles as they looked round for some means of having their apprehensions dispelled. Their teachers and accompanying adults, as well as the Macclesfield officials who were receiving these evacuees, did all they could to give the reassurance so desperately sought.

The local newspapers reported the following week that one group of children were from Gorton Mount School, Manchester, and had been sent to the desirable residential area of Prestbury. While the children waited to be taken to their new homes, a sing-song was arranged in the large village hall of the village. Two volunteers, Mr Stoker and Mrs Barker, were Master of Ceremonies and pianist respectively. They performed their task well, claimed the reporter. But, as we read this account, we realised that the artificial atmosphere of joviality could not have deceived the children into thinking that evacuation, no matter how necessary, was anything other than a devastatingly unpleasant experience.

So it was that several hundred children from each special train waited in almost a dozen centres to be redistributed to their host families. A total of 3,769 evacuees, mainly children escorted by teachers (although quite a few mothers had accompanied their children), arrived in Macclesfield on Friday 1 September and Saturday 2 September 1939. For many inhabitants of the town this sudden influx confirmed that a state of war, rendered almost imminent by the German invasion of Poland, was now unavoidable.

The local newspapers of the following week praised the efforts of all concerned in this huge undertaking, not least Mr A.L. Collinson, headmaster of Athey Street School, who had been appointed Chief Billeting Officer. A list of potential hosts had been drawn up early in 1939 by a group of schoolteachers who, under the instructions of the Town Clerk, Mr A. Bond, had apparently 'walked round the town' canvassing householders. The evacuees had been installed in their new homes by the evening of Saturday 2 September.

But scores of parents came to Macclesfield on the Saturday and Sunday to see their children; and many of them had to make enquiries at a specially manned Post Office in order to discover where their children were. Some hosts were in difficulties over beds. It was reported that, in one or two cases, husband and wife were sleeping on the floor so that their guests could share the only bed they possessed. The Town Clerk quickly assured householders that camp beds would be available the moment government stocks arrived.

Sunday 3 September came. There was no shortage of places of worship in Macclesfield, a great centre of the Wesleyan Methodist Revival since the 1740s. There were 11 huge Methodist Chapels; there was an imposing Congregational Church, two Roman Catholic Churches, two Baptist Churches and several large Sunday Schools and Missions. There was the Salvation Amy Citadel in Mill Street. There were no less than seven Anglican churches, two of which looked after ' daughter ' churches. Altogether there were 29 major religious establishments in Macclesfield in 1939, for the most part large buildings, quite capable of taking in at least one third of the total population of the whole town, reckoned to be about 36,000. (The arrival of evacuees and billeted troops was to push that figure to over 40,000)

The churches on 3 September were unusually full. Many people hoped that their prayers might contribute to the avoidance of war. The congregations were boosted by a not inconsiderable number of evacuees, especially those brought along by newly appointed host families who were wont to worship on Sundays. I was a boy chorister in the choir of St George's Church, High Street (a building that still stands but is now no longer used for normal worship). There were about sixteen boys and ten men in that choir in 1939. There was also a girls' choir which functioned at the Sunday morning Children's Church, held in balcony pews directly over the clock at the west end of the main aisle. Children's services were taken by a Church Army Chaplain called Pritchard helped by Lay Reader James Arnold. (The Arnolds were an extensive family, not a few of whose members were attached to the Silk Trade. Many of them were also conspicuous members of St George's Church, so much so that the waggish would refer to the church as St George's and All Arnolds!)

Many of the children who lived in that part of Macclesfield would attend the Children's Church on Sunday mornings, and then join the senior choir for Mattins, attend Sunday School held in St George's Church of England Elementary School opposite the church in the afternoon, and, after Sunday afternoon tea, sing again in the senior choir at Evensong, which had a larger congregation than Mattins.

It was mainly on Sunday evenings that the sides of the balcony were quite full of people in addition to those who preferred to use the pews downstairs. As we stood in the choir stalls at Mattins on Sunday 3 September we looked with great interest at the new faces in the congregation. From my particular position (I was at the top of the Decani side - opposite those in the Cantori choir stalls) I noted that the Lay Reader James Arnold, now a member of the congregation at Mattins after the Children's Service upstairs, and his wife Annie, were this week accompanied by two elegantly dressed girls of about my age. My heart leapt. I had never imagined that anonymous and therefore dull evacuees could be transformed into these lovely creatures. For the next five months I dressed more carefully, sang more loudly and tried to speak to this pair of girls whenever the opportunity occurred. But James and Annie chaperoned their charges well.

I never found myself able to speak to them in any way which might have given relief to the feverish stirrings I felt within myself. Even now I think of them as a pair. What were their names - Marjorie and Joyce? And yet I knew that only one of them - I think it was Marjorie - had really won my affections. I had caught a glimpse of infinite possibilities of joy and happiness. I worshipped this magical creature from afar. I suppose that I was only to exchange a dozen words with her at various church functions in the five months I knew her. I still remember her face. I have not forgotten her or what she represented to me at that particular time.

My mind came back to the morning service we men and boys were leading. I tried hard to concentrate on the psalm we were singing but remembered that the world around us was in turmoil. Then we were into the Te Deum, with its strong and lively and joyful trio of chants. I risked glances during the alternate verses (when it was up to the Cantori side to sing) at the two girls whose existence I had just discovered. Were they singing? What was going on in their minds? Had they spotted me? It was now about five minutes past eleven. We were just about to kneel in prayer. Instead we found ourselves congealed in a bent position, shocked by footsteps coming down the central aisle.

It was the 'vicar's warden', the tall Mr Crowder, who walked purposefully but solemnly towards the choir. Total silence prevailed and craned necks were visible everywhere as he approached the vicar, the Reverend Edwin Smith, sitting in his special place at the nave side of the choir. He gave a little cough and whispered something which we strained to overhear. He then turned and retraced his footsteps back down the aisle. We waited expectantly as we looked at the chubby and ruddy face of the Reverend Smith, who was prepared to take his time. It was now his turn to cough. *'I have just been informed'*, he said, *'that the Prime Minister has spoken on the wireless. We are now at war with Germany.'* We continued to stare at him. He went on, *'If any of you would wish to go home now, please do so. We shall continue with our service here. Let us now sing.......'* he searched amongst the books in front of him........ *'O God , our help in ages past, our hope for years to come.'*

There was a pause as Mr E.G.Gulliford, our organist and choirmaster, flicked through his Ancient and Modern hymn book. Then that solemn and dignified music began and we all sang firmly and with determination although both shock and awe were in our voices. My mother had often told me what a mournful hymn this was. She had heard it and sung it endlessly throughout the First World War when Macclesfield had been emptied of its menfolk. She could only associate it with pain and grief and suffering. This impression had been so fixed in my mind that I required decades to accept it for the great hymn that it was and is.

Very recently we discovered an old photograph of my mother and a girl friend. They were dressed in overcoats, suggesting that there was a chilly breeze around and reminding us that variety and plentifulness of clothing have not always been with us. They were sitting on a stile and smiling happily. On the back she had written *'Whit Monday 1914'*. She would have been just fifteen years old. She was not to know what appalling things were to happen in Europe within a few months and what bereavements Macclesfield was to suffer. Perhaps as well. She looked lovely on the threshold of womanhood.

I think that on that very first morning of the War we also sang the hymn *'Eternal Father, strong to save, whose arm hath bound the restless wave...'*. For the rest of the War the last verse of that hymn - *O Trinity of love and power, Our brethren shield in danger's hour; From rock and tempest, fire and foe, Protect them wheresoe'er they go: Thus evermore shall rise to thee Glad hymns of praise from land and sea* - was to end every choral service at St George's. Within hours on that first Sunday this particular hymn received relevance with the news of the sinking of the British passenger ship Athenia by the U-boat 30.

It was probably the presence of evacuees in the town rather than the shock of the news bulletins which most impressed itself upon the inhabitants. The new faces were not reassuring; they betrayed great anxiety, the pang of sudden separation and a pessimism over the future. By as early as the 6th September a number of evacuees had returned home, the shock of being uprooted proving too devastating an experience.

On that same day the evacuated teachers from Manchester met the local teachers to discuss arrangements over school buildings and the time of their use. In order to keep evacuated children occupied until schools were open for this potentially difficult Autumn Term, visits of educational interest to historic places and beauty spots were arranged. Catering, especially at lunch time, was likely to be problematic, not least where both householders upon whom children had been billeted went to work. So plans were speedily made to institute a Communal Dining Centre on the site of an old mill in Longacre Street, at which the evacuated children would be able to get a two-course meal for 2d.

The Local Education Authorities were also much exercised over their provision of air raid shelters for the extra numbers of schoolchildren. As early as April 1939 their Schools' Air Raid Precautions Committee had recommended that 53 arched steel shelters should be provided to cover the needs of all schools under Borough control at an estimated cost of £3,700. Now the presence of 3,000 evacuated children led to a re-assessment of the adequacy of the 53 shelters.

The Borough of Macclesfield was responsible in 1939 for the majority of the schools in the town. Its top tier consisted of the two allied Central Schools, one for boys and one for girls, aged 11 to 15, which had had a combined number of pupils of 422 in December 1937. They were situated in Byron Street, beyond Byron Street Primary School. Pupils from all Elementary/Primary Schools in the Borough took an examination at the age of 10 for entry into the Central Schools. If not successful they went to an Elementary school - or continued in their present Elementary School until the age of 14. There were 9 Primary Schools (ages 4-11) and 6 Elementary Schools (ages 4-14).

There were other schools in the town. First there was the independent King's School for Boys, which had been founded in 1502. By the autumn of 1939, 580 boys attended the school, a third of whom had been selected after examination from the Primary and Elementary Schools in and around Macclesfield by the Cheshire County Council Education Committee, which paid for their fees and school books.

The only comparable school to the King's School in Macclesfield was the County High School for Girls. But whereas King's provided facilities for those boys nominated by the Cheshire Education Authority, the High School was the County's means of providing Grammar School education for all girls in the town and surrounding area it considered suitable.

The sharing of facilities between local schoolchildren and Manchester's evacuees meant that the 'double-shift' principle had to be followed. The normal arrangements were that evacuated children had a three and a half hour session in the mornings of the first week, while local children did their three and a half hours in the afternoon. In the second week they all switched times.

The King's School shared its facilities with the boys of Stretford Grammar School. Both schools were fortunate to be able to use Westbrook House, a large mansion owned by the King's School, situated at the side of the West Park, and hence very near to the school. The boys of both the King's School and Stretford Grammar School thus divided their time principally between the King's School's Cumberland Street premises and Westbrook House.

In addition the King's School (and therefore Stretford Grammar School) acquired the weekday use of St Michael's Church Parish Rooms - the 'Tin Tabernacle', so-called because it had an outside cover of corrugated iron. These rooms were opposite the school's main gates in Cumberland Street. Moreover both schools were granted the use of the Trinity Methodist Chapel in Riseley Street, a large building with a balcony but which was not easily adapted to schoolteaching purposes.

The High School for Girls, situated in Fence Avenue, which links Buxton Road to Hurdsfield Road, received the Stretford High School for Girls and acquired the use of the Stanley Hall in Castle Street, so both schools were spared the disadvantage of squeezing into one building.

The Central School for Boys, under its headmaster Mr R.E. Houseman, re-opened on 14 September 1939 on the 'double-shift' principle with St Margaret's School, Manchester. A few days later Mr Houseman had obtained for both his school and the Girls' Central School and their evacuated equivalents the use of St Barnabas Church on the Moss Rose Estate. In November he secured in addition the use of two rooms in the Brocklehurst Memorial Hall, some distance away but another means of easing the problems caused by lack of teaching accommodation.

The Infants' department of St George's School, High Street, managed to obtain the use of 'Canton Street', a wooden hall in the tiny street of that name, some three hundred yards further down High Street.

This initiative of obtaining buildings, halls, huts in order to allow the continued education of Macclesfield children together with their evacuated counterparts, was exercised by all the schools in Macclesfield and reflected great credit on all concerned.

Judgements on the evacuees were quickly made and, of course, these judgements varied enormously. It was perhaps surprising that the editorial of the *Macclesfield Courier and Herald* as early as the 14 September, 1939, when the town had only had two weeks' experience of evacuees in its midst, made this assertion: *'Much more discipline is needed than can be exerted by hosts and hostesses, for we hear of conduct in many directions and by no means confined to elementary scholars, which, to say the least, does not add prestige to our educational methods.'*

The writer, a few lines later, developed his thoughts, and perhaps changed tack a little - *'How can we expect boys and girls from, say, Ancoats and Gorton to be completely happy in a mansion where the domestic organisation is completely foreign to them? .....Likewise children from High Schools who have found themselves billeted in a small working-class home?'* The remedy suggested was the transference of evacuees to *'homes more in harmony with those which they have left'*.

The first remark concerning the behaviour of evacuees, distasteful and unfairly subjective as it may perhaps seem to us, was being echoed throughout the country and, in some places, was to gain in momentum. The second about incompatibility of some evacuees with some homes reflected a phenomenon which again had much greater intensity in other areas. For example, Harold Nicolson wrote about the evacuation of children to his country mansion in Sissinghurst, Kent. He thought that, where children had been evacuated along with their schoolteachers, everything had gone well, but that, when the mothers had also come, there had been trouble. He wrote in his *Diaries and Letters*: *'Many of the children are verminous and have disgusting habits. This horrifies the cottagers upon whom they have been billeted. Moreover the mothers refuse to help, grumble dreadfully, and are pathetically homesick and bored. Many of them have drifted back to London. Much ill feeling has been caused. But the interesting thing is that this feeling is not between the rich and the poor but between the urban and the rural poor. One thing that they say is that these children were evacuated at the end of the holidays and were therefore more verminous and undisciplined than if they had been taken in the middle of term. But the effect will be to demonstrate to people how deplorable is the standard of life and civilisation among the urban proletariat.'*

Oliver Lyttleton, who was to become a member of Churchill's government, had volunteered to put up ten evacuees in his spacious country house - and had received thirty one. He wrote, *'I got a shock; I had little dreamt that English children could be so completely ignorant of the simplest rules of hygiene and that they would regard the floors and carpets as suitable places upon which to relieve themselves.'*

R.M. Titmuss quoted a Glasgow mother who had accompanied her six-year old child to the Scottish countryside and who remonstrated with her in the following words, *'You dirty thing, messing up the lady's carpet. Go and do it in the corner.'*

Few criticisms of the habits and behaviour of Manchester schoolchildren in Macclesfield can be remotely compared with the remarks quoted above. The people of Macclesfield generally regarded the evacuees as being on a similar social level and of a similar social mix as themselves. As early as 22 September 1939 *The Macclesfield Advertiser* had reported that complaints had been made at the meeting of the Macclesfield Education Committee two days earlier that members of the Committee had seen evacuees about in the black-out after 10pm.

One week later an indignant correspondent to the Macclesfield Courier and Herald complained about 'the black-out rowdyism'. He wrote, *'One night this week I had occasion to go across Park Green. All the seats around the Fountain* (which was near the old public library and has long since been demolished) *were occupied by girls and youths of anything from 14 to 20 years. One of the girls was singing a popular song.......... and others were shouting and laughing and generally behaving in a disgraceful manner'* The writer appealed to Church leaders and to parents to *'solve the problem of young people who are at a loose end'*.

All the evidence is that the state of affairs of which the writer complained was, if anything, to become even worse as the War wore on. But most inhabitants would have recognised that some local schoolchildren also qualified for the sort of rebukes levelled at a small number of the Manchester evacuees they saw around them. *The Macclesfield Courier* and Herald of 2 November 1939 reported that nearly 4,000 children and mothers had by this time been billeted in Macclesfield. Since 2 September some 300 adjustments had been made after *'faulty billeting'*. Another 300 adjustments had been made through the illness or change of circumstances of householders. There were still some 30 cases outstanding where transfer appeared desirable.

The evacuees and their parents were the butt of many criticisms according to *The Macclesfield Courier*, '*....the criminality of going home at week-ends; the audacity of parents; the impudence of children; the meagreness of evacuees' wardrobes; verminosity; parental parsimony,'* and so on. An Evacuation Tribunal was set up to hear Evacuation complaints. Nevertheless some householders refused to abide by the laws concerning evacuees. *The Courier* and *Herald* of 23 November 1939 reported that a well-known local draper had been fined £5 for refusing to take evacuees. He said that the ill health of his wife and his lack of accommodation caused him to commit the offence.

The Macclesfield School Management Committee had been told on 24 November 1939 that only about 100 evacuees would be left during the Christmas holidays. This meant that the others would be returning to Manchester at the end of the Christmas Term. There was clearly some misgiving over this; and the Education Committee which met on 20 December 1939 was told that the evacuated Head Teachers in Macclesfield had been asked to do all they could to ensure that Manchester's evacuated children remained in Macclesfield. A commitment was also given that evacuated teachers would be on duty, at certain times, in each school attended by evacuees, every day except Sunday during the holidays.

A tragic incident reported in the local press on 4 January 1940 illustrates several aspects of the phenomenon of evacuees and the arrangements made for them. A sister and brother aged 9 and 8 had been billeted on a couple on the Moss Estate. They had decided not to go home for the Christmas holidays since they were very happy to stay with their foster-parents. They asked permission to go for a walk, were warned not to go near the frozen canal but did so - and were drowned. Their parents, even though grief-stricken, wrote extraordinarily sensitive and appreciative letters to the local paper about the way their children had been received by the people of Macclesfield.

Of course the evacuees varied in their behaviour, cleanliness and habits, just as much as the Macclesfield children; and the experience of evacuation was confusing for all concerned. Some evacuees were extremely grateful for the love they received, as can be seen from many letters sent at a later date and now kept in the Heritage Centre. One correspondent wrote of her host family: *'Their first names were Jim and Mary. I stayed with them a few years. I grew to love them and they loved me. I had a wonderful home with them. They asked my mother could they adopt me. She refused. But I visited them for many years till sadly Mary died.'*

But another experience was described in the following terms, *'They had two children who I wasn't allowed to mix with. I was never allowed to play out with my sisters. I was made to eat my meals alone in the kitchen and had to do lots of polishing, scrubbing floors, I was there about six weeks. My mother found out and requested I be taken away.'*

Another girl wrote, *'I hated Macclesfield...... not that there was anything wrong with the town. I think I would have hated anywhere at that time. All I wanted was to be at home with my family.'* Another seemed to have summed things up very fairly. She wrote, *'All in all, like most children, I adapted and, as was quite usual then, accepted the situation as it was and remember it with no feeling of unhappiness or regret. I know my mother must have felt more distress, being without both her children. Had she still been alive she would have been able to give me more specific dates and the duration of my stay. She declared it a nightmare she would never forget.'*

One mother of four children wrote to the billeting authorities with a request for her two sons of five and eleven years to have a change of billet. *'The reason for this is that at their present billet there are only two bedrooms and they have to sleep in the same room as a married couple, the other bedroom being occupied by two other children.'* She went on to talk about her two daughters who had also moved to another billet: *'Susan is O.K. and quite comfortable but I am not satisfied with Angela at all. It is only a two-bedroomed house and they have two boys of their own and I don't want Angela where there are only boys. I definitely think they ought to be together. I have had a talk with Mrs....... and she tells me they were two good girls and they agreed quite well together. I hope you will look into this matter as the moving has made me ill. I have got one of the little boys at home for a few days and if Angela is still at the same billet when it is time for him to come back I am afraid I will have to bring them all home as their dad who is in the army says she must not stay there.'*

There are many pleasant references in these letters to *'the glorious countryside'*, acceptance by the local people, snow up to the bedroom windows, blackberry-picking, the gardens, the bees, cakes in a tea-room in Chestergate, expeditions and half-day schooling. But the fact remains that not many stayed more than six months to widen their experiences. It is certain that most mothers were relieved when their children returned.

One interesting item appeared in the *Manchester Evening News* supplement of Tuesday 5 September 1989. The supplement was concerned with the outbreak of war 50 years earlier. Valentine Gardner was evacuated in November 1939 to Macclesfield, turning up on a Saturday morning, thinking that he was going on a picnic. Giving full details of roads and streets (Park Lane, Newton Street etc) where he stayed, he had nothing but praise for his hosts and their families. He spent five years in Macclesfield and attended a V.E. Day Street Party.

It was known that, throughout Great Britain, there was a steady trickle of evacuees returning home from the earliest days of evacuation. By 5 November 1939, for example, 63% of mothers and children had returned home to Scotland. The Macclesfield Borough Education Committee, meeting on 24 November 1939, considered Circular 1913, issued by the Ministry of Health. This circular urged local authorities to do all they could to lighten difficulties by, first, the development of communal services, and second, the re-distribution of billeting in the receiving areas, on the grounds that *'evacuees are beginning to drift home.'*

The Committee again met on 20 December 1939. There had been correspondence with the Director of Education, Manchester, who had given particulars of the steps being taken over the re-opening of certain schools in that city. He said that the evacuated Head Teachers in

Macclesfield had been asked to do everything possible to ensure that children evacuated from Manchester remained in Macclesfield. It was clear that a crisis was occurring in the Manchester - Macclesfield Evacuation Scheme.

On 26 January 1940 the Education Meeting was informed that, in December 1939, only 771 children (of the original 3769) from Manchester remained. Moreover more schools in Manchester were being re-opened. There had clearly been a significant opting-out. The Education Committee was at pains to point out that this state of affairs, however deplorable from a national point of view, now released a number of rooms to Macclesfield teachers and children. The Manchester and Stretford Evacuation scheme to Macclesfield was crumbling.

So the Spring Term 1940 passed with a very much reduced number of evacuees in the schools of Macclesfield. These first six months of the War had turned out to be the 'phoney war'. Little had happened so far - no bombing of cities; no civilian casualties; no attack on the snowed-up Western Front. But here in Macclesfield there had been disrupted education, disrupted lives, many human problems, much frustration, some resentment felt by hosts and guests alike. The fact that the threatened terror from the skies had not arrived seemed to make what had been an enormous effort of no avail.

And so the evacuated schools decided to go home. It is true that a certain number of both official and private evacuees stayed on, and more were to come later; but for the moment the bulk had gone. The town felt empty. Sighs of relief mingled with regret and a sense of nostalgia. When German planes bombed Manchester very heavily on 22 and 23 December 1940 the people of Macclesfield, contemplating the vivid red sky to the north, thought of all those who had spent the previous winter with them. The danger which their temporary guests had tried to avoid, which they had deceived themselves into imagining had disappeared, had now become a reality. There was much dismay in the town.

But the Manchester evacuees were not the only strangers living in the town in the early part of the War. Many military units were drafted into Macclesfield. There were numerous reasons for this, one of which was that the town had been long accustomed to having soldiers in its midst. The 7th Battalion of the Cheshire Regiment, both regular army and Territorial (part-time soldiers) had for long been associated with Macclesfield and were based on the Crompton Road Barracks and the Bridge Street Drill Hall. In September 1939 the Territorial soldiers were immediately called up as first reservists on the outbreak of war and sailed to France on 27 October with their professional colleagues. By 5 November they had taken over a section of the French line near Armentières under the command of the 51st French Division. They were to serve later mainly as a machine-gun battalion in India, Burma, Sicily and Italy.

But the facilities for billeting afforded by Macclesfield were quickly exploited by the military authorities upon the departure of the 7th Battalion. Indeed it was soon essential to expand them. The factory belonging to Neckwear Ltd at the junction of King Edward Street and Chestergate, and Tytherington Hall, were commandeered for billeting purposes.

The unit which took over from the '7th Cheshires' was the '6th Loyals', which came to Macclesfield in October 1940. They had been formed in North Lancashire in April 1939 and by the end of July 1939 numbered 18 officers and 480 men. They occupied the mill belonging to Neckwear Ltd, the Drill Hall and (for the recruits) Tytherington Hall, which was a mile outside the town - at Tytherington, in fact.

The Loyals stayed in Macclesfield until May 1940. But these were not the only troops sustained by the town in the first few months of the War. Macclesfield was filled to overflowing by troops of the so-called 'crack' Y Division, who occupied all conceivable premises and who, in some cases, were allowed to have their wives staying with them in private billets. The soldiers of the Y Division used the Bridge Street Drill Hall as their Headquarters and, of course, occupied the Crompton Road Barracks. The additional buildings they used were Lord Street Sunday School and the Parochial Hall, Roe Street (this building, when occupied later by the Americans, was known as 'The Abbey' - its ecclesiastical windows gave rise to this name).

Other premises used were 259 Park Lane and the old St Michael's Vicarage, Chester Road (both used as Officers' Messes), Highfield House in Park Lane, the Charles Roe House in Chestergate and certain shop space in Chestergate, the latter occupied by medical orderlies. This Y Division was, in fact, the 5th Infantry Division. The reason for the popular nomenclature Y Division was that its insignia consisted of a white 'Y' on a khaki background. It is assumed that the Y stood for Yorkshire, the division having been stationed in that part of the United Kingdom in the pre-war years.

When this Division left Macclesfield in December 1939 its members had been more responsible than any other troops for the sudden transformation of Macclesfield at the beginning of the War. The Loyals, departing in May 1940, were replaced by others so that on 31 December 1940 there were still 813 soldiers based on the town. Clearly the presence in Macclesfield of additional inhabitants, all in uniform, had a considerable effect on the town. First there was an atmosphere of vigorous wartime activity. All conceivable places were used for marching and drilling and general military training. Army vehicles were constantly seen on streets and roads. The Royal Artillery practised gun drill in the South Park, often, in the early days, without even dummy ammunition, simply rehearsing the drill of loading and unloading. Secondly, in spite of rationing shortages, an air of sudden prosperity was around. Large shops were not usual in most towns at that time. The bulk of trading was carried out in small shops, often corner shops. The demand for food, drink, domestic and consumer goods in general increased. The consequence was that most retailers found their profits and income enhanced. The numerous tiny public houses, already well patronised by the male inhabitants of their areas, now found their clientele enlarged by young men in uniform.

Thirdly, the 'night life' of the town underwent a series of changes which it had hardly seen before the War and which it certainly has not seen since the War. Before the War Sunday evening in Macclesfield had a characteristic which it shared with other similar towns but which, in view of the locality in which it was displayed, possessed its own individuality, perhaps uniqueness. This characteristic was given the name of 'the monkey-run'. A large number of young unattached men and women paraded up and down the major thoroughfare of Macclesfield, which is Mill Street and Chestergate, eyeing each other and occasionally talking to each other.

Once war started in September 1939 a new spirit was abroad - so far as meetings between the sexes were concerned speed now became important. Relationships had to be built upon flimsy acquaintance, often artificially contrived. With young men departing for the Forces and being replaced by others whose presence in the town would probably be of short duration, this main thoroughfare of the town became the most important meeting place for all seeking members of the opposite sex. Whereas the pre-war Monkey-Run had been a weekly event, it now became, with the population explosion of the Y Division and of the 6th Loyals, a nightly phenomenon. Large numbers of young men and women walked up, large numbers walked down. Conversations were easily started; couplings were easily made.

At the bottom of Mill street was the Public Fountain outside the Municipal Library. This was the starting point of the Monkey-Run. Various landmarks on its route sustained the whole backwards and forwards flow of human beings - the Majestic Cinema near the bottom of Mill Street, the Milk Bar a hundred yards higher, the Market Place where signs indicated that the traffic should turn left and go as far as the Picturedrome Cinema near the end of Chestergate. No fewer than 22 drinking establishments existed on the route or very close to the route, offering refreshment, warmth and an opportunity to strengthen a friendship. These were The White Lion, The Bear's Head, The Green Dragon, Beresford's Wine Vaults, Norton's Wine Vaults, Yates Wine Vaults, The Black's Head, The Angel, The Bate Hall, The Old King's Head, The Swan with Two Necks, The Spread Eagle and The Grove Inn. All these were situated on the Monkey-Run itself. But there were others just a few yards off the beaten track - The White Swan, The Hole i'th Wall, The Post Office Public House, The Derby Arms, The Castle Inn, The Bull's Head, The Pack Horse, The Feathers, The George.

The crowds were usually made up of young girls from the town and young militiamen, strangers to the area for the most part. Respectable people in the town began to shun the Monkey-Run and its activities. Here I have to make a confession. My friend Ken Allen and I, both proud of our mature age of thirteen, thought that our education would be advanced if we were to enjoy personal experience of this phenomenon. So on several evenings we joined the throng. It was noisy, intriguing, cheerful. The women walked in pairs, arm in arm as if protecting themselves from the dishonour they had come to avoid. A loud hello, especially if repeated as a follow-up, might lure them to walk a little more slowly. But unless the males involved immediately responded by coming closer and making some polite remark, such as - *'that's a nice hat you've got on'* or *'it's nice to see you, young lady, come and have a drink'*, the ladies would hasten on as if the last thing they wanted was conversation with young men. If the men, often soldiers, were polite and persistent, the girls would then pause, a conversation would start and all would consider that they had successfully 'clicked'. Their evening was made.

People today would hardly believe that for most pairings the evening would consist of a drink, a chat, an offer to walk the girl home and then a kiss or two. Doubtless some went further than that. Ultimate achievements became more frequent as the War wore on and, when the Americans arrived from 1942 onwards, they and their partners were perhaps more ambitious, leaving proof of their liaisons in fields, streets and especially in 'entries' - the little covered alley ways which divided terraced houses.

At our age Ken and I hardly expected to be taken seriously and, to be honest, we were hardly looked at. But we took great pleasure in examining the nature of this grown-up sport. We went into the Milk Bar on one occasion and bought a milk-shake. Two girls of about sixteen or seventeen were sitting next to us and looked at us disdainfully, even pitifully. Two men passed us on the way out and one of them said to the girls *'like a walk?'*. The girls shrugged nonchalantly. The men stood by the door and the question was repeated. One girl whispered, *'Come on, now's our chance'*. They slowly rose, took a last sip from their coffee cup and made their unhurried way to the door and disappeared into the night with their new companions. They had 'clicked'.

Observing all this Ken and I decided that we had perhaps learned valuable lessons for the future and made our way home. Certainly if we had been taken seriously by a couple of girls we would have been bewildered. The following Easter Monday another friend Bernard Lovatt walked with me to Prestbury. At the side of the river Bollin we met two girls of our own age. We had a sort of conversation. We suggested that we should all meet outside the Picturedrome in Chestergate that very evening and 'go to the pictures'. Bernard and I turned up and stood fifty yards away at the corner of Bridge Street at least an hour before the 'house', the showing of the programme, started.

Soon we saw the two girls on the other side of the road and on the other side of the cinema. They looked in our direction. We looked in theirs. We laughed quietly to each other. They were clearly doing the same. So we talked earnestly. They did too. We all kept looking at each other. Bernard and I gradually realised that we were terrified of embarking upon our assignation. The girls did nothing to encourage us. Then we realised that the 'house' must have started. So we went home. That was our first date. We never saw either of the girls again. And if we had, we would certainly have looked away.

There were five cinemas in Macclesfield in 1939 and they were to benefit considerably from the increased population of the town throughout the War. The most splendid, the Majestic Picture House, had absorbed into its management, in the course of the 1930s, three of the others - the Picturedrome, the (New) Cinema, and the Premier (Picture House). The remaining and totally independent cinema was the (New) Regal, which had been the first to be built. It had been erected in 1910 on a site in Duke Street where there had been a silk mill.

On 21 October 1911, the Picturedrome in Chestergate opened its doors to a packed house and gave excellent service throughout the First World War. The (New Electric) Cinema was built at the bottom of the steep Buxton Road on 13 July 1913. The Premier Picture House was erected in 1919 in Vincent Street. This was a beautiful single-floored cinema, built to accommodate 800 people. Finally, in 1922, William Higginbotham, who owned a china and brush shop in Mill Street, converted and extended it into the magnificent Majestic Cinema, with a balcony, an orchestra pit, good ventilation, central heating and tip-up seats. It was built by the firm Gorton and Wilson of Elizabeth Street in hardly more than four months.

At 4-30 pm on Sunday 3 September 1939 the Air Raid Precautions Department of the Home Office issued a memorandum for the *Guidance of Owners and Occupiers of Places of Entertainment*. It stated: *"In view of the great danger involved in the assembly of large numbers of persons in places where it is not feasible to provide adequate protection against the effect of bombs, it has been decided that, during the initial stages of a war, all the theatres, music-halls, cinemas and other places of entertainment shall be closed throughout the country."*

However, the panic which had led to the sudden closing of places of entertainment began to recede in the course of the first week of war and modifications were slowly introduced into the Home Office Regulations. Cinemas in the 'reception areas' (those, like Macclesfield, receiving evacuees) and 'neutral areas' (those not receiving evacuees but not in imminent danger of air attack) were allowed to open again until 10 pm from Saturday 9 September. Then permission was given for half of London's West End cinemas and theatres at a time to open, provided that they closed at 6 pm. Finally from December 1939 all were allowed to open simultaneously, closing between 10 and 11 pm.

Three busy Macclesfield cinemas during the War.

The Regal Cinema, with facade now cemented over.

The Premier Cinema, Vincent Street,

and The (Picture) Drome.

The Majestic Cinema.

SUNDAY MATINEE AT MAJESTIC

THERE has been such an overwhelming demand for tickets for Sunday's show at the Majestic that the organisers, after repeated requests, have decided to run a matinee at 2-30 p.m.

The Directors of the Majestic have kindly lent the Theatre free of all cost, so that members of the Services who happen to be in town may visit the show. The remainder of the tickets will be sold to the public.

An official welcome will be given to American visitors, who will also provide some of the turns in the programme, along with Jos. Clowes and his orchestra, Vera Demonte's Majestic Girls, Sylvia and her Xylophone, Paul and Paulette, Beth O'Dare, Barton and Bowen, Jimmy Charters and, last but not least, Stanley Mercer's Musical Patriotic Cavalcade.

Programmes for the special effort will be on sale at both performances (price 1s. each), and even if you have already had one, "try another" and send it to your relative serving with the Forces, whether they be at home or abroad (as many have already done) and give them a little breath of old Macclesfield just to show that they are not entirely forgotten.

Tickets may be obtained at the Bull's Head Hotel, Market Place, or from Blackburn's, Chestergate. The charge for admission (excluding Services) is 2/- downstairs and 2/6 balcony.

Macclesfield at War

There was a stampede when the cinemas were re-opened on 9 September 1939. The sudden stress of wartime living prompted people more than ever to seek solace in the entertainment provided by the cinema. For a time it had seemed that the film industry, and hence the cinemas, were under threat as a result of the outbreak of war. Patrons in Macclesfield were told that they had to carry gas masks and that the cinemas would close at 10 pm. But cinema-going in Macclesfield, with minor hiccups, continued to rise throughout the War and reached a peak in 1946.

There can be no doubt that the cinemas generally in the United Kingdom in this 'phoney war' period reflected the position of the Macclesfield cinemas and the attitude of the population of Macclesfield towards cinema-going. The great need was to be entertained, to have one's mind taken off the War, to have a night out. If severe air attacks had been launched on the country by the Luftwaffe in September 1939, it is probable that the closure of all cinemas and places of entertainment would have continued long enough for their prospective resurrection to have been questioned.

The lively evening life in Macclesfield during that first winter was pursued in spite of severe black-out regulations embodied in the Lighting Restriction Act, and enforced by both police and air raid wardens. A haulage contractor foreman was summoned for having used a motor car in Beech Lane on 4 September with a light which did not comply with regulations. This light was a powerful near-side headlamp which was not screened in any way. He had been warned the previous morning by the same policeman. His offence was compounded by the fact that, when challenged, he had used indecent language. He complained that the policeman had been harassing him and his firm for months; *'What with heavy vehicles and one thing and another, you can't go about town'*, he complained, *'I admit flashing the headlamp but it was only to find the white line'*. The case was dismissed by the magistrate, but by October fines were being imposed, as many as four in one week in November.

Not a few young boys profited from the black-out. They went to a builder's yard carrying a bucket, bought one pennyworth of lime, added water and stirred it well, obtained a whitewash brush and charged householders 2d or 3d to whiten the kerbstones outside their house. They thereby all contributed to lessening the risk of accidents large or small to people who could not avoid moving around in the black-out. The mayor publicly complimented these boys on their initiative. More elaborate whitening was being carried out by the local authority in public areas.

My brother Norman, some three years my junior, was adept at whitening private kerbstones. I accompanied him, sometimes in the black-out, as often as I could. This was a lucrative occupation; people were only too willing to have this job done for them; and twopence or threepence a time, according to the length of their pavement, was regarded as being of very good value. When our bucket of lime was getting low we would ask one of our customers for some water which we simply poured into the bucket and then swished it around with the stick we kept with the brush in the bucket for this purpose. We worked out a theory that the thinner the mixture the whiter the result. We failed to ask ourselves whether a thicker mixture might have lasted longer on the kerbstones. However, thinning down the mixture certainly prolonged our evening's work, and hence our earning time. Norman received special individual praise from the mayor, Councillor Mowbray, for his efforts.

Nevertheless the black-out clearly contributed to a large number of accidents. In the first few months of the War at least five fatal road accidents in and around the town were attributed to the black-out. Much advice was given to pedestrians - smoke a cigarette, wear something white, walk on the left hand side of the footpaths, only cross the road at recognised crossings, direct the light from your torch onto the ground - and so on. But many small accidents took place. My mother, for example, walked into the metal protection round a tree on Park Green, as she walked away from the public library. She had two black eyes for weeks.

In September 1939 Norman and I were very conscious of the need to buy food that would last. This was, of course, being impressed on the whole population by the government. We saw our first opportunity during the blackberry season of September 1939. We had been told that there were wonderful blackberries to be had on the 'Shooting Butts'. The Shooting Butts themselves had been available for shooting practice by army personnel since before the First World War. They were situated at Rulow Hollow at the Old Buxton Road end of a lovely sweeping hill which stretched almost to the famous gorse-covered Noah's Hill on the Hollins. They consisted of wooden structures embedded in sand and with their backs up against hillocks of land. On the lower slopes of the hill, several hundred yards from the butts themselves, were enormous blackberry bushes upon which grew enormous blackberries.

It was essential to carry a walking stick in order to bring the branches laden with berries down to one's picking height. You also needed to have an appreciation of what exactly constituted a perfect blackberry, so that you did not waste time on inferior material. Patience was of course extremely important; so too was an iron constitution. We had to walk for at least an hour, up over the Iron Bridge onto the Hollins, over the mighty Noah's Hill and down on the other side before rising up again to where the blackberry bushes were. At the end of our blackberrying session we would then have to return, often just before dusk - for this was normally an after-school activity - the same way, carrying our baskets which contained eight or ten pounds of luscious appetising fruit.

We had not finished when we arrived home in Lord Street. We now hurried to ask Mrs Jackson, baker par excellence of pies and oatcakes at her grocery shop in Coronation Street, if she would like to buy some blackberries. She always agreed - everybody knew that her blackberry and apple pies were wonderful creations. We left her with smiles on our faces and money in our pockets. We used any blackberries left over to make blackberry jelly, a skill we soon acquired. Then we would place the jars of this jelly on shelves in a cupboard, ready for future use, especially when the inevitable shortages we were all being warned about began to make themselves felt.

The money Mrs Jackson had paid us we would spend on tins of cocoa, fruit, tea and coffee. We received congratulations on our achievements from our mother and our feelings of self satisfaction were unbounded. Our smugness was terrible. Looking back I wonder why neither Norman or I, as adults, ever displayed any business-like qualities which might have made us a fortune. Certainly our carol-singing on Christmas Eves from 1939 to 1941, even in the black-out, was so well organised that we could hardly carry in our pockets the rewards for our efforts. We would, for example, place ourselves at opposite ends of a backyard of, say, 6 or 8 houses, and sing - with solos - Good King Wenceslas, Silent Night and While Shepherds Watched, making sure that each house was at least aware that we were singing. Then we quickly knocked on doors and joyfully received the pennies that were forthcoming. Some people were generous and grateful; most were supportive; some laughed at us and closed the door. On one occasion we were kept waiting while the owner of the house claimed to be looking for money. He then returned to drop, into our hands, from his handkerchief, a red hot penny which we quickly threw away. We left in disgust. Such a trick nowadays would warrant a summons for assault.

But that first winter of the War in Macclesfield was marked by what the local newspapers referred to as *'the worst freeze-up for a century'*. Because of ice and heavy snowfalls trains were unable to get through Macclesfield for four days in early February. The surrounding hills were totally white. Langley was isolated. Roads were blocked, schools were closed. Fuel was scarce and hardly any private houses had central heating. Whole families, and in many cases their evacuee guests, had to huddle round one fire in most dwellings. A large number of households had frozen pipes. The continued use of outside toilets - and most inhabitants of Macclesfield at that time only had outside toilets - could just about be guaranteed by small oil lamps which managed to keep the temperature fractionally above freezing level.

One striking tragedy illustrated the severity of the winter of 1939-1940. A 19 year old youth from Hurdsfield and a 35 year old man, a fellow member of the Manchester Youth Hostels Association, met at the Macclesfield bus station and set out together for Rainow via Kerridge in an effort to get to Windgather Youth Hostel. They were overwhelmed by a blizzard and the younger man collapsed and died from exhaustion and exposure.

Inside the town there were many other reminders that we were at war apart from the black-out and the presence of evacuees and billeted troops. There were wardens, first-aid parties, ambulance drivers, Report Centre staff, the Auxiliary Fire Service and decontamination squads. Altogether in Macclesfield there were almost three thousand Civil Defence workers, one third of them women. Most of these Air Raid Precautions members were part-time. When war did break out, 12 Corporation (public) air raid shelters were in the process of being erected in the parks and open spaces of the town. In May 1940 the decision was made to build six more shelters. Later many communal domestic shelters, created from strong cellars and basements, were set up.

Throughout the first nine or ten months of the War Macclesfield during the day was very busy, except when the frosts and snow took a grip on the town. In the evenings only the Monkey-Run, the cinemas and the pubs were active. Outside those centres of social density few people moved around. By April 1940 the days were becoming longer, the sun was beginning to shine and optimism was in the air. Not for long. That first tedious, uncomfortable, disturbing but, on the whole, peaceful chapter of the War was over. On Tuesday 9 April 1940 both Denmark and Norway were invaded by Germany. Little could be done by the Allies to help Denmark, since its border was shared with Germany. But the Royal Navy had been active along the Norwegian coast in an effort to prevent Germany from shipping iron ore from the northerly port of Narvick for use in its war machine.

The fact of invasion, proof yet again of Hitler's desire for conquest, was nevertheless extremely alarming. We expected Britain and France to send ships and troops to help the Norwegians to resist German forces but we were fearful that Norway was too far away for our efforts to be of much avail. On Saturday 13 April, four days later, I found myself at home in the evening with my parents. My younger brothers had gone to bed and my older brother was to come in later. We were listening to the wireless, as was our wont on Saturday evenings. First we listened to the popular *In Town Tonight* which started at 7-30 pm. The format was well known and appreciated. So-called 'Visitors' to London, coming in from the noise of the city, spoke about their life or some particular experience or experiences and, between each personal story, a record was played. The unmistakable signature tune of the programme was taken from Eric Coates' *Knightsbridge March* which was part of his London Suite.

Now I have to confess that only a few vivid memories of what else was broadcast on the wireless that evening remain fixed in my mind. So I have checked with the BBC Archives at Reading and am now able to fill in the gaps. In spite of the dismal war news, we had now accustomed ourselves temporarily to what was happening in Scandinavia; there was a nice fire burning in the grate and everything seemed warm and cosy and relaxed. We heard a sea captain giving details of his experiences over 50 years at sea. We listened to the father of an evacuated boy as he described his fears for his son as well as his confidence in the evacuation scheme. A ballet dancer, a football referee, and a flower seller in Piccadilly Circus also spoke. Most interesting perhaps was an interview with the Norwegian born wife of an English doctor.

Quite suddenly the programme was interrupted by a news flash which informed us that an important communiqué was expected from the Admiralty shortly. Our hearts started to beat rapidly - what could this mean? Was it good or bad? But *In Town Tonight* finished at 8pm and was followed by *The Garrison Theatre* which was being broadcast from Clifton Parish Hall, Bristol, for the next hour. This was a traditional Variety Concert, including comedians Jack Warner and Naunton Wayne, with orchestral items and songs and audience participation. No further reference had been made to the expected Admiralty communiqué. Then came the famous Nine o'clock News. We waited expectantly but yet again we only heard that an important news bulletin from the Admiralty was on its way. What on earth could it be?

We were on tenterhooks. For 15 minutes Clement Attlee, speaking 'From the Front Bench' gave an assessment of the progress of the War. Surely the announcement, whatever it was, would come soon? But no, the BBC Theatre Orchestra playing at Evesham came on, then Her Majesty the Queen (the now deceased Queen Mother) spoke for 5 minutes. But...... no further announcement concerning the Admiralty. We could hardly claim to have listened to Clement Attlee or the Queen very intently. When would our minds be set at rest?

Now gramophone records were played - dances from Edward German's Merrie England, a selection from Gilbert and Sullivan (music only - the copyright for the words and music combined had not yet run out), and, most appropriately perhaps, a selection from HMS Pinafore. At that time I had not realised just how deliberately silly were the words of *For he is an Englishman* - '*For he is an Englishman! And it's greatly to his credit, That he is an Englishman. For he might have been a Roosian, A French, or Turk, or Proosian, Or perhaps Itali-an! But in spite of all temptations To belong to other nations He remains an Englishman!*' The music which Sullivan composed to fit these words is superb - a military march, dignified, inspiring, morale-boosting and intensely patriotic.

This music seemed to sum up the whole evening for me. With those Sullivan notes still ringing in our ears we heard at last the following statement at 10-15 pm. 'No official announcement regarding the landing of Allied troops in Norway has yet been issued but one is expected shortly and we hope to be able to give it at midnight'. We looked at each other with disappointment but still tingling with the expectation of some thrilling news. There was nothing for it but to wait until the midnight news. We listened to *Lighten our Darkness* from Bristol Cathedral and then to Henry Roy and his band. Finally midnight struck, the sound died away and the newsreader spoke: *'Just over one hour ago it was officially announced that there had been a fierce naval engagement today in Narvick Fjord. Seven German destroyers were sunk. As a result of the engagement the Allies have gained control of Narvick'.*

Our hearts leapt. Further clarification followed: *'This morning, about noon, the battleship Warspite, accompanied by a strong force of destroyers, advanced up the Narvick Fjord to attack the German destroyers, which were sheltering in the harbour. The attack was extremely successful. Four German destroyers were shattered and sunk in Narvick Bay. Three others fled up the Rombaks Fjord, a small inlet eight or nine miles long behind Narvick town. These were also pursued, engaged and destroyed. The destruction of seven of the enemy's destroyers was not achieved without some loss. Three destroyers were damaged in the fight but not seriously, and the British loss of life is believed to have been very small. The operation is still proceeding.'*

We went to bed thrilled, feeling that the War had taken a turn for the better. It was a moment of rejoicing which I tried to preserve - as we all try to preserve such moments. But we were soon to learn that the War was far from over. British troops landed in Norway on Monday 15 April, two days after the above broadcast. French and Polish troops arrived on 19 April. But German occupation of the country was being strengthened . In any case, from the Allies' point of view, the contemplation of their responsibilities in Norway was overtaken by the German onslaught on 10 May 1940 upon the Netherlands, Belgium, Luxembourg and, soon afterwards, on France itself. The position of Great Britain, not least the possibility of a German invasion of its shores, was soon to be critical in the extreme.

Dad puts the finishing touches to the Anderson shelter.

These building s were used for the billeting of troops during the Second World War.
Above: The Large Sunday School in Roe Street, now the Heritage Centre.
Below: The Parochial Church Hall (now the Salvation Army), also in Roe Street, was particularly used by
American troops who referred to it affectionately, presumably because of its windows, as the Abbey.

Frost's Silk Mill, Park Green, overlooking the War Memorial Cenotaph, was extremely busy in the War producing silk articles, especially parachutes, for the war effort.
Below: Lord Street Sunday School is seen in the middle of the picture. Now used by the Macclesfield Amateur Dramatic Society, was also used for the billeting of troops.

Above: Anti-tank obstacle on bridge over the Macclesfield Canal : Map ref. SJ927759.
It was the duty of the Home Guard to man the pill boxes around Macclesfield
and to supervise anti-tank obstacles in case of invasion.

Pill box near Macclesfield.

CHAPTER 2
Macclesfield's Home Guard, its birth and activities
April-May 1940

As we have seen, at the beginning of April 1940, before the Germans invaded Denmark and Norway, the majority of the official school evacuees from Manchester and Stretford had left Macclesfield to resume life in their native localities. The phoney war had reduced general fear of air attack upon the British Isles.

Understandably many people, in Macclesfield and elsewhere, were asking openly if the complex and expensive Civil Defence system so vigorously set up in the previous year or two could be justified. Possibly there was a greater hesitation in the expression of these sentiments after the invasion of Norway from the 9 April 1940. But it was the German onslaught on Holland, Belgium and France on 10 May 1940 which totally reversed the descent into complacency which had begun to affect most British people. On that same day Churchill succeeded the ousted Chamberlain as Prime Minister of the United Kingdom.

On 15 May the Dutch Army capitulated. That very morning Churchill received a message from the French Prime Minister Reynaud. *'We are beaten,'* Reynaud said, *'we have lost the battle.'* Brussels fell to the German Army on 17 May and, by 18 May, the Germans were moving towards the Channel Coast from Abbeville to Antwerp. By nightfall on 25 May the British Expeditionary Force was, like the French and Belgian troops, cut off and withdrawing towards Dunkirk. The evacuation from Dunkirk began on 26 May and was completed on 4 June. A total of 338,226 Allied troops were rescued and transported by boats of all shapes and sizes to England.

In the face of the rapid advance of the German forces, the re-formed British Administration took speedy precautions against the sudden danger of invasion. Churchill made his famous 'blood, toil, tears and sweat' speech on Monday 13 May. On Tuesday 14 May, Anthony Eden, the new Secretary of State for War, broadcast over the radio to *'men of all ages, who are for one reason or another not at present engaged in military service and who wish to do something for the defence of the country. '* He went on, *'Now is your opportunity. We want large numbers of such men in Great Britain who are British subjects between the ages of 15 and 65, to come forward now and offer their services.'*

Within 24 hours a quarter of a million volunteers had signed up at local police stations. By mid July a million men had put their names forward. At the end of July the decision was taken to change the original name of the new force - LDV (Local Defence Volunteers) - to The Home Guard. This name became popular throughout August.

By Wednesday 15 May, less than two days after Eden's appeal, some 500 Macclesfield men and youths had given in their names to the local Police Station, which occupied part of the southern side of the Town Hall in the Market Place. Several days later about six of the men who had registered assembled at the Macclesfield Police Station and selected, from the full list of volunteers, the names of 250 ex-Servicemen of the 1914-1918 war, inviting them to a meeting at the Drill Hall in Bridge Street the following day. They came and were addressed by Colonel G. N. Heath on the aims of the new force.

Further volunteers were joining all the time. This total group of men were to become, at the end of July, 1940, the Macclesfield Home Guard Battalion, which eventually expanded into Numbers 1, 2 and 3 Battalions of the Macclesfield and Congleton Group, with Headquarters for Numbers 1 and 2 at Macclesfield, while Number 3 was based on Wilmslow. Their final nomenclature was to be the 8th Cheshire (Macclesfield) Battalion, the 9th Cheshire (Macclesfield Forest) Battalion, and the 10th Cheshire (Wilmslow) Battalion. These three Battalions constituted the so-called Number 9 Sector, Cheshire Sub Area.

The 8th Cheshire (Macclesfield) Battalion was formed principally from those men who had put their names forward in the first batch. They were organised under the leadership of Colonel Heath and soon joined volunteers from Congleton (under Captain A. Gaunt) to form the Macclesfield-Congleton Group. The Congleton men (E Company) looked after the town of Congleton. The Macclesfield men (A Company) looked after the south part of Macclesfield and the country to the south of it between Macclesfield and Congleton.

As early as the end of May 1940 (only two weeks after their enrolment) volunteers were guarding vulnerable points in the town - public utility works, railway yards and the like - as well as manning observation points in the country. The 9th Home Guard Battalion became responsible for the protection of much high rough moorland and of villages and townships within the general area of the 'Macclesfield Forest', especially in the triangle of Bollington, Rainow and Kettleshulme. The western fringes of the Battalion's responsibilities were also part of the Cheshire Plain.

There were rigorous training programmes, proficiency tests and courses for officers and NCOs. Home Guard Training Camps took place at Bowmere and Tarporley, and weekend camps were specifically started for the training of officers and NCOs of the 9th Battalion.

On 23 August, 1941, the whole Battalion assembled on the Bollington Cricket Ground, a piece of land generally known as The Recreation Ground, and was inspected by Colonel Heath. In November 1942 a demonstration took place, at Styperson Range, of Home Guard weapons.

The average combined strength of the Macclesfield and Congleton 8th Home Guard Battalion and the Macclesfield 9th Battalion throughout the War was 2,500. The total number of all who served (allowing for call-up into the Forces and its repercussions) was at least twice this figure. Each member was called upon to spend a considerable amount of his spare time training, parading and doing guard duty near important utility installations, which normally involved one sleepless night a week. So far as the population of Macclesfield was concerned the presence of civilians in uniform became an accepted part of normal living.

A noteworthy phenomenon took place in Macclesfield and other towns during the War. There was a succession of fund-raising activities, which started in 1940 with the Spitfire Fund, followed in 1941 by War Weapons Week. Then came the massive Warships Week in 1942. In 1943 the town had its Wings for Victory Week and, in 1944, the Salute the Soldier Appeal.

Now each of these Special Weeks had a mass of activities attached to it - in Macclesfield there were military parades, processions, bands, dancing in the parks round the bandstands, demonstrations, public meetings, film shows, whist drives, variety shows, religious services, sports fixtures and the inevitable ceremony of the 'Indicator', which stood in the Market Place in front of the Town Hall and marked the amount of money raised.

The Home Guard was always called upon to parade, no matter what other Regular

Forces' units in the area appeared. This meant that the 8th and 9th Battalions, getting smarter and smarter by the month, were seen frequently by the local population. No one would have claimed that they could have repelled a fully armed German Panzer Division, but the members of the Macclesfield Home Guard were not the figures of fun which the admirably humorous television series 'Dad's Army' have implied to later generations. They did a great deal to emphasise to the population of the town that a large number of people were doing their bit towards the enormous war effort. The result of all this was a tremendously heartening esprit de corps, a sense of togetherness which will probably not be experienced again.

The Home Guard certainly played its part in the creation of that morale-boosting spirit. So too did the lovely South Park. When nowadays I take a stroll in that park and walk past or round the crumbling cement of the Band Stand, I often think of the one or two occasions - or were there more than that? - when, on a long summer's evening favoured by Double British Summer Time, I was part of the crowd enjoying the music of a locally based military band. It is probable that such occasions were part of a fund-raising week's activities. There were people of all ages in that crowd, many in uniform, and they listened or danced and sang as they danced. The dancing circle itself was filled almost to capacity. People would meet acquaintances and have a chat. Small children had been given special dispensation to be out with their parents so that they could enjoy the sunshine and the long evening with its sweet-smelling air. They shrieked with delight and felt very grown-up. Adolescent boys and girls sought each other out and, having danced, walked in other parts of the park.

The South Park holds other memories. There was, for example, the enormous air raid shelter which had been dug out at one end of a football pitch not far from Ryle Street in September 1939. There were sandbags at the two entrances which were linked together apparently by a series of passages and benches. It was rumoured that courting couples found the shelter extremely comfortable. But other intruders caused damage and raised questions of safety. Suppose the sandy shelter caved in? There were doubts too about how hygienic it was in there. Would people actually advance into its darkness if they heard the air raid siren? There was something sinister and extremely distasteful in the thought of finding ourselves in that shelter and not being able to get out.

In the summer of 1941 I walked round the park with some friends and met others who were accompanied by a young boy in RAF uniform. He looked desperately unhappy. He himself never said a word but his companions explained that he was a rear-gunner in a bomber and just had a few days 'leave'. I felt embarrassed on behalf of the young man. His friends pointed out the dangers of his job with nonchalance, almost mockery. My thoughts went to another rear-gunner of my acquaintance, Ronald Entwistle, whose riddled body had been found strapped into his place when his bomber returned to base.

The story of a very young member of the Macclesfield Home Guard

Maurice Winnell was 15 years old at the beginning of the Second World War and lived in Barton Street, Macclesfield. He had been one of the first to acquire a gas mask even before war was declared. The moment he heard that gas masks were to be issued at St John's Church Rooms in South Park Road he resolved to be at the head of the queue. Indeed, his greatest fear was that the possibility of war would evaporate before he had the chance to try out one of these fascinating novelties. So he found himself hurrying away, full of excitement and anticipation, clutching the brown cardboard box which contained his latest possession.. Once home he fitted the mask, not without some difficulty, round his head and tried to accustom himself to using it. It smelt strongly of the rubber it was made of; and breathing in and out of it was not at all comfortable. Nevertheless Maurice was utterly thrilled.

He worked in Hollindrake's Garage at Prestbury, one of his jobs being to fit V. Hartley headlamp masks to the headlights of cars, an effective hooding device for black-out purposes. He also helped to paint white strips along the side running boards and bumpers of cars. Just before petrol became rationed he was intrigued to see frantic people rushing to the garage with containers of all shapes and sizes, eager to build up a stock of this now invaluable commodity before supplies dwindled. The regulations, which came quickly, limited the ration to 5 gallons a month, although some people - doctors and specialist war workers - were able to qualify for more. But some of Maurice's customers decided to lay up their car 'for the duration'. They raised the vehicle onto wooden blocks, took the wheels off, unfitted the sparking plugs and squirted oil into the bores, turning the engine over by hand to spread the oil inside the cylinders. These precautions were wise and the cars emerged at the end of the War in good condition.

Maurice remembers the first air raid warning which wailed eerily one night shortly after the outbreak of war. Frightened residents of Barton Street and Vincent Street rushed out of their houses almost without clothes in their frenzy to reach the nearest shelter, leaving doors open and lights on. Of course, they quickly became accustomed to the sound and frequency and significance of sirens and the chugging drone of German aircraft. Briefly awakened in their sleep, they simply turned over - albeit a little guiltily - and continued to snore and dream, knowing that it would be the people of Manchester or Liverpool who would be receiving the bombs. In the winter of 1940-1941, when German air raids on Manchester became heavy, Maurice was called upon to mend many car tyre punctures. These had been caused by the anti-aircraft shrapnel picked up in the streets of Manchester by Prestbury residents who worked there.

Maurice joined the Air Raid Pecautions (ARP) services as a Messenger Boy at the beginning of the War, using his own cycle, as was the practice, to deliver messages to and from various posts in the town. Messenger Boys were expected to turn out each time the siren sounded. But as the air raids gained momentum the strain imposed on the boys was unsustainable. Maurice, at work in the garage, found himself 'asleep on his feet'. The ARP authorities drew up a rota which resulted in each boy only having to turn out on alternate air raid warnings. This was still demanding, of course, but did help to reduce extreme fatigue.

As a member of the Civil Defence set-up Maurice took part in an exercise at Westbrook House in the West Park. He found himself lying prone on a metal stretcher in an upstairs room. Round his neck was a label describing his 'injuries'. After a lengthy discussion amongst officials of the rescue team about knots and their correct positions he was swung out of the window on the stretcher, each corner of which was roped to a pulley on a beam. He now dangled some fifteen feet above the ground. He had just sufficient time to note that the air was rather cold before falling heavily, still flat on his back on the stretcher, onto some paving stones below. He was immediately surrounded by concerned officials who pointed out that the pillow underneath his head had saved him from serious injury. He was escorted by a large group of concerned colleagues to the nearby Infirmary where he was pronounced fit and healthy, with no broken bones and hardly a bruise worth mentioning. He was surprised to hear that the whole exercise, which involved most ARP members in the town, had been called off as a result of his fall.

When Maurice became 17 years of age in July 1941 he joined the Home Guard and wore his uniform with pride and joy. It may seem astonishing now that part-time soldiers were trained as thoroughly as Maurice was trained when he was still little more than a boy. The weapons he was taught to use at this tender age (and which were, of course, issued to his Home Guard Unit) were, first, the long Canadian P.19 Rifle (a First World War rifle), complete with bayonet; second, a Sten Gun; third, a Browning automatic rifle. But the 'pride and joy' of his unit was a Thomson sub-machine gun. In addition there were Mills grenades with 4-second fuses for throwing and with 7-second fuses for firing from rifle cup-dischargers - a blank cartridge was fired in the rifle and threw the grenade some 120 or 130 yards.

The Home Guards also had 'sticky bombs' - for sticking on the sides of tanks. These consisted of a glass dome covered in a sticky substance which was encased in a metal cover. A handle was screwed into the contraption and became the detonator. Once the metal casing had been removed, the soldier (or Home Guard) was free to run towards the tank and smash the glass against it. In theory he then walked away calmly - clearly easier said than done. There were also anti-tank grenades for rolling underneath tanks. These latter grenades were round cans, about twelve inches long, with a tape round the top which unwound as they rolled, thus releasing the striker pin. Again, easier said than done. But since the whole purpose of the Home Guard was to repel an invading force, anti-tank weapons of this kind were very important.

Maurice was also taught how to use a 'Molotov Cocktail'. The official version of this weapon was called the 'Number 76 Self-Igniting Phosphorous (SIP) Grenade'. It consisted of a smallish bottle which was filled with phosphorus and other chemicals. These substances were ignited by the breaking of the glass. A problem was that the man who was throwing the bottle was likely to receive the full force of the chemicals.

Whilst Maurice was a member of the Home Guard his unit never possessed the so-called Spigot Mortar, but he and his colleagues were trained in the use of it. Indeed he still has his note-book containing the notes he took at a lecture on this weapon, which also had its problems. Its accuracy was far from certain, and one authority claims that Général de Gaulle was almost killed by it when he attended a demonstration of the way to use it.

Eight Home Guard Officers and nine other ranks were, by the end of 1944, officially recognised as having been killed in training throughout the United Kingdom. Quite separate is a list of 14 officers and 16 other ranks killed in bomb disposal and similar duties.

The throwing of grenades by the Home Guard of Macclesfield was practised at Styperson Quarry near Pott Shrigley, three miles north of Macclesfield and just beyond Bollington, very much on the western end of the quite precipitous Pennines, which at this point overlook the Cheshire Plain. A thick steel dome was erected in the quarry to house observers who plotted the distances achieved by the grenade throwers. This very convenient quarry (remote, protective, 'safe') was the venue for frequent demonstrations to Home Guards of all sorts of weapons by the so-called 'travelling wings' of the Regular Army. The outline of a tank was painted on the quarry face and provided a convenient target. Maurice relates that, on one occasion, a man just in front of him fell to the ground having been hit on the shin by the tail fin of a missile. He suffered a fractured leg and this incident taught all Home Guard members present that they could not take any risks over what were laid down as 'safe' distances from explosions.

With his Company, (D), Winnell carried out his target practice (rifles, Sten guns, Browning automatic rifles) at the firing range at Rulow Hollow on the Buxton Old Road (where my brother and I had picked so many blackberrries in September 1939). This firing range (now utilised for clay pigeon shooting) was used by regular troops and by the Territorial Army. The normal square-bashing training was carried out on any convenient plot of land in the town. Maurice remembers drilling in the quadrangle of Athey Street School and at the top of Barton Street, which was very close to the Home Guard Headquarters of 'D' Company at 231 Park Lane (one of twelve strongly built red-brick houses which have always been known as the Twelve Apostles). The cellar of this house was used as an ammunition store for 'D' Company and was looked after by an armourer. Maurice was not the only member of his unit who had nightmares about the possibility of an accidental explosion.

Most members of the Home Guard were either 'lads of 17' like himself or men over call-up age or men in reserved occupations. *We also had one or two ex-army soldiers who had been discharged for medical reasons and I remember how they impressed us by their smartness on parade,'* he says.

But there was a great deal of patrolling and observation to be done in the hilly area to the north and east of Macclesfield covered by the 9th Battalion. Maurice participated in activities at Rainow and in Wildboarclough, especially near Crag Hall. He remembers particularly a week-end Home Guard operation in a disused quarry on the (new) Buxton Road, half a mile down the road from the Walker Barn/Setter Dog Public House. He had only been in the Home Guard for a few days and had been ordered to stand at the door of a stone building in the quarry. His unit was visited by the GOC Western Command, General Sir Robert Gordon-Finlayson, and he found himself having to put together an awkward salute to honour him. He remembers the little smile with which the GOC returned his salute.

On other occasions he helped to man an observation post on top of Windyway Quarry, with its magnificent view over the Cheshire Plain, and situated near Windyway House on the Old Buxton Road just above Tegg's Nose, site of yet another quarry. Maurice had the job of driving his squad up to this Observation Post and then driving them down again to their Park Lane Headquarters. He was also called upon to do Guard Duty at Tytherington Hall which was used for the billeting of regular troops but needed Home Guard supervision at change-over periods.

Maurice reached the age of 18 on 19 July 1942. At the earliest opportunity he reported to the recruiting office in Dover Street, Manchester, to volunteer for the armed forces. Eventually he became a driver/wireless operator in the 108 LAA (Light Anti-Aircraft) Regiment RA, part of the 52nd Scottish Lowland Division. After training in various locations in England he was posted to the Dundee area of Scotland. The régime was harsh, the weather in winter a challenge, his fitness extreme. His regiment was issued with Arctic clothing, including snow goggles. It was trained for mountain warfare. The soldiers slept in windproof tents five feet high, six men to a tent. The entrance was an igloo-type tunnel, drawn shut by those inside. All slept fully clothed for warmth, each boot covered by a sand bag and pointing to the central pole. Mules, mountain howitzer units, a Norwegian Field Battery, and

Norwegian liaison officers were all part of a division of 20,000 men, trained in mountain warfare. Their presence in Scotland, apart from any future campaign that might be envisaged, was part of a plan to keep 160,000 German troops firmly fixed in Norway. The Germans had to take into account the fact that the expected Allied invasion of Europe might start there.

After D-Day, 6 June 1944, Maurice's division stood by to help in three operations with the 1st British Airborne Division and the 101 US Airborne Division. The first was an attempt to cut off the Brittany Peninsula, the second to open the road to Paris, the third to close the Falaise gap. In each event their assistance was not required. So the 52nd Scottish Lowland Division was moved to Newark in September 1944 in a plan to support Operation Market-Garden (the Arnhem scheme).

Just when the troops were about to board aircraft bound for the 'captured' airfield at Deelen, near Arnhem, they were ordered to hold back. The operation had been a gigantic disaster and there was nothing extra forces could do about it. Maurice witnessed the return to Newark of some 20 or 30 survivors out of the 200 who had shared his particular camp's facilities a week or so earlier.

Thereafter Maurice was sent to Belgium and Holland, where he had to fight alongside many others, wading up to his chest in water from breached dykes. Moved back to a suburb of Antwerp as a rest from fighting, he experienced the continuous bombardment from V1 flying bombs. (More V1s fell on the recently liberated Antwerp than on London. One of them killed 200 British soldiers in a cinema there)

His unit was then transferred to the area of Maastricht, very close to the German frontier, where shelling from the Siegfried Line had to be endured. It was here that British troops saw distant V2 rockets from South Holland being launched towards their targets. During the day several seemed to rise together, trailing smoke.. At night they streaked as single units like blurred red dots high above the upturned faces of the troops below. The nearer the front Maurice was the more he witnessed the burial of troops killed in action. These burial places were only temporary and often they were sited in the corner of a field. (Later the bodies were

British troops in the Ardennes -
Battle of the Bulge

disinterred by a group specially formed for this purpose and re-interred in war cemeteries). In his Scottish Division a piper would play a lament as the body, stitched up in a blanket, was lowered down. There would almost always be a small group of the soldier's comrades present at the burial. Such events and the continuous ambulance traffic to and from the forward aid posts destroyed once and for all any sense of the glamour of war which Maurice or any of his companions may have entertained.

The Battle of the Bulge, Hitler's last great offensive of the War in December 1944, shattered the temporary winter peacefulness which, with the snow and the cold, had descended upon the Ardennes in Belgium and Luxembourg. Maurice and his colleagues, within close range of the fighting, had to dig sloping ramps into the ground and drive their trucks nose first down them in order to protect them from shell fire. Every two hours they warmed up the engines in preparation for a quick move.

One temporary blessing of the cold weather was that the mines left by the retreating Germans on the verges and roads were rendered harmless by the freeze-up. But the thaw of January 1945 brought them to life again, and many vehicles and troops were blown sky-high. There were some fiendish types of mines, not least the so-called S mines. If you trod on one of these it would leap up behind you to a height of three feet, explode and shower you with 300 ball-bearings. You were unlikely to survive that fateful step.

The Germans had to retreat after their defeat in the Battle of the Bulge and Maurice found himself driving his truck into Germany itself. His unit now was entering villages at one end knowing that the Germans were leaving it at the other. But enormous care had to be taken over mines and booby traps. He was a member of a party who on one occasion were trying to find billets for the tired troops. They went into a farm which looked very promising, especially since it was clearly abandoned and deserted. They took notes and made plans and then withdrew. As they looked back they saw a vivid skull and crossbones sign, left by fellow soldiers hours before, pointing out that the farm was in the middle of a minefield. They moved as quickly as they dared to put some distance between themselves and this innocent-looking refuge.

But by this time German women and children were choosing to stay behind in villages which were unlikely to be recaptured by the Nazi war machine. They were fearful of what might happen to them but could not contemplate moving with their own soldiers into further battle zones. They had decided to let the War leave them behind and to trust that they would be well treated by the British troops. This was a bold decision for them, because Goebbels' propaganda machine had painted a fearsome picture of all Allied troops. Maurice comments that the relief of the women was enormous when 'they found that we behaved like gentlemen'.

As the British forces contemplated the task of crossing the Rhine at Wessel, Maurice became aware that Montgomery and other high-ranking officers were paying frequent visits to the locality. On one occasion Monty was just departing in his jeep accompanied by two Military Policemen armed with Tommy guns, when Maurice stepped from between two trucks and saluted. The policemen immediately swung their guns round to cover Maurice, who thought that his end had arrived. This was rather different from giving his first Home Guard salute to the GOC Western Command in the quarry above Macclesfield in 1941 nearly four years before. Monty smiled - just as General Gordon-Finlayson had done - and returned his salute, and the policemen relaxed.

During the days prior to the crossing of the Rhine there was a massive build up of men and weapons and materials. 'Ducks' (Dukhs) and 'buffaloes', amphibious craft for the transporting of men across the river, appeared in their hundreds. A huge number of artillery regiments moved up and increasingly deafening barrages of shelling left everyone tense and feverish. Maurice was aware that on his right were very well-equipped American forces whose heavy guns gave enormous comfort to the British troops. He confesses to feeling sorry for the German soldiers who were at the receiving end of this assault. As he drove his truck, Maurice noted frequent signs, erected by the Engineers, which read 'Drive slowly - dust means death'. The German mortar crews were observing the western side of the Rhine and were able to pinpoint as targets any vehicles which raised dust behind them.

But the Engineers too were trying to hide all details of preparations from the enemy by creating gigantic palls of smoke which hovered above and around. Maurice and many other truck-drivers found themselves blinded by the smoke and there were numerous accidents, some vehicles driving off the road and into ditches. One or two hit mines and blew up. In one of the quiet moments Maurice looked out across the Rhine and noticed a church spire which was surely a German observation post. Quite suddenly several Typhoon aircraft appeared and, firing rockets, demolished the spire and much of the church below it.

On 22 March 1945, the evening before the Allied crossing of the Rhine, the artillery attack against the German army on the other side was awesome. The following morning an airborne armada passed low overhead, hundreds of Dakotas and Horsa gliders. They were immediately attacked by German Ack Ack fire and several Dakotas came down in flames, with paratroopers bailing out in a chilling descent - where would they land? Maurice watched in silent horror as one plane hit the ground very close to him and exploded.

On the sides of the Rhine the scene was one of complete devastation. The fields were littered with dead cattle, killed by mines or shells or bombs or stray bullets. Their bodies were swollen into grotesque shapes like inflated balloons and were in various stages of decomposition. There were also many uniformed bodies, mainly of German soldiers, lying prone and muddy and sickeningly still. There had been no time to bury them. Abandoned weapons and military equipment of all kinds were strewn without any semblance of order and British troops moved warily, ordered to touch nothing until the area was totally free of mines and booby traps.

Eventually Maurice was sent to the battered Bremen in the latter days of the European War. The Germans still occupied the centre and on one occasion Maurice, driving a reconnaissance officer, overran the front line and caught a glimpse of German anti-tank guns at the end of the street. Frantically he spun the steering wheel round and had just disappeared into a side street when the guns burst into life.

Maurice then served in the British Army of the Rhine in its duties as an occupying force in Halberstadt, Magdeburg, Dusseldorf, Hanover, Hamburg and Dortmund. He saw the devastation of Germany, its starving adults and children, the total breakdown of the infrastructure of the country. Moreover most roads, damaged beyond belief, were full of displaced persons and refugees, with carts - some lucky ones had a horse as well - and sometimes bicycles, wretched and forlorn and miserable in spite of their relief that the War was over. Poles and Russians, assuredly not the best of friends, were travelling east. Most others were travelling west in an effort to avoid the Russians.

Advertisement for Home Guard Volunteers in Macclesfield
Below is reproduced the second advertisement for Home Guard volunteers.
This appeal appeared in the Macclesfield Courier and Herald of 3 July 1941.

There is a special need within the Western Command for young men under 19 to join the Home Guard. The General Officer Commanding in Chief, Western Command (General Sir Robert Gordon-Finlayson, K.C.B, C.M.G, D.S.O.) is most anxious that these young men should offer their services, and he points out some advantages that accrue to the youth of the nation between the ages of 17 and 19, who enlist in the Home Guard. -

a. It is their chance to help to save England.

b. It will help them to get quick promotion when they join the Navy, the Army and the R.A.F.

c. They will find that service in the Home Guard will keep them in good health and that it will be full of interest.

d. They will make good friends in its ranks, for serving together is the best foundation for comradeship.

c. The weapons with which the Home Guard is being armed include the Tommy Gun and modern anti-tank weapons.

f. Scouts will have every opportunity of using their skill at stalking and concealment.

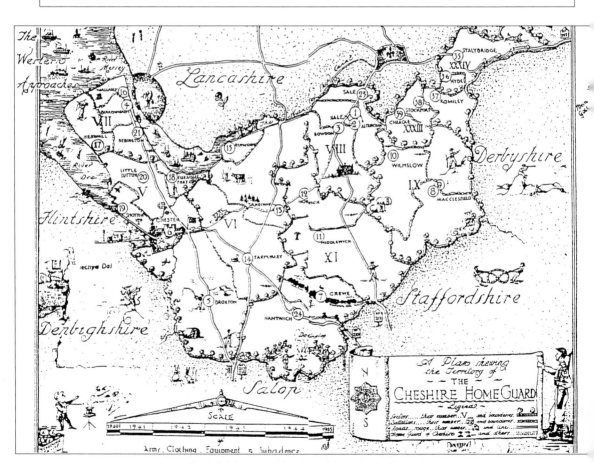

Official Map of the Cheshire Home Guard
From *History of the Cheshire Home Guard*, Gale and Polden Ltd, 1950

In the very cold winter of 1946-1947 Maurice served with the Anti-Tank Regiment of the Guards Armoured Division at Husum in Schleswig-Holstein. He was manning a telephone exchange and was assisted by an ex German prisoner of war. The latter was aged about 23 or 24 and was extremely good at his job, especially considering that he had lost all his fingers and the tops of his thumbs. He had been a soldier on the Russian front and had suffered his injury through frostbite. When Maurice or his companions thoughtlessly complained about the cold in Germany, the young German quietly looked at his hands.

Maurice was demobbed in May 1947 and had to report to York with thousands of others from the north of England in order to obtain his civilian clothes. He handed in his knife, fork and spoon, items to which he had become particularly attached and which represented his last remnants of army equipment, and was issued with a demob suit, shoes, and a wide-brimmed trilby hat. He also received £50 demob pay, which he regarded as a fortune. He returned to Macclesfield and was relieved not to be asked this time by relatives and friends when he would be returning to army duty.

He married Edith in 1948 in Carnoustie, Scotland, the place where they had met in 1943. Maurice went back to the motor trade, joining Simisters' garage in Macclesfield. He and Edith settled down in the town and brought up their family. They still live there and are immensely energetic, pursuing many interests and activities.

Portrait of an Older Macclesfield Home Guard

When he heard, on 3 September 1939, that war had been declared, his heart sank. His young son, trying to console him, reported with some satisfaction that, according to one report quoted on the wireless, people in Germany were so dismayed by the prospects of yet another war that many had committed suicide. *'And there will be many in England doing the same thing'*, he replied as gently as he could.

He had volunteered at the age of 16 immediately war was declared in August 1914. Like many others he claimed to have reached the age of 18. In April 1915, just before his 17th birthday, he found himself, totally bewildered, in the water off Gallipoli with hundreds of others who were trying to make their way to the shore, bayoneted rifles held high above their heads. The noise was appalling. From behind him came the boom-boom of shells from the mighty British naval vessels. All around him were struggling men, trying to keep their rifles out of the water. But many were already caught up in barbed wire and they yelled as the hail of machine-gun bullets from the shore cut them down.

The screams of the wounded and dying, the gurgles as they sank below the surface of the sea, the incredible multiple deaths taking place before his eyes, deaths of young boys he had been joking with the previous day..... he was living a nightmare and the only thing he felt able to do was to wade on towards the sandy beach in accordance with his orders. He was utterly breathless, completely exhausted and absolutely terrified. So, choking and gulping and sobbing, amazed that he was still alive and intact, he reached the sand and collapsed onto it.

He remembered little of his subsequent time in the Dardanelles. He seemed to avoid the diseases which left many of his colleagues sick or dying. He felt no gratitude for his continued existence, rather he felt guilt that so many of his friends and compatriots had gone for ever. Life had little meaning for him. He was trying to come to terms with an experience which left him empty in body, mind and spirit.

He eventually served in Egypt and Palestine, and lived through some difficult moments, but nothing remotely compared to the horror of his Gallipoli landing. When he was demobilised he had reached the rank of sergeant. In 1938 and 1939 he had trembled with anxiety for his family as Britain found itself on a collision course with Germany. Yet his anger swallowed up his anxiety and channelled his energies into a determined opposition to Hitler.

He was one of the first in the town to queue up to join the Local Defence Volunteers in May 1940. He was amongst the 250 chosen First World War Macclesfield veterans who were addressed by Colonel G.N. Heath in the Drill Hall as the preliminary step to putting the force onto a proper footing. He paraded in civilian clothes and drilled with a stick for several months, but he felt at home - he realised with a shock that military discipline appealed to him. He was short and stocky and had acquired the habit of moving in an erect and soldierly way.

He was a little surprised to find himself being held up as a model of military smartness. Within a short time he was appointed Sergeant in A Company of the 9th Cheshire Battalion. At least once a week he spent the night taking charge of a small unit guarding water supplies, or electric generators or gas installations or manning an observation post in the country. He had training evenings and week-end exercises. The camaraderie he had enjoyed in the First World War came back to him and gave him a sense of purpose and morale. His great joy was the regular public parades of the Home Guard for wartime fund-raising events. He quite often found himself leading his whole Company through the streets of the town. He never smiled, but kept his eyes firmly fixed ahead, his shouldered rifle motionless. His orders were given in a clear and authoritative voice. Every move he made was sharp and urgent. The sense of duty, of loyalty and commitment in everything he did was exemplary. He was one of fourteen men in A Company to receive a Certificate of Good Service.

When he heard on 6 June 1944 that British and Allied troops had landed on the Normandy beaches he saw himself once more staggering up the Turkish shore at Gallipoli and his heart went out to all the young men involved in the landings. He could imagine the intense naval bombardment behind them, the frightful noise, the screams and staccato hissing of the machine guns. He felt his heart pounding, his breathing laboured and was astonished to find himself sitting in an arm chair- and felt great relief!

The conquest of the beaches and the victories in Normandy took a great weight from his mind. He no longer needed to share the sufferings of men hurling themselves against coastal defences. And he kept telling himself that soon the War would be over.

Certainly the activities of the Home Guard could now be curtailed. The stand-down ceremony took place on 3 December 1944 and the 8th and 9th Battalions paraded in Macclesfield. Our sergeant played a prominent part. He still could not understand how his horrific First World War experiences had allowed him, had possibly encouraged him, to take such satisfaction in the town's Home Guard in the Second World War. When he heard the words 'As representatives of the 8th and 9th Battalions of the Cheshire Home Guard we, in symbol, hand back for safe custody the arms we have been proud to bear' he shuddered with emotion but, conquering this, stood even more erect. In some peculiar way he seemed to have come to terms at last with the loss of life he had witnessed in the eastern Mediterranean in 1915. By his renewed service he had paid a belated tribute to the sacrifices of his young companions.

UNITS OF THE MACCLESFIELD HOME GUARD
Above; at the Macclesfield Gasworks.
Below, on the playing fields of the King's School.

A large group of the Macclesfield Home Guard, also photographed on the playing fields of the King's School, which played an important part in Home Guard and Cadet activities during the War.

Anti-tank obstacle on bridge over the Macclesfield Canal : Map ref. SJ927791.

Pill boxes: The Home Guard were to man these in the event of an airborne invasion. Top, by the A54 Congleton to Buxton road, map ref. SJ903663, and bottom, overlooking Bosley Reservoir

Photographs courtesy of Maurice Winnell

Gunner Maurice Winnell, R.A. 52nd Scottish Lowland Division.

"D" Company, 9th Cheshire Home Guard.

LIVE GRENADE THROWING — THURSDAY 23rd JULY, 1942.

Parade at 2000hrs. punctually, at Simister's Garage, Hibel Road Station, for train to Adlington.
Dress: Clean Fatigue — with Steel Helmet.

Signed............E.H. Seeley, 2/Lt

231, Park Lane,
Macclesfield.
21.7.42.

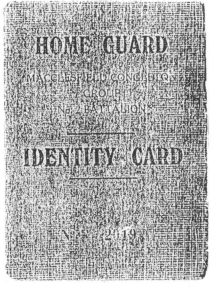

Mementoes from Maurice Winnell's service with Macclesfield Home Guard

The Bearer

MAURICE WINNELL

is an enrolled member of

D C. **No. 2 Battalion**

of the Macclesfield/Congleton Group

of the Home Guard

Signature of
Holder   M Winnell.

Signature of
O. C. Company

Company Commander.

Date 3RD. NOVEMBER 1941.

This Card must not leave your possession and must be given up before leaving the forces.

'WINGS for VICTORY'
MAY 8th to 15th

OUR AIM—

10 LANCASTERS

10 HURRICANES

10 SPITFIRES

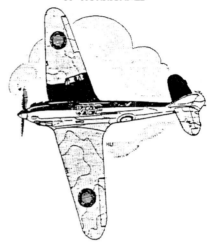

OVER Sixty Entries have been received for the "Wings For Victory" Week Slogan Competition, the closing date for which was Monday. Judging will take place this week-end, and the results will be announced next week.

Another Competition, which is creating considerable interest, is that for Aero-Modelling. There has been a big demand for plans, and intending entrants are reminded that the Closing Date is Monday Next, May 3rd, at 4 p.m. Every Entry must be accompanied by an Entry Form duly completed.

Eight Groups have expressed their willingness to participate in the Inter-Group League Competition, and the Committee propose that the first Competition shall be for the period May 3rd to July 31st, so including "Wings For Victory" Week. The Challenge Shield, which will be for competition, will shortly be exhibited.

LOG BOOK

which will record the operational activities
of an Aircraft
is a tribute to the success achieved by

Macclesfield

SAVINGS COMMITTEE

in the

WINGS FOR VICTORY

NATIONAL SAVINGS CAMPAIGN · 1943

Target :-£ 500,000,

Achievement :-£ 533,236,

REPRESENTING
THE COST OF :- { 10 Lancaster Bombers
16 Spitfire Fighters
10 Hurricane Fighters

King's School Cadet Corps in front of the War Memorial Library and Cricket Pavilion, on the Front Playing Field, in 1943.
Centre: Headmaster TT Shaw. To his left, masters, RG Squibbs and JAV Richards, then senior boys K. Finch, FH Bradley, J Coates, K Bradley.
To his right, major JWE Ransley, then Mr ML Harvey, then senior boys, JB Gardiner, PF Robinson, MF Crowder

CHAPTER 3
The Second World War and the King's School in Macclesfield

Sir John Percyvale, a native of Macclesfield, was elected Lord Mayor of London in 1498. In 1502 he set up a Grammar School in Macclesfield attached to the chapel which was to become St Michael's Church. In 1552 the school was re-established by the Charter of King Edward VI, re-organised, re-endowed and became known as The Grammar School of King Edward VI in Macclesfield. In 1748 it moved to new buildings in King Edward Street and by 1802 there were 72 boarders and 19 day boys.

It became increasingly necessary to move to larger premises and this was eventually achieved in 1856 when the school acquired its present main site in Cumberland Street. In 1938 the Governors decided upon the full title of 'The Foundation of King Edward the Sixth, or The King's School in Macclesfield', but the contracted form 'The King's School in Macclesfield' became the normal title.

In 1939 there were 23 members of staff and 540 boys in the school. The standing of the school in the town increased considerably during the Second World War. The primary reason for this was the great use made of the school's facilities by local wartime organisations, not least the Home Guard which held many of its training and demonstration evenings and week-ends on the school's playing fields. It was here too that Home Guard Companies assembled before their big parades in the town.

T.T. Shaw, headmaster of the King's School, particularly encouraged the local Air Training Corps to use classrooms as well as playing fields for instruction and parading purposes respectively. From 1942 the school's Cadet Force became known as the Macclesfield Junior Training Corps and was affiliated to the 9th Battalion of the Cheshire Regimental Home Guard. Shortly afterwards it received the title of the Second Cadet Battalion, the Cheshire Regiment, and included the Macclesfield Company (C), the Broken Cross Company (D) and the Wilmslow Company (E). Hence many boys in the surrounding area became aware of the King's School and its facilities.

There were 3 Companies in the School Cadet Corps and boys were expected to take the Certificate A Examination (a basic military exam) and were encouraged to join the Home Guard when they became 17 years of age. There was now a special platoon in D Company of the 9th Battalion Home Guard into which all present Old Boys and current pupils of the school would be placed. The Officer in Command of this platoon would be a master of the school and the NCO's would either be Old Boys or senior boys of the school.

Major Ransley, officer commanding the school's Cadet Force, presided over all cadet companies in the area and in 1943 was given the title of Honorary Colonel (Cadets), the only person in Cheshire to receive such a title. The cadets received a uniform in the Lent Term of 1942. This meant that they had to come to school on Fridays dressed in khaki and wearing heavy boots. Uniforms were now seen so frequently that no boys felt embarrassed to walk through the streets wearing one. Perhaps the most tedious part of belonging to the Cadet Corps was parading on the front field of the school. It seemed to go on for so long - 'Atten ... shun!' - 'Stand at... ease!' - 'Stand..... easy!' Then a long wait, at the end of which we heard

- 'Atten..... shun!' - 'Stand at..... ease!' - 'Stand.... easy!'

From time to time we would march - and discover those boys who swung their left arm in unison with their left leg and hence looked uncoordinated. The harder they tried to put themselves right the worse it became. I once saw this happening to an older friend who was leading the parade. It was impossible for most of us, including the officers, to keep a straight face. The more we tried the worse it became.

On Friday afternoons the regular activity for senior boys before the parading of the Cadet Corps was 'current affairs'. This normally involved a talk by a member of staff or invited speaker on some serious topic, often relating to aspirations for a post-war society. Then would follow an open discussion. One Friday in late 1944 the discussion concerned the continuing value of the Cadet Corps as a school activity. The stern Under Officer and Captain of the school Michael Crowder rose and sang the praises of the Cadet Corps. He finished off by claiming: *'The Cadet Corps makes you think'*. A rebellious boy called Dick Gates stood up and, rather to the astonishment of us all, seemed to support Michael; *'Yes'* he began, *'the Cadet corps does make you think. Every Friday afternoon..... .on parade..... I find myself thinking.... the whole time!'*

In August 1942 the Cadet Corps had a week's camp at Seven Springs, Disley. For most boys this was a novel and interesting experience. We climbed into a train at the Central Station and, some 25 minutes later, got out at Disley Station. Now we had to march through the roads just outside the town. At this time the senior Officer Cadet, Captain of Rugby and Captain of the School was Gus Gardiner. He was a neat, compact, lithe figure, the epitome of military smartness in his movements and especially knowledgeable as a result of some months spent in the Home Guard. As we marched, his crisp clear orders kept our arms swinging and our head and shoulders erect. Then, quite suddenly, he started singing; *'Roll out the barrel, we'll have a barrel of fun, roll out the barrel, we've got the blues on the run!'* We turned in amazement, but only for a split second, for his next order was *'Sing..... Sing... Blast You!'* Even more astonished we again snapped our eyes ahead and began with embarrassment to sing, tentatively, shyly, half-heartedly.... *'Roll ...out ....the .....barrel'*. We knew that our efforts were feeble but at least we were obeying orders. We sensed a rattling storm emerging from the mouth of Gus. He erupted, *'I said'*, he bellowed, *'I said Sing..... Sing, damn you.... Sing!'* We suddenly felt all mature and soldierly and we began to sing loudly and with enjoyment. Gus was clearly happy with our response and, as we continued to sing, he reverted to *'Left, Right, Left, Right! Well done, well done! Left Right, Left right!'*

There are many forms of leadership. At the age of 17 or 18 Gus Gardiner revealed himself as a born leader, confident and direct. He was soon to obtain a commission in the Indian Army and to find himself fighting the Japanese. But he lost an arm in battle and this brought his military endeavours to a close. He spent his career teaching agriculture at Reading University. When I met Gus again some ten years ago he had the round smiling face he had always displayed. The zest and eagerness which had always served him so well in his youth had been replaced by the gentleness and courtesy which had also been part of his make-up. Whatever achievements he enjoyed after he left school, they could hardly have matched the charisma and authority with which a whole generation of King's School boys associated him.

But we are still with the school Cadet Corps on its way to Seven Springs Camp at Disley in August 1942 After 'breaking step' to climb a rather steep hill we finally arrived at our camp. Our advance party had done its stuff, even though they had only been there for a few hours. Like all advance parties they gave the comforting impression that they had arrived days before. Indeed their particular occupation at the moment of our going through the main gate of the camp (simply a normal five-barred farm gate) was splashing green paint onto perfectly white canvas in order to camouflage the numerous bell tents dotted around.

We were allocated a tent, told how to sleep with our feet towards the middle and how to store our belongings (which had been brought in kit bags by lorry) in a way which made the most of the small amount of space available. We had taken over a Scouts' camp which already possessed several wooden huts for administration, feeding, ablutions and toilets. Indeed we could not complain about lack of accommodation in spite of the cramped space in our tents. Our Cadet Force authorities had made their preparations well.

After a meal we paraded and were given various duties to perform. My friend Vic Hall and I received instructions to carry out a late evening guard duty by the main gate to the camp. Presumably we were to guard our companions and military equipment from hostile encroachment. We were given elderly rifles (no ammunition, of course,) and ordered to challenge any suspicious prowlers. By this time the darkness was complete, save for a few torches flashing in the tents, which now seemed strangely distant. Rain was in the air and there was a chilly breeze whistling over the top of our hill. Suddenly we heard some sluggish footsteps. Vic and I blinked at each other across the blackness of the gate and its surroundings. The footsteps came nearer. My heart was beating ferociously. But Vic resolved the situation by thrusting his rifle aggressively forward, advancing his left foot and shouting out, *'Halt! Who goes there?'* An elderly farmer blurted out, *'It's only me, it's only me!'* Vic was not to be trifled with. *'Step forth to be recognised!'* he yelled. The frightened figure edged nearer and explained that he worked on the nearby farm and just wanted a stroll. *'Go back where you came from!'* ordered Vic, still pointing his rifle. The man meekly obeyed.

Strangely Vic and I did not laugh over this incident until much later. The gravity of the situation and of our responsibility had filled us both with alarm. In daylight there would have been no real concern. But here, on moorland, in the darkness, when most people around were asleep, we were astonished by our own fears. In many ways the old farmer had frightened us more than we had frightened him.

Two nights later we found ourselves on night manoeuvres. I was never clear whether we were supposed to be stalking enemies or waiting to be attacked. We still carried rifles which were rather harmless, unless we decided to use them as clubs. We had to crawl on our bellies on grass which was very wet. We had no waterproofs and our khaki uniforms were soon sodden. We cocked our ears, cocked our rifles, lay silent or moved cautiously. After two hours of this I whispered to Vic, near whom I had stayed for most of the exercise, *'Shall we go back?'* He nodded and, noiselessly we found our way back to our tent, laid our rifle at the side of our mattress and crept under our blankets. Nothing more was said about the exercise.

The whole week it rained and our tents were not comfortable. This meant that many of our proposed activities were curtailed or abandoned. One afternoon, for example, Sergeant Ken Finch, large and congenial, grinned as he gathered together the unit to which I belonged into a small space in the administration block. He got us to sit down if and where we could and, continuing to grin, asserted that every man should be able to defend himself. He produced two pairs of boxing gloves and gave us a very elementary lesson on the way to use them. Then, with a renewed grin, he asked for two volunteers. Before anyone had the chance to respond he pointed to me; and then to a burly chap whose name I cannot remember. We slugged away at each other without any pretence of finesse for what seemed at least ten minutes but perhaps was only two minutes. Our colleagues the spectators, delighted that they had not been nominated to demonstrate the principles Ken had endeavoured to impart to us, were the only ones who seemed to enjoy the occasion - apart from Ken, of course, who continued to grin as he always did.

In a strange way we enjoyed our first taste of cadet camp because of the camaraderie. But we could hardly have claimed anything near the sort of military fitness and proficiency young men a few years older than us were acquiring up and down the Country. At least we felt that we had done something *'to help the war effort'*. We did realise, too, that it was easy for any of us to criticise the efforts of those who were responsible for organising our training and activities, a task which called for considerable ingenuity, skill and persistence, especially when the weather was not on their side.

Our Commanding Officer, Major (as he still was then) Ransley, took full charge of that camp. You would not have described him as a distinctly military person although his neat figure, his moustache and his general bearing were much to his advantage. He was a quiet and courteous person, a teacher of chemistry and much respected. He was supported in his Cadet Force duties by three other masters, Messrs M.L. (Len) Harvey, R.G. Squibbs and J.A.V. Richards. Eight other members of staff (out of a total of 23 in 1939), who would doubtless have given him additional assistance, were already serving in the armed forces by 1942.

Len Harvey, eventually to become Second Master, was a short, dark-haired, smiling and business-like teacher of French. He was very wiry and strong, and gave excellent coaching to the school's Rugby teams. For a time he assisted Mr Squibbs ('Squibby') in the coaching of the 1st XV until the latter left the school in 1943 to return as a master to Bedford School. Len then took over the 1st XV and had a series of remarkably successful seasons. From time to time when he was refereeing a scratch game between the 1st and 2nd XV's as part of training, he would pick up the ball and sidestep his way through our outstretched hands. Since he was smaller than most of us there was a tendency for us to hold back lest we should injure our mentor. No need for this; he was elusive and powerful and he easily broke our tackles. Fortunately, too, he never allowed such incursions to last for long - our exasperation might have persuaded us to tackle even more decisively and risk upsetting the main objectives of the practice. Len also took over - with conspicuous success - the production of school plays from F.C. Milner, a celebrated teacher of the French language who died in December 1943.

In the early years of the War Squibby laid the basis for the school's extraordinary achievements in Rugby in 1944, 1945 and 1946, by elevating his coaching of the game into an art form, almost a philosophy. His quiet thoughtful manner, the shrewdness of his comments, especially in his 'post-mortems' on matches, inspired a zest for the game and a resolution to reach high standards in all those boys who played it.

T.T. Shaw, a first-class mathematician, had been appointed headmaster of King's in 1933. Two years later, rugby, a game in which he excelled, became the school's major winter sport. TT was responsible for a tightening-up of general discipline and morale and for his pupils' successes in many spheres of activity in the years up to the War and well beyond - he eventually retired in 1966. Certainly he was a big man in every sense. He was referred to sometimes as 'The Boss', sometimes as TT but the most popular nickname used of him by the boys was Chimp. His lower lip protruded (as it does for a considerable number of people) beyond his upper lip and this had been seized upon from his early days at King's. Some bright youngster sent an entry to the school's magazine late in the War shortly after the birth of TT's son Jeremy. It ran, *'We congratulate the headmaster on the birth of his son. We hear that he is a little monkey'.*

The task of TT during the War was immense. The arrival of evacuees from Stretford Grammar School was the first major task but this was followed by many others, not least the replacement of those masters who went into the Forces. There had been 540 boys in the school in September 1939, the beginning of the War. In July 1940 this figure had increased to 568. Some 60 private evacuees from all over the country (but especially London and Manchester) swelled the numbers starting the new academic year in September

T.T. Shaw

1940 to 630. By the Autumn Term of 1943 and in each following war-time year there were approximately 700 boys in the school. Hence the increase in the War years was from 540 to 700, 160 boys, the school population swelling by almost one third in the course of the War.

There had been 23 members of staff (including the Headmaster) at the beginning of the War, that is one teacher for every 22 boys. If this quite generous proportion was to be maintained, the total staff number for the rest of the War would have to be 31. The major factor was the call-up of permanent members of staff. Eight masters served in the Forces. A problem for T.T. Shaw was that he never knew exactly when the call-up of any one member of staff would take place. Mrs Howarth was the first woman to be appointed to the staff in the first year of the War and 12 other women were to follow her before 1945. Altogether, apart from the Headmaster, 50 teachers were active in the Second World War years at the King's School, 37 men and 13 women. Very different from the settled staff of 23 in September 1939.

A personal tragedy rocked TT when his wife was killed on their Christmas Holidays 1940-1941 as the result of a German bombing raid on the south coast, where they were staying. His later second marriage happily proved to be enormously successful.

Mr M.W. Davies was Second Master during the War and beyond. He was always referred to as Ben Davies by the boys and indeed by his colleagues. He had studied classical languages at Oxford but had chosen to teach English Literature and History to the senior form on the Arts side, the Upper Six Modern. There was a long and wide refectory table in that room and, in order of seniority, we would sit around that table, the most senior sitting on each side at the top next to Ben who, of course, had the seat of honour. Ben was tall and slim and bespectacled and often wore a frowning expression of surprise, raising his eyebrows and puckering his forehead. This resulted in our looking at him with apparent rapt attention when he was investigating the art of Francis Bacon's essay-writing or the causes of the French Revolution. But Ben was a great teacher, stressing that what he taught would provide us with the ability to use our leisure time well. His extra-curricular activity was cricket and he took charge of this sport in the school during the War. Indeed he played the game himself until he was well into his sixties. As well as running the cricket he also had to be groundsman, since the War had claimed any professional groundsman we might have had. He carried out this role with the help of the boy cricketers who spent hours during the Easter holidays patiently rolling the heavy roller over the proposed square.

Mr G.C. Bartindale, like T.T. Shaw an excellent mathematician, was a celebrated school character. He was tall, dark, scraggy, stooping and with his academic gown swirling round him he looked a cross between Batman and some elongated bird of prey. (In those days the wearing of gowns by staff was expected) In fact he was known to the boys as Jim Crow. His mannerisms were so exceptionally idiosyncratic that he had to struggle to achieve any sort of discipline, certainly with junior forms. He was genuinely bewildered by the failure of some of his pupils to understand concepts which to him were simple. But all his pupils recognised his humanity and good will. Indeed, in spite of his sometimes unruly classes, his pupils always seemed to do themselves justice in examinations. He was an ardent Communist, a fact which did not make him generally popular in the town. Indeed he once wrote to the local newspaper to complain that he had been fined the maximum amount of money (rather than the normal nominal amount) in the magistrate's court for a black-out offence, simply because of his Communist leanings. In special current affairs classes for senior boys he explained Communism from time to time and was received with great respect. These boys were well aware of the fact that arguably the greatest English treatise on Russian communism, *The Socialist Sixth of the World* of 1939, had been written by an old boy of King's, Dr Hewlett Johnson, Dean of Canterbury, who was known as 'The Red Dean'.

There were a large number of outstanding personalities amongst the boys. I have already mentioned Gus Gardiner. An earlier school captain in the first years of the War was Pip Fairhurst. He too, slight in build, was a good games player and a strong personality and exerted a very effective sense of discipline upon the boys. When I was in Five Modern (the third year) he came in to take us for a Latin period, our Latin master being absent. He stared at us, asked for the book we were using and the page we had reached and then stretched himself out sideways upon the master's desk and facing us. He asked me to translate. I started but came to a word I didn't recognise. *'What does it mean?* 'I asked him. *'I don't know'*, he replied, *'get on with it'*. So I did. Still leaning on his right elbow and following our translation in apparent total absorption he had us eating out of his hand for the whole of the period.

Pip received a bullet in his knee on D-Day but recovered well. He died a couple of years ago after a long illness. I played both rugby and cricket with him for several years after the War and we remained great friends.

Roger Wood was a later School Captain. After the War I got to know him quite well at college. He returned to the King's School and taught geography there until he retired. He died suddenly some eight years ago. Only then did I discover that he had been one of the few to survive the Market Garden operation - the disastrous attempt in September 1944 to take the bridge at Arnhem on the Lower Rhine after the capture of two other bridges over the River Maas and the River Waal. Roger had never once mentioned to me his participation in this fateful battle, despite many opportunities to do so.

I should like to pay tribute to those members of staff who went off to War. With two exceptions, I saw them all again from time to time after the War.

A.A. (Tony) Arnold had been appointed to coach rugby and cricket in addition to teaching geography. He had an impediment in his speech which left him open-mouthed at frequent intervals as he struggled to get his words out. He turned this apparent defect to advantage by imbuing important words with a sort of oratorical emphasis. He was a lively and encouraging person. He returned after the War having reached the rank of Lieutenant-Colonel and claiming that the higher he had risen in the Army, the less work he had been called upon to do and the more his ability at billiards had improved. He played some magnificent cricket for the Maxonians Cricket team, which consisted of staff and old boys and flourished after the War.

Selwyn Russell-Jones was a large stocky, articulate, friendly Welshman. He had come to teach art at the school; he taught it well and stood no nonsense. He loved games of all kinds, although his physique fitted him mainly for the position of front row forward in Rugby. We realised later that he was a poet of some distinction. He was a superb raconteur of incidents - let one story suffice as an example. In the army he had found himself, at the age of 35, competing with youngsters of 18 or 19 in his officer-training unit. Because he was far from slim he was normally left behind on all exercises which called for athletic prowess. Whenever he and his colleagues were called upon to run, Selwyn was always way behind the others. Whenever an obstacle had to be surmounted it was always Selwyn who was left stuck at the top. If water was being crossed it was always Selwyn who lost his balance and fell in. If a rope had to be climbed it was always Selwyn who, arms aloft, failed to lift his feet off the ground. Perhaps it was not surprising that one particular physical training instructor took advantage of Selwyn's predicament and made him the butt of all his jokes. On each occasion that Selwyn distinguished himself for his sheer incompetence this PTI would call out, *'Ah, Jones again!'* or *'Come on, Jones!'* and all other would-be officers fell about with laughter.

They may well have got the impression that Selwyn did not mind being held up to ridicule. Not so. Selwyn seethed with suppressed resentment. But one day there was rain and the PTI, quite a robust man himself, took his trainees into the gym to teach them the rudiments of boxing. He put on boxing gloves and, for some minutes, demonstrated with sudden jabs the art of both attack and defence. Then he said, *'Now I need a volunteer - Jones, you'll do!'* His colleagues roared with laughter, particularly out of relief that they had not been asked to step forward. The PTI threw a pair of boxing gloves at Selwyn, who put them on with surprising ease. (He had not revealed that he had been heavyweight boxing champion at Cardiff University!) The two boxers eyed each other; the instructor threw a decoy punch but, before he had time to consider the next move, Selwyn let go with his right hand and floored his instructor and tormentor. He turned round casually to his gaping colleagues and said, *'You will have noticed that he dropped his guard'*. He explained *'one should never do that, you know. Now what he should have told us was.......'* and Selwyn went through a list of do's and don't's. He then stretched out a friendly ungloved hand to the PTI who was sitting on the floor, rubbing his chin. This was his one moment of glory in the army, he claimed afterwards. He felt as if a weight had been lifted from his mind and soul. He was not teased or tortured again.

Selwyn returned to King's after the War, designed a splendid new Art School and continued to enjoy his life as a schoolmaster. He played regularly with the Maxonians' Cricket team for some time.

Almost certainly the finest additional member to the staff King's acquired during the War was A.S. (Paddy) Haresign, who arrived in September 1941 with his first class honours in modern languages from Cambridge. He was said to have a medical condition which prevented him from joining the forces. The King's School was to gain enormously over many years from his personality, his ability and his abundant good will. He was slight, dark, pale, very young, scarcely older than a senior boy. His hair was neatly parted but on the right side it flopped down over his temple and this meant that, unconsciously, he kept putting his right hand up to his head to push it back. This gesture was particularly effective when he was teaching; it seemed to give him an air of deep thought as he spoke.

Paddy immersed himself in the life and work of the King's School. He was a real gem of a schoolmaster, helping in all aspects of school life where he felt able to make the slightest contribution. He even wrote a history of sport at the school. After his retirement he visited the Staff Common Room, where he had his own chair, every day.

On the whole the wartime games players at King's were extremely fortunate. They had ample opportunity to demonstrate their skills, although the variety of games played was small; rugby, cricket and fives (two outdoor courts behind the Science Block) with a certain amount of swimming (at the Municipal Baths in Davenport Street) and athletics, especially for an annual sports day. The rugby results steadily improved in the early years of the War. By Christmas 1944 it was clear that the Rugby XV was having an exceptional season; *'The achievements of the Rugby team of 1942-1943, which broke the school record, have been equalled and even excelled by succeeding teams. The present XV have won every school match they have played'*... was the summing-up in the school's magazine for the Lent Term 1945. The final results of the season were: Played 12, Won 12, Points for 408, Points against 41. The team went on to win the Manchester Seven-a Sides in 1945 and 1946.

The War gave the school's rugby players the opportunity of additional playing experience. For example they played Ringway Aerodrome (now Manchester Airport) which was the home of many wartime parachutists. One of the results of the special dispensation during the War by the Rugby Union authorities, that Rugby League players could now play amateur Rugby Union matches, was that the Ringway team was exceptionally strong, most of its members being former professional Rugby League players. Unusual opportunities for playing extra cricket matches were also opened up. The Lancashire and Cheshire Cricket League, to which the Macclesfield and Bollington Cricket Clubs belonged, was suspended for the duration of hostilities. As a result many scratch matches were organised by those clubs and, through Ben Davies, many King's players were invited to play during the long summer holidays on the Macclesfield Victoria Road ground and on the Bollington Recreation ground. During the late War years I began to know and love the cricket fields of lovely Cheshire.

The record of the King's School 1st XI Cricket team was almost as exceptional as that of the King's School 1st XV. Some boys played in both teams, of course. The school

King's School Rugby 1st XV 1943-44

King's School Rugby 1st XV 1944-45

magazine recorded, *'Only three school matches have been lost by the 1st Xl in the last two seasons'*.

The wartime duties of both staff and senior boys were increased by the burden of fire-watching, set up during the Easter holidays of 1941. A rota of duties was arranged for boys in their final year, and their task was to put out and report on any fires caused by incendiary bombs. This normally meant that two boys slept the night on the premises, usually in the First World War Memorial Library (and cricket pavilion) on the front playing field. Two masters would sleep in the Staff Common Room. The system was to continue until well into 1944.

A national message, 'Dig for Victory', received a strong response from the school. The military events of May/June 1940 had resulted in a greater concentration on the needs of defence and on the sustenance of the population. The Battle of Britain, with its images of air battles and crashing aircraft, had associated quite clearly the prosecution of the War with the countryside, farm workers, Land Army girls and fields of corn. In the Summer holidays of 1940, 14 King's School boys, led by two masters, Messrs Bosley and Underwood, departed on 12th August to Meadow Bank Farm, Siddington, where they lived in huts which had been previously occupied by hens. They gathered corn into stooks, stacked it into ricks, picked early potatoes and looked after pigs. This was the start of considerable involvement of the school in agricultural activity throughout the War.

In the Autumn Term of 1940 the decision was taken to plough up 'The Rock' (the upper and elevated part of the school grounds behind the school, beyond Coare Street) as well as part of the lower field. Potato-picking in the Autumn Term to help local farmers also started. A circular from the Board of Education was read out in March 1941 to the governors. It requested that schools should attempt to modify their holiday arrangements wherever possible to enable children at the school to be employed in agriculture. The Headmaster and governors responded and the Editorial of the school magazine of the Summer Term 1942 stated; *'It is to be hoped that a large number of boys will take advantage of the Summer Holidays to help the country with farm work, as many did last year'*

The Cheshire War Agricultural Committee had its headquarters in a building opposite the Town Hall and next to the Bull Hotel in the Market Place. Here all kinds of agricultural innovations were conceived, not least the ploughing-up of the side of Shutlingsloe, the highest hill for miles around, situated between Langley and Wildboarclough. The Committee based its work on Shutlingsloe on Lower Nabbs Farm, Wildboarclough. During the Summer Holidays of 1942 a group of boys from the school did many jobs here. I was part of this group.

Our routine was, first, to meet a van driven by an employee of the Macclesfield branch of the Cheshire War Agricultural Committee, at 8.00 am each morning in the market place in front of the Town Hall. We then drove to Lower Nabbs Farm via the Hanging Gate Inn and the steep hill called Greenway.

Our greatest complaint was that, having arrived at the farm we had to spend one or two or more hours waiting to be told what to do. However, two particular jobs remain in my memory. First I spent most of one Friday with others weeding a walled area near the road and not far from the Crag Inn. (This large walled area has now disappeared) We must have worked very hard considering that we were not used to bending down in the way required by this particular activity. The next day I happened to be playing for Bollington Cricket Club and, when I was called upon to bowl (and at that time Bollington was playing the system of 8-ball overs), my back made what to me seemed audible protests. I did not bowl very well.

The other job which remains vividly in my mind was spreading lime from a tractor-drawn cart on the higher reaches of Shutlingsloe. The objective in both tasks was, of course, to prepare the land for cultivation. I never discovered whether the objective was achieved or not. The slope on Shutlingsloe was a demanding phenomenon for a tractor of those times and, looking back, we were lucky not to have finished up under the cart or even the tractor. What I do know is that the clothes we were wearing were so covered by lime that future use of them was impossible. My friends Peter Kearsley, Vic Hall and I received 15 shillings each for two weeks' work. (A labourer's wage was in the region of £2 to £2.10 shillings a week)

In the Christmas Term of 1942 there was considerable emphasis on potato-picking; *'Officially our only holiday this term was the usual half-term one on 26 October but most boys, including certain members of the Upper 6th, have enjoyed two or three weeks' holidays-with-pay helping with the potato-harvest.'* reported the school magazine in December 1942. Two years later the magazine for the Christmas Term 1944 reported that 300 boys had been helping the local farmers in potato-picking and that the Harvest Camp in the Summer Holidays had been a great success.

During the lunch-hour near the end of term in December 1944, a fourteen year old pupil, Colin Foster, went out into Cumberland Street and down Hibel Road towards the railway station, where he joined others watching the unloading of American tanks in the station's goods yard. As the tanks came out into the road through a gate in the high surrounding wall, one lost direction and crashed into the wall. Colin had his back to this wall and was killed.

In this astonishing way a young boy also became the victim of a conflict which claimed the lives of no fewer than 44 former pupils of the School who were serving in the armed forces. Their short lives came to an end in different ways.

In the first year of the War Geoffrey Mellor, at the school between 1928 and 1936, died in a military hospital after only three weeks in the Royal Engineers. He had won a place at Merton College, Oxford four years previously. K.R.Dean, at school from 1930 to 1938, a Leading Aircraftman about to take a commission, was killed after attacking German naval objectives. His bomber had come down 'in a sea accident' 30 miles from the English coast. He had won an Oxford place to train for the Church. And every year of the War further names were added to the list: A.C. Hamman, at school from 1933 to 1936; P.K. Green, who lived in Leek, left school at the age of 16 to join the Merchant Navy and went down in his first ship; Norman Brocklehurst hit by a propeller on an RAF Station; Bernard Connor, who lived in Brook Street Macclesfield, became an RAF Pilot officer and died shortly after the War when his transport plane crashed in Belgium.

196 Macclesfield men and women lost their lives in the Second World War. The following names of King's School boys appear on the Macclesfield War Memorial at Park Green.

Harold Chesworth	Geoffrey Mellor
Bernard Connor	Kenneth Potts
Thomas W. Etchells	John N. Smith
John Hutchinson	Edward G. Warrington
Philip Latchford	

Of course, not all King's School boys lived in Macclesfield - the names of those who lived in other towns and villages will be on the War Memorials of those places. 35 who lived elsewhere, also died - confirmation of the very widespread intake from East Cheshire enjoyed by the King's School. 297 Old Boys served in the Forces. So one in every seven who served was killed. One in twenty was decorated.

The full Roll of Honour of Old Boys of the King's School killed in the 1939-1945 War:

Adams B.F. (1927-1933)	Atty J.C. (1939-1940)	Banks R.A. (1932-1938)
Basnett W. (1930-1935)	Bowyer J. (1933-1937)	Brocklehurst N. (1933-1937)
Burt W.H. (1932-1938)	Chesworth H. (1918-1924)	Clayton H. (1915-1920)
Connor B. (1933-1938)	Davies L.R. (1935-1942)	Dean K.R. (1930-1938)
Etchells T.W. (1931-1937)	Green P.K. (1940-1943)	Hale K. (1932-1936)
Hallworth F. (1932-1937)	Hamman A.C. (1933-1936)	Hampton P.J.L. (1932-1941)
Harrap F.S. (1930-1935)	Harrison P. (1927-1934)	Healey P. (1936-1938)
Highfield D.C. (1933-1937)	Hutchinson J.E. (1934-1938)	Jolliffe D. (1934-1939)
Kershaw L.H. (1928-1937)	Latchford P. (1931-1935)	Mellor G. (1928-1936)
Moffett A.O. (1929-1934)	Owen J. (1932-1936)	Owen S. (1933-1940)
Pendlebury N. (1933-1937)	Porcher F.C. (1935-1940)	Potts K. (1934-1939)
Prosser P. (1930-1937)	Sherratt J.R. (1933-1937)	Shore J.E. (1934-1939)
Slingsby H.T. (1928-1933)	Smith J.N. (1928-1935)	Stanier A. (1927-1933)
Storey A.E. (1938-1941)	Taylor C.G. (1931-1937)	Warrington E.G. (1924-1929)
Whittaker A.W. (1927-1934)	Woods D.S. (1928-1935)	

Postscript: It is impossible to read the History of the King's School during the War without becoming aware of the wisdom and competence of its governing body, led by its Chairman, Brigadier-General Sir William Bromley-Davenport, KCB, CMG, CBE, DSO. The Mayor of Macclesfield was always an ex officio governor, and there were some half-dozen other governors, and a dozen representative governors appointed by the Cheshire County Council and by the Town Council of Macclesfield. Their support of the Headmaster and his staff was exemplary. In spite of staffing difficulties, and the extra commitments by all the boys in their own contribution to the War effort, the scholastic attainments of the school remained impressive.

I am grateful to the Headmaster and Bursar of the King's School for letting me sit in the school library and read the their archives.

King's School in 2002

A VOLUNTARY SCHEME

AT the monthly meeting of the Borough Education Committee on Friday, Alderman F. Wood presiding, the secretary (Mr. T. Mellor) stated he had received various circulars and regulations in regard to the employment of children in agricultural work. The Board of Education envisaged the employment of children over twelve years of age where necessary for ten school days in a year. Exemptions were to be granted only to meet urgent seasonal needs. The fact was stressed that holidays might have to be adjusted in the national interest. Wages must be not less than the statutory rate.

A.T.C.

(CONTRIBUTED BY F. BELFIELD)

ON SUNDAY I was one of 50 cadets of 201 (Macclesfield) Squadron chosen to pay a visit to an R.A.F. station. We packed into a 32-seater bus and duly arrived at the station.

First we were shown two films which impressed upon us the importance of keeping to ourselves whatever we saw inside the camp. The 25 cadets privileged to be taken for flights left us at this stage, whil the remainder of us were shown some useful films on aircraft recognition.

The parachute section next held our attention, for here we were shown how the airman's life-line (the parachute) opens, and how it is periodically examined and folded One cadet had a parachute strapped on, and was allowed to pull the rip cord to illustrate to us the actual opening of the parachute.

Next, the meteorological office captivated our interest. Here we were shown several different instruments what purpose they served, and how they were used; then listened to a short lecture on meteorology.

After examining several different types of aircraft we went to the firing range, where we joined the party who had been flying, and who had many varying experiences to relate. A machine-gun was loaded and we were shown how to handle it; then we were allowed to fire a short burst each at a target, behind which was a very necessary bank of sand.

By this time we were all feeling rather hungry, having been out in the keen weather all afternoon. The airmen's mess-room was a very welcome establishment, and here we had tea, after which a few words were addressed to us by the officer who had taken great care to see that our afternoon at the camp was really worth while.

Some cuttings from
the Macclesfield Express 1942

School Children To Help Farmers

Education Committee Agree
SCHOLARS MUST CARRY RESPIRATORS

What do I do . . .

to go "all out" for victory?

I SAVE everything I can for my local salvage campaign — paper, metal, bones, food scraps.

I SAVE gas, electricity, coal, paraffin and water.

I SAVE money wherever possible and put it into War Savings.

I SPEND every ounce of energy and every minute I can spare in War-winning work. I help local voluntary organisations and if I can, I dig for victory.

I KNOW that everyone, including *myself*, can do *something*.

Cut this out and keep it!

Issued by the Ministry of Information

Parachute workers in Macclesfield.
The caption for the middle one was
"RAF PILOTS WHOSE LIVES HAVE BEEN SAVED"

CHAPTER 4
The Population of Macclesfield during the Second World War
'At Work'

In 1939 Macclesfield was regarded as a fairly large town, certainly not so vast as Stockport to the north - with a population of about 130,000 and itself a huge adjoining suburb to Manchester - and not so large as Crewe to the south (with a population of some 48,000), but distinctly larger than many towns in the vicinity, such as Congleton, Leek and Buxton. It was an important industrial town, the pivot of a famous silk industry shared not only with Congleton but also with neighbouring Leek in Staffordshire.

This prominence in the silk industry resulted principally from two factors, one geographical, the other climatic. The first was the situation of the town in a strikingly beautiful bend of Pennine hills to its east and south. From those hills descended streams which provided the water for factory wheels at the beginning of the industrial revolution. The second was a dampish climate ideally suited to the prevention of frequent snapping of silk and cotton thread.

Macclesfield silk became famous. The streams which ran westward from the hills emptied themselves into the River Bollin, narrow and shallow, hardly a beautiful river but without it the town of Macclesfield through which it flowed would not have earned its living. The streams which left the hills in a south-westerly direction flowed into the attractive River Dane, which sustained the less pretentious silk mills of Congleton to the south of Macclesfield. Both rivers continued into the flat Cheshire Plain, discharging their water into the River Mersey (via the Manchester Ship Canal and the River Weaver respectively). So Macclesfield had steep hills in the east and a gentle plain in the west.

The silk industry started in the seventeenth century with the making of silk buttons. Soon cotton manufacturing followed but never recovered from the slump which occurred after the Napoleonic Wars. In the 1820s there were over 10,000 Macclesfield people engaged in the manufacture of silk. They worked a 62-hour week for a reward of eleven shillings, according to a report presented to the House of Commons in 1832 by the MP for Macclesfield, John Brocklehurst. Many of them did their weaving in the attics of specially built houses; and one can still see many houses in the town which boast the extra storey.

There was a decline in the silk industry as the nineteenth century progressed, and the work became concentrated in the mills themselves, but there were still many silk mills in Macclesfield in 1939, both large and small. Among the most prestigious were the Royal Depot Mills in Park Green, owned by Messrs J. Swindells Limited, and built on the site of Charles Roe's original mill erected in 1744 for the making of silk buttons. The water power for this mill, as for many others, came from the so-called Dams Brook or 'Water of E' (the medieval name for it, from the Scandinavian word 'ea' meaning river), a stream which emerges from the west of the town onto the fields behind Chiltern Avenue. There the stream clarifies itself, goes underground through man-made culverts and joins the River Bollin a few hundred yards beyond the Royal Depot Mills.

A nearby mill, also originally powered by the Dams Brook and a stone's throw away from the Royal Depot Mills, was the Pickford Street Mill of Messrs G.H. Heath & Co Ltd. In Park Lane, west of Park Green, were the mills of Josiah Smale and Sons Ltd, Messrs A.W. Hewetson, (Silk Embroiderers) and the Paradise Mills of Messrs Cartwright and Sheldon. These mills were also powered by the water of the Dams Brook.

In London Road, erected at the side of the River Bollin between 1840 and 1850, were the magnificent single Wilshaw Mill, owned by the Macclesfield Silk Manufacturing Society, and the dual Albion Mills. Just below them was another, Hewetson Mill. The same Bollin water had turned the wheels of the elegant factory of Messrs William Frost and Sons, which had been erected in 1785 and which, surmounted by a prominent black and white clock, looked down in 1939 upon the Great War Memorial in Park Green - and still does.

In Hurdsfield were the mills of Brocklehurst-Whiston Amalgamated Limited, a combination of silk throwsters and weavers with the Whiston hand-block and screen-printing firm at Langley, a village through which the young River Bollin flows on its way to Macclesfield. There was also Henry Leigh-Slater's in Chester Road, although this factory specialised principally in the production of cards and paper. In Elizabeth Street and St John's Road, the 'Dams Area' liable to flooding and surrounded by the Dams Brook, was the Dams Mill.

The Bollin Mills, owned by Josiah Smale and Brother, were situated in an area bounded by the River Bollin in the east, Brook Street in the south, Pickford Street in the north and George Street in the west. On Waters Green were the tall premises of Mr Edmund Lomas, opposite the Central station. The total number of silk factories and associated industries was in the region of eighty or ninety.

The production of silk, indeed of any fabric or manufactured article, has always depended upon the availability of raw materials. At first the sole source of supply for silk was the silk-worm. Sericulture was the name given to the process of silk-worm breeding and the production of pure silk. The 'pure silk' which this worm produced came to Great Britain, and especially to Macclesfield, from the Far East. In 1900 the Brocklehurst-Whiston Hurdsfield Silk Mills manufactured the first artificial silk fabrics ever made in the United Kingdom. The material used was called rayon.

When the Second World War broke out the silk mills of Macclesfield were using both pure silk and artificial silk in their production of fine material and clothing. The major supplier of the raw silk was Japan, which, in 1938 produced 38,000 metric tons out of a total world supply of 50,574. In addition to the general supply of raw silk Japan also provided the United Kingdom with the delicate light-weight silk fabric which was used for electrical insulation.

At the very beginning of World War ll, the Silk and Rayon Control, Ministry of Supply, was set up in Macclesfield under the Emergency Powers Act. At first the establishment of 15-16 employees, led by Mr Oswald Hamberton, worked in a mill in Elizabeth Street, but in 1940 moved into the Brocklehurst Memorial Hall, Queen Victoria Street, where it stayed until the summer of 1949. The government requisitioned all existing stocks of raw silk in September 1939 and, enlisting the careful management of the Silk and Rayon Control, stored it in two places - first in certain mills in Lancashire, second in some Cheshire Salt mines grouped around Northwich. Supplies continued to come into the Country throughout the War, their source depending upon the wartime relationship of Great Britain with the supplying countries.

Macclesfield at War

From 7th December 1941, Japan, attacking Pearl Harbor and thereby entering the War against Britain as well as the United States, ceased to send raw materials to the United Kingdom. It was now a question of seeking supplies from America, China, India, Cyprus, Syria and the Lebanon. Peter Gaddum of Macclesfield was seconded from the army to work during the remainder of the War for the Ministry of Supply. His responsibility was to obtain supplies of raw silk. He was based mainly in Beirut and necessarily travelled widely in the Middle East and India. In 1942 he bought from Turkey almost all its crop of silk cocoons and despatched them to Syria for reeling. After the fall of Italy he was sent to Rome to obtain further supplies of raw silk. His replacement in the Lebanon was Eric Whiston, another Macclesfield man. Their names are immediately recognisable as leaders of the Macclesfield Silk Industry. Peter Gaddum's experiences resulted in the eleven printings between 1948 and 1989 of the book *Silk*, under the auspices of H.T. Gaddum and Company, Silk Merchants of Macclesfield.

Not unexpectedly several ships bringing the raw silk to Great Britain were sunk by enemy action. The members of staff of Silk and Rayon Control monitored, by ciphered messages, the movements of all relevant transport ships and their varying ports of entry. They were also responsible for arranging the transportation of raw silk from the port of entry to mills throughout the country, to throwsters, spinners, weavers and knitters. Apart from the concentration of silk firms around Macclesfield, at Leek and Congleton, there were also factories in East Anglia and some in the west country, while Nottingham and Leicester prided themselves on the production of silk stockings.

Mainly the Ministry of Aircraft Production dictated what was to be produced - articles such as parachutes, parachute cords, and airmen's clothing, including gloves. Mr Wallace Ellison of Brocklehurst-Whiston Amalgamated gave a radio talk in November 1946 about the value of Macclesfield silk to the war effort. He gave details of dinghies, life-saving jackets (the so-called 'Mae Wests'), and slow-dropping flares for the detection of U-boats, all manufactured in Macclesfield. In addition he spoke of the bonded paper and silk discs which were used extensively as components in aircraft rockets which did so much damage after D-Day. He also praised the silk fabric oil-proofed saline bags used for the treatment of severe burns, silk mittens being less cumbersome to burned airmen than heavy bandages. In the jungle swift application of this saline oiled-silk helped check the dreaded blood poisoning. He also spoke of the more mundane uses of silk ribbons in naval uniform and gallantry decorations. Items demanded by other government agencies included surgical sutures, bolting cloth (used in the sieving of flour), silk maps and gunpowder packs. The latter, like many crude but necessary articles, were made from silk noils (short silk combings), the residue from low-grade silk-waste.

But the primary use of Macclesfield's silk was for the manufacturing of parachutes. Silk was strong and light and could be folded up into a very small space. Eighty square yards (67 square metres) were required to make a single parachute. The tasks of Peter Gaddum in his quest for raw silk in the Middle East during the war, and also of Oswald Hambleton and his staff at Silk and Rayon Control in Macclesfield, would have been easier if the United Kingdom had been able to develop the production of nylon - a high quality artificial silk made from chemicals - before the War. The U.S.A. developed a huge production of nylon during the War through the Du Pont Company. Indeed its GI's became famous for their presents of nylon stockings to young British women. Great Britain benefited more and more from supplies of American nylon as the War approached its end and the decision was taken to make parachutes out of this new material. An interesting factor was that such parachutes could only be used by bomber crews, nylon not having the qualities to fold tightly enough into the cockpits of fighter aircraft. On the other hand nylon parachutes were excellent for droppimg supplies and equipment over enemy territory.

Clearly the Silk and Rayon Control, based in Macclesfield and manned by some fifteen people, carried out a valuable task during the War. In 1946 it became part of the Board of Trade and the distribution of supplies of silk was gradually taken over by the Raw Silk Allocation Committee, under the direction of Mr Peter Gaddum. The Silk and Rayon Control was finally discarded in 1949.

Since silk was the fabric most suitable for the manufacture of parachutes, most of the parachutes used by the R.A.F. were made in Macclesfield, home of the British Silk Industry. The workers employed in the production of parachutes were faced with steady relentless work with occasional peak demands, such as those during the weeks and months after Dunkirk when replacement supplies wcre urgently required. One of the most vivid memories of these employees was the heat of the factories, not so much in the summer as during the blackout when the material used to keep in the light also excluded the cool air from the outside.

But many Macclesfield factories produced other essential items apart from silk during the course of the War. For example. although Messrs J.Dunkerley & Son Ltd of Oxford Road had been founded in 1837, and had become another famous Macclesfield silk mill, it was not parachutes which demanded its vigour and skills during the Second World War, but rather, at least in the first place, the so-called Frank's Flying Suits. Dunkerleys combined with the Dunlop Rubber Company in the production of these suits which were designed to lessen the effect of 'black-out' upon fighter pilots when they pulled out of power dives.

The expertise which Dunkerleys acquired led to the new development of Frogmen's suits under the direction of Departmental Manager J. Hagger, especially in the run-up to D-Day. Many experiments were necessary to perfect an undersuit absolutely watertight and ideal for the task of under-water investigation. Special machines were imported from the USA under the Lease-Lend agreement. Once all production decisions had been made, Dunkerleys combined again with Dunlop to produce these frog-suits.

Messrs E. Scragg & Sons, well known local engineers, based at premises in Sunderland Street, employed 300 workers during the War in various workshops scattered around Macclesfield. Their Shaw Street works produced thousands of 18lbs smoke shells and 6lbs practice shells. They also made many tank parts, including 'eccentric axles', which were used to tighten up the tank's tracks.

During the War itself Mr Vernon Sangster, Chairman of the Vernons' Organisation, started a new company, Vernon Industries Ltd, using premises in Athey Street and Wardle Street and employing several hundred people. The articles they manufactured were many and various and included complex equipment such as special containers and labelling, and sophisticated packaging for RAF use particularly. Vernons also produced 'Angels' Hair', which was the name given by German children to the streamers of aluminium foil released over enemy territory to confuse enemy radio-location instruments. This foil was known to Allied services as 'window'.

The well known Sutton firm Backhouse and Coppock, rising high above the River Bollin and the railway line to London produced a varied selection of articles, all of which contributed to the war effort. They too produced 'Angels' Hair'. They also manufactured bomb noses in their Mechanics' Shop. But their specialities were paper and board coatings, and cigarette and chocolate wrappers. The emphasis on tobacco is perhaps astonishing to human beings in the 21st century but during the War almost all men and many women smoked. Indeed smoking was generally regarded as a major comfort and morale-booster to all adults, let alone servicemen.

Many London firms like Messrs M. Belmont & Co, V. and E. Plastics, and Osband Brothers, came to Macclesfield with a nucleus staff and then recruited locally. Before the War Belmont and Co had been furriers and their speciality now became, not unnaturally, thick warm clothing. They sent 50,000 sheep-skin lined coats to the Red Army and designed these coats for other firms to produce. They provided 100,000 suits of battle-dress for the Forces, flying helmets for the RAF, scarves and tunics for the ATS, and sheep-skin coats for British transport drivers. Belmonts also took over part of the Macclesfield Courier and Herald building in King Edward Street. Here 100 employees worked far into the night making clothing for both men and women members of the forces - fireproof tank suits, paratroops' knee pads, Denim overalls, RAF trousers, ATS smocks, khaki battle-dress and greatcoats, and jungle suits. At the end of the War they switched their production to hundreds of 'demob raincoats'.

Shoes were also produced in Macclesfield. The best known shoe company in Macclesfield was the Castle Shoe Company, Waters Green and they produced 1,295,000 pairs of very varied type during the War The firm of Hovis - wholemeal bread manufacturers - had always been associated with Macclesfield, but when the Second World War broke out the Macclesfield premises, having stopped baking bread, had become the principal administrative centre of the firm. Then came the bombings of Manchester on 22/23 December 1940 and the Trafford Park Hovis buildings, where much Hovis bread was made, were totally destroyed. The decision was made to re-equip the Macclesfield premises for the manufacture of Hovis flour. Members of the Manchester Staff joined newly recruited local labour, and Macclesfield now became the source of supplies for almost all northern England. Hovis also ran a Van and Motor Works in Macclesfield during the War, producing vehicles for ENSA (Forces' entertainment), GPO vans, and ARP rescue vehicles and wheelbarrows.

All local firms found that their workforce was affected badly by call-up of both men and women. But, especially by enlisting the services of more and more women, (a policy which was to have a great influence not only on the postwar employment of women but on women's rights) these companies succeeded in maintaining a very high level of output. Throughout the War there were constant advertisements in the local press for new employees. Altogether the industrial vitality of Macclesfield during the War, combined with postwar developments such as the Hurdsfield Industrial Estate, propelled the town into the prosperous manufacturing base it now enjoys.

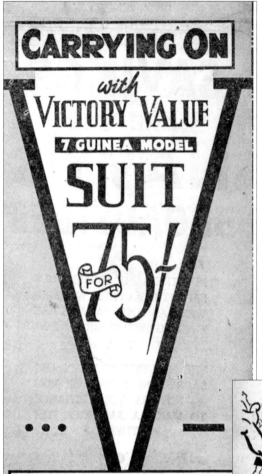
IRON RAILINGS DEMOLITION

THE WORK of removal of unnecessary iron and steel railings, etc., in the borough by contractors acting on behalf of the Ministry of Works and Buildings, will commence on or after 8th June, 1942.

It is hoped that owners will be prepared to make a contribution of their railings to the nation, but property owners and others whose interests are affected by the removal, and who desire to claim compensation, may obtain the appropriate form from the Senior Sanitary Inspector at the Town Hall.

The rate of compensation is 25/- per ton.

'Take my case'

says

Mrs. Faraway

" Keeping house for forty-five million people, as he does, is no joke, I'm sure,' says Mrs. Faraway. 'But all the same I do think Lord Woolton might have left our eggs alone. We country people never seem to find as much in our shops as you townsfolk do in yours—we can't make up with a tin of this or that. But we could, most weeks in the year, get eggs from the farm. Now you've taken even those from us. Is it fair? "

Do you remember, Mrs. Faraway, that in the winter of 1917-18 eggs cost as much as 9d. each? A very few could afford them. The others had to go without. In this war, too, in the towns, many people never had sight of an egg before the present scheme. Is it fairer for a very few people to have as many eggs as they please, or for everybody to have his two or three a month?

And as for buying 'a tin of this or that'—well, Mrs. Faraway, the Ministry of Food has made that possible for you now with the Points scheme.

Mind you, we don't pretend that everything in the garden is always lovely, Mrs. Faraway. Things are bound to be difficult in war-time and we have our troubles and make our mistakes too. We know you're doing a grand job on the Kitchen Front — so

 thank you, Mrs. Faraway!

FOOD FACTS No. 77.   THE MINISTRY OF FOOD, LONDON, W.1.

BLACK-OUT TIMES

THE following are the black-out times for to-day (Friday), Jan. 16th, to next Friday, Jan. 23rd:—

Jan. 18th—5·55 p.m. to 8·44 a.m.
Jan. 17th—5·53 p.m. to 8·45 a.m.
Jan. 18th—5·55 p.m. to 8·45 a.m.
Jan. 19th—5·56 p.m. to 8·43 a.m.
Jan. 20th—5·58 p.m. to 8·42 a.m.
Jan. 21st—6·0 p.m. to 8·40 a.m.
Jan. 22nd—6·2 p.m. to 8·39 a.m.
Jan. 23rd—6·3 p.m. to 8·38 a.m.

UNARMED COMBAT

You've seen her—she's knocked at your door. Her weapons are a note-book, a supply of Savings Stamps— and her grim determination to help win the war. Ask her in and she will convince you that the savings of every one of us are a vital part in our fight. Give her a hand. Join her group. Don't spend a penny on anything you can do without, and with the money you save every week buy Savings Certificates. Buy them through a Savings Group —or, if you prefer, through a Post Office or Trustee Savings Bank.

BUY SAVINGS CERTIFICATES

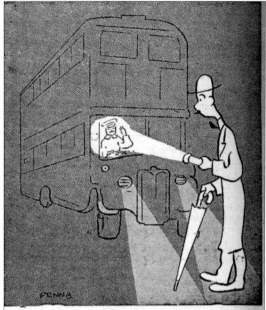

Ophelia Snodkins loved to ride
On the crown of the road instead of the side.
No signal she gave as she swerved to the right,
So a sprightly young life met its end that night.
Let Ophelia's ghost be a warning to you
If you wish to live to a hundred and two.

LOOK OUT IN THE BLACK-OUT!

A careless man, Ezekiel Clowne,
He would not keep his torchlight down!
He flashed it in the Driver's face,
Really a most regrettable case.
Ezekiel now will never see
The Brave New World that's going to be.

LOOK OUT IN THE BLACKOUT

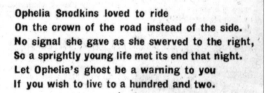

Mis-Use Of Petrol Alleged

Gawsworth Fete Sequel

A NUMBER of defendants appeared at the Macclesfield County Petty Sessions held at the Town Hall on Tuesday, for the mis-use of petrol, and in every case fines were imposed. In three of the cases the defendants were summoned for attending the Oak Cottage charity fete at Gawsworth on August 3rd. Another appeared for taking a dance band to an Aid-to-Russia effort at Eaton, while another was summoned for taking his car a short distance for the purpose of testing the engine after it had been de-carbonised.

For your TRAVEL COMFORT

HAVE YOUR TICKET READY—The fumbler is a travelling highwayman—he holds up fellow travellers and robs them and the Railway of time.

⋆

GET YOUR WEEKLY "SEASON" ON SATURDAY EVENING OR SUNDAY MORNING and cut out the Monday Morning queue.

⋆

CLOSE THE CARRIAGE DOOR—this will help the depleted platform staff to get the train away quickly.

⋆

KEEP SEATS FREE OF L yourself and other passe

and

Travel only wh

BRITISH R

G W R   L M S

MINISTRY **MF** OF FOOD

SOAP RATIONING

FROM MONDAY, FEBRUARY 9TH, soap may be bought only against a coupon or buying permit. The oils and fats used in soap manufacture occupy much shipping space, and some of this must be saved for food. You will have 4 coupons in each 4-weekly period, and will be able to use these how and when you like within the period. There will be no registration, and you may buy from any shop stocking the kind you require.

Each of the four coupons which make up a four-weeks' ration will entitle you to any one of

either
4 ozs. Hard Soap (common Household Soap in bars or pieces)
or 3 ozs. Toilet Soap
or 3 ozs. Soap Flakes or Chips
6 ozs. Soap Powder No. 1
12 ozs. Soap Powder No. 2
6 ozs. Soft Soap.

to shaving soaps or dental iquid soap, or scourers.

re those in the frame at the LLOW BOOK (RB 9)—the pon numbers and periods will nd tea, *so that you will start* he first period—February 9th -28 are of no value.

out, but must be cancelled ink or indelible pencil.

RVICES, ETC.

ration Card (RB 8 X) will use the m of page 4. Holders of Leave ill use the coupons marked "Y" ill be issued to other members of holding Ration Book RB 6 will on the last green page (leaf 11).

Always
ON ACTIVE SERVICE

IN the long armistice which followed the "cease fire" in 1918, British Railways instituted developments and improvements which could not have been more wisely planned had they known beyond doubt that hostilities would be resumed in 1939.

Many millions of money were expended on widening tracks, improving signalling, removing bottlenecks and in a hundred and one other ways which gave the public the fine trains and high speeds

prevailing before the war The railways carried through these improvements during a period of acute depression when they were suffering grave loss year after year.

Their courage and foresight have stood the Nation in good stead — for these years of intensive development have made it possible now for British Railways to carry smoothly and efficiently the vast burden of additional freight and passenger services so vital to the war effort.

BRITISH RAILWAYS
GWR · LMS   LNER · SR

Police Flash-Light Patrol

Couples Before Court For Indecency

AS the result of a Police flash-light patrol that has been instituted by the Chief Constable (Mr. R. Alderson) following complaints of the conduct of young people in the streets of the town late at night, a number of persons appeared at the Borough Police Court on Friday. There were two cases of intercourse to the annoyance of passengers. In the first, fines were imposed, but in the second the defendant was given the benefit of the doubt.

Prison Sentences

FOLLOWING a police raid on a house in Bridge Street—No. 69,—in the early hours of last Saturday morning, two women and a girl appeared at the Borough Police Court on Wednesday. The house had been under observation for several days, and the raid followed frequent visits to the house by American soldiers.

Three Moss Estate People Heavily Fined

FINES totalling £80 were imposed on three Moss Estate persons at the Borough Police Court on Friday for over-charging. The offences took place at a grocery and provision shop at 2, Stamford Road, and the excess charge was 3d. in one case and a halfpenny in each of three others.

9-30 'Bus Curfew

How Macclesfield Is Affected

DRASTIC CURTAILMENTS HAVE BEEN MADE IN THE LOCAL AND DISTRICT 'BUS SERVICES BY THE NORTH WESTERN ROAD CAR COMPANY, LTD.

This decision, which was fully expected, has been made following negotiations between the Company and the Traffic Commissioners to effect petrol and rubber economies, and to bring this area into line with other parts of the country.

A 9-30 p.m. curfew has been imposed on all routes, while on Sundays very few services will commence before 1 p.m.

The new times become operative as from Sunday next, December 20th, and we publish below a summary of the time-table alterations:—

Notice signs in the countryside were
painted out to fool invaders.
Ration books and identity cards

Issue of *new* RATION BOOKS

YOU NEED 1. Your present Ration
Book with Reference leaf filled in.
2. Your Identity Card.

WHERE TO GO

MACCLESFIELD

	Monday to Friday, May 18th to 29th.	Saturday May 23rd and 30th.
The Food Office, King Edward street, MACCLESFIELD.	9 a.m. to 9 p.m.	9 a.m. to 4 p.m.
The C. of E. School, BROKEN CROSS.	6 p.m. to 9 p.m.	Closed.
St. George's Schoolroom, London Road, MACCLESFIELD.	6 p.m. to 9 p.m.	Closed.

1. This Identity Card must be carefully preserved. You may need it under conditions of national emergency for important purposes. You must not lose it or allow it to be stolen. If, nevertheless, it is stolen or completely lost, you must report the fact in person at any local National Registration Office.

2. You may have to show your Identity Card to persons who are authorised by law to ask you to produce it.

3. You must not allow your Identity Card to pass into the hands of unauthorised persons or strangers. Every grown up person should be responsible for the keeping of his or her Identity Card. The Identity Card of a child should be kept by the parent or guardian or person in charge of the child for the time being.

4. Anyone finding this Card must hand it in at a Police Station or National Registration Office.

...IONAL REGISTRATION

JJO 15 3

...rown William

DO NOTHING WITH THIS PART UNTIL YOU ARE TOLD

Full Postal Address of Above Person :—

(Signed)

Date

NATIONAL REGISTRATION IDENTITY CARD

Land Girls

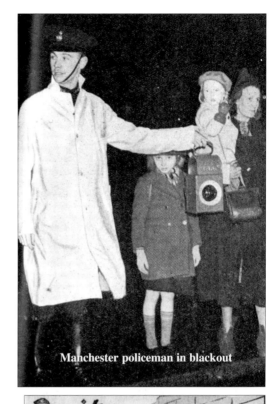

Manchester policeman in blackout

Tanks for Attack

THIS TANK'S READY

Will it go into battle bearing your district's name?

Everything you put into —
National Savings Certificates, Defence Bonds and
the Post Office or Trustee Savings Bank counts

Do it NOW!

CHESHIRE COUNTY SALVAGE DRIVE

May 30 · June 13

KITCHEN WASTE

RUBBER

PAPER

METAL

RAGS

BONES

Warship Choice

A DESTROYER

THE SHIP that Macclesfield and District are out to purchase during Warships Week is a destroyer. This decision was made at a meeting of Macclesfield National Savings Committee on Monday evening, when Alderman T. M. Abraham, J.P. (Chairman of the Committee) presided. He was supported by the Hon. General Secretary (Mr. T. Meade), the Hon. Secretary (Mr. J. Upton), and the Hon. Treasurer (Mr. M. Poloway). Apologies were received from the Mayor (Alderman C. W. Kirk), and the Deputy Mayor (Councillor F. Baron).

Now that the Macclesfield Rural District Council have announced their intention of joining the Borough, it is expected that Bollington will do likewise, and a resolution was passed at the meeting recommending that the target should be £700,000, the complete cost of a destroyer. Another important item discussed was the date —and the suggested week is March 14th to 21st.

MACCLESFIELD & DISTRICT
WARSHIP WEEK
MARCH 14th to 21st

TARGET - £700,000
Help Us To Provide That Destroyer!

SIR EARLE PAGE
(Australia's Representative in the Imperial War Cabinet)
will speak on
"THE FAR EASTERN SITUATION"
AT THE
MASS MEETING
IN THE
Drill Hall, Macclesfield,
Saturday Evening, March 14th,
at 7-30

HE WILL BE SUPPORTED BY—
Mr. W. GARFIELD WESTON,
M.P., AND OTHERS.

WATCH THIS SPACE FOR FURTHER ANNOUNCEMENTS.

Warship Target Well Beaten

March 14th — 21st
MACCLESFIELD BOROUGH R.D. & BOLLINGTON
OBJECTIVE £700,000
The cost of a Destroyer

Turn Out Every Pound

Then 'Teazer' Will Be Ours

MACCLESFIELD and District and Bollington are within striking distance of their target of £700,000 for Warship Week, and with four days to go are little more than £250,000 short of their objective. This is magnificent progress, but though the "half-way house" has been well passed, there is still a large amount to be raised, and it will only be by a united effort of the whole of the people in the town and districts that H.M.S. Teazer, the destroyer that has been allocated, will be completely purchased.

CHAPTER 5
The Population of Macclesfield during the Second World War
'At Play'

The five Macclesfield cinemas were the most striking source of the town's entertainment in the 1920s and 1930s. They did, however, receive considerable competition from within the town, not least from the Repertory Theatre, based on the Liberal Club premises in Victoria Street, and taken over by the Bancroft Players after the Theatre Royal (later known as the Opera House) in Catherine Street had been burnt down in 1931. Various other stage performances took place in several halls - the Stanley Hall in Castle Street, the Beehive Café in Sunderland Street and the Town Hall itself.

Many churches and chapels had regular social evenings ('socials') or whist drives, concerts or parties. Regular dances were held in dancing schools, the Brocklehurst Memorial Hall in Queen Victoria Street, the Stanley Hall and in other halls and church halls.

Competition for the cinemas was also provided by the huge number of public houses in the town. Virtually every street had its pub, small, cosy, intimate, especially attractive to the menfolk of Macclesfield. Altogether there was more than a little entertainment available in the evenings in pre-war Macclesfield. However at least one half of the inhabitants of Macclesfield went once a week to the cinema before the War. This habit continued during the War itself and, indeed, increased in intensity as the town became filled with evacuees and billeted troops.

It so happened that the War years marked a significant peak of excellence for British films. Although American films were far more plentiful and did much to entertain Macclesfield's swollen population, some outstanding British films of the period have stood the test of time and, in some cases, have become known to generations who were not born until after the War. Such films include *The Battle of the River Plate*, *Coastal Command*, *The Stars Look Down*, *Love on the Dole*, *Convoy*, *The 49th Parallel*, *One of Our Aircraft is Missing*, and *In Which We Serve*. All of these were released in the early part of the War.

Of course, not all films, American or British, were good. But a wartime Social Survey discovered that three quarters of adults went to the cinema, and about a third of them went at least once a week. Most teenagers between 14 and 17 went once a week and nearly half went twice a week.

In the autumn of 1939, once the initial panic over the probability of bombs falling on packed cinemas had evaporated, the cinemas of Macclesfield, like most in the country, settled down to providing excellent relaxation and entertainment for the town's population and for the troops and evacuees billeted in the town. To impress a girl friend a young man had to buy tickets in the balcony of the prestigious Majestic. He would never offer to take her to the Regal Cinema in Duke Street, the so-called 'Bug Hut', for although there was a balcony of sorts and although seat prices were low, there was little comfort. In the pit the seats were benches and leaning back was a hazardous occupation. The Picturedrome held second place after the Majestic. Although there was no balcony, the floor rose gently towards the back, where the most expensive seats were. The Premier Cinema resembled the Picturedrome in structure and was indeed a lovely building but did not quite possess the cachet of the Picturedrome or the Majestic. The New Cinema, at the bottom of Buxton Road, was also similarly constructed with a sloping pit and no balcony but it was less central than the other four cinemas.

Outstanding films normally made their first appearance in Macclesfield at the Majestic and then returned perhaps two or three years later to one of the other cinemas. One corollary of this was that not a few pre-war films were shown at the Regal and the New Cinema during the War itself. There was doubtless a pecking order of cinema preference, recognised by the people of Macclesfield - Majestic, Picturedrome, Premier, New Cinema, Regal. Comfort, type of films, cleanliness of the building, noise level of unwelcome participation by the audience, graded costs of admission to a variety of seats - and perhaps other criteria - confirmed this pecking order.

The Regal was not a great financial success. It is noticeable that, once the War was under way, it never advertised itself in the *Macclesfield Courier and Herald*, only in the *Macclesfield Times and Observer*. Before the War the cheapest Regal seats were 2d - prospective clients thought in terms of 2d, 4d and 6d, whereas for the other four cinemas they thought along the line of 3d, 6d, 9d. The Majestic prices again were always higher than were the prices at the Cinema, the Picturedrome and the Premier. In May 1942 the Regal prices made the psychological jump to 6d, 9d, and 1/- (including tax) - at that time the prices of the superior seats at the Majestic were 1/6 -and 2/-, while the cheapest seats, at the very front of the stalls, were 9d.

It must be mentioned that, in practice, the directors of four cinemas - the Majestic, the Picturedrome, the Premier and the 'Cinema' - were the same, even though the Premier nominally had its own Board of Directors and issued its separate minutes of its meetings. A phenomenon associated with this unity of the four establishments was that a boy on a bicycle was hired to take the newsreel (be it Gaumont British or Movietone, forerunners of modern television news) from one cinema to another twice an evening. Of course this meant that each programme had to be individually planned to harmonise with that of the others.

Several factors need to be mentioned in connection with national cinema-going. First the big London cinemas, together with those of other cities, normally provided a continuous three-hour programme which included live organ-playing - in the interval a huge organ, complete with organist, would rise up well in front of the screen. This did not happen in Macclesfield but inhabitants of the town were aware that some Manchester cinemas enjoyed the privilege. In Macclesfield there would normally be two separate two-hour programmes (called 'houses') each evening - 6-30 pm to 8-30 pm and 8-30pm to 10-30pm. Although there would be, in addition to the main film, local advertisements, the news, a documentary and small governmental war-time films, the Macclesfield programmes were less full than those in the big cities, where an additional supporting 'B' film was expected.

The Majestic and the Picturedrome benefited from the outstanding films being shown. It was usual for the cinemas except the Majestic, and often the Picturedrome, to have one programme for Monday, Tuesday and Wednesday; and a separate programme for Thursday, Friday and Saturday. On the whole the Majestic had first choice of the most recent outstanding releases, second choice going to the Picturedrome. In 1943 *Mrs Miniver* was booked for a 6 days' continuous run at the Picturedrome. It had already had one week at the

Majestic in the week ending 14 November 1942 . This film, starring Greer Garson, told most effectively the story of the wartime hardships, but stern resolve, of a British family and was regarded as an excellent morale-booster. The booking of *In Which We Serve* - an outstanding film about the Royal Navy - received triumphant mention at the meeting of the Majestic Directors on 29 January 1943 as did the American *Gone with the Wind* on 14 May 1943 - *'hired for two weeks from 31 May at £600 per week'*. In the week beginning Monday 10 August 1942 the Majestic Cinema was showing the important war film, *One of our Aircraft is Missing*, starring Eric Portman and Googie Withers, and directed by the powerful combination of Michael Powell and Emeric Pressburger. This film was a British National production which had only been released one month earlier, in July 1942.

The Regal was showing in the first part of the same week a gangster film 'Double Cross' with a virtually unknown actor, Kane Richmond. In the second part of the week it showed *Old Mother Riley in Paris*, with Arthur Lucan and Kitty McShane, one of a series of very popular slapstick comedies, shown at other cinemas in the first few months of the War. The films shown at the Regal Cinema, entertaining though they may have been to a large number of people, were not so recent or of such good quality or in such demand as those shown at the Majestic. In spite of its unprepossessing appearance both inside and out the Regal enjoyed a certain jocular affection amongst the people of the town. It closed on Saturday, 24 March 1962. Briefly it became a Night Club but is now a derelict building.

In 1956 the New Cinema closed; two years later the Premier showed its last film. The Picturedrome became a Bingo Hall in the course of the 1970s - and still is. The Majestic looks exactly the same - a resplendent building with a striking façade. But it stopped showing films in 1997 and, in 2000 became a huge bar and restaurant called The Litten Tree, part of a growing chain throughout the country.

It was usual to have all five cinemas well attended during the winter, less so during the summer, not least because many outdoor attractions existed. One advantage of living in a town the size of Macclesfield was that it was possible to get into the country quickly. Both the hills in the east and the plains in the west inspired most families, especially in the spring and summer, to indulge in country outings.

Then there were the town parks. The ornate and landscaped West Park with its 16 acres was opened in 1854. The less popular and more isolated Victoria Park (12 acres) was presented to the town in 1894 by Francis Dicken Brocklehurst JP. The land bought by John Ryle, silk and cotton manufacturer, in 1787, eventually became - in 1922 - the spacious and lovely South Park.

The firm link in the Macclesfield area between town and country had been strengthened during generations by the regular week-end markets in the town. The Market Place itself was sited around the Town Hall and the 'Parish Church' (St Michael's), on the prominent hill which towered - and still towers - above Waters Green and which, with its ascent of 108 steps, has been the major feature of Macclesfield since its earliest days. The low-lying Waters Green opposite what was the railway's Central Station and what is now the town's only railway station, also housed week-end market stalls The farmers from the outlying villages, hills and plains were known for their milk and eggs and chickens; and for the places they occupied in the market stalls from week to week.

A considerable amount of sport took place in the town before the Second World War.

The Macclesfield Football team, first founded in 1873, had joined the Cheshire League when this league was first formed in 1919 and had enjoyed conspicuous success in the league championships as well as in the Challenge Cup Competitions. The Macclesfield Cricket Club, already established by 1845, had acquired the reputation of being formidable competitors in the Lancashire and Cheshire League well before 1939. Rugby Football, first played in the town in 1873, but discontinued, became firmly established in 1926, and in 1939 was playing full fixture lists at its Fallibroome ground. Golf, tennis, hockey, fishing, cycling and swimming had their strong adherents in the town.

Clearly the two privileged secondary schools in the town - the King's School for boys and the High School for girls - were able to offer their pupils a much wider choice of more intensively pursued and coached sports than were the Central, Elementary and Primary schools. Rugby, Cricket, Athletics, and Fives dominated at the King's School; Hockey and Netball at the High School. These activities resulted in the greater ability of the pupils of these two schools to practise sport in later life, not least in the town itself. But the Central Schools and even Primary Schools gave their pupils the opportunity to swim (at the Public Baths in Davenport Street), to play football (inter-school matches were organised) and cricket (alas, usually without the advantage of good pitches, rough wickets in a park being the norm).

A most successful annual event was the inter-school athletics competition on the Moss Rose Football ground. Inter-school football matches were plentiful. The three principal venues were the Cottage Street ground, the Central School playing field and the Puss Bank ground. Schools like Mill Street, Athey Street, St George's and the Central School, played matches which attracted many pupils. I remember watching a final played between the Central School and Athey Street School on the Puss Bank ground which was watched by hundreds of people. A boy called Hyde played wonderfully for the Central School. Another boy called Davies, a member of the Mill Street team, had the reputation amongst Macclesfield's schoolchildren which Beckham now enjoys internationally.

Like many Midlands and Northern towns Macclesfield had its specific holiday week or, in some cases, fortnight. But unlike most other towns, whose holiday periods were usually referred to as 'Wakes', Macclesfield had its own name for this holiday period, 'Barnaby', based on St Barnabas Day, which was originally 11 June but which was pushed back to 22 June by the Gregorian Calendar of 1752. Traditionally this was when all silk and other mills closed down and many workers went on holiday. A large number went to Blackpool in Lancashire or to Rhyl in North Wales and helped to fill the thousands of boarding houses in those two resorts. One disadvantage of the boarding house was that you were expected to be out of the house from breakfast to supper time. Those depressing photographs of coastal resort holiday makers, huddled together in shelters to protect themselves from the wind and rain, stemmed at least partially from this boarding house regulation. Comfort existed much less in those days than now. People who professed to enjoy quieter holidays chose Southport. The discerning and adventurous went to Scarborough.

Not a few, remembering that the countryside around Macclesfield was extremely beautiful, contented themselves by staying at home, punctuating their freedom from work with bus trips to Langley or Rainow. Some walked to Prestbury in order to sit at the side of the River Bollin, where it was possible to obtain for one penny a jug of tea so long as you had brought the necessary amount of dry tea leaves in a little paper bag. Of course you had to bring your own drinking vessels too. Others caught the bus to Langley and then walked on into the Macclesfield Forest or even climbed up and over Shutlingsloe, dropping down into Wildboarclough.

What was astonishing about the sport in wartime Macclesfield, particularly cricket, was that it continued so successfully. Sports throughout the United Kingdom were hit in September 1939 by the government's decree (first issued in a memorandum on 3 September, less than six hours after the declaration of war) against large crowds, gatherings and audiences - lest they should become scenes of carnage from air raids. At first this injunction was carried out meticulously - for example, *'Macclesfield Wednesday FC'*, reported the local newspaper on 7 September 1939, *'who were to have played the Pawnbrokers on the Puss Bank ground* (by the canal on Buxton Road) *yesterday in their first match of the season, cancelled the game in view of the government's decree on football'*.

Official football and cricket leagues were discontinued; in any case national call-up was soon to render maintenance of standards impossible. But the feeling was strong that participation in sport was 'good for the war effort', providing release from the commitments of Civil Defence, the care of evacuees, Home Guard duties, and the production of industrial and war weapons.

In May 1940 it did not seem that much had changed on the cricket scene. *The Macclesfield Courier and Herald* of the 16 May 1940 gave details of friendly matches played by Macclesfield, Bollington and Stand, all previous staunch members of the Lancashire and Cheshire League. Macclesfield had defeated Stand who understandably regretted the recent departure of some of their best young cricketers into the forces. Ironically - for this was the time of the rush of the British and Allied armies to Dunkirk - the same newspaper reported two weeks later: *'Peace time, with its professionals and other luxuries, has produced no more thrilling climax to a Macclesfield - Bollington match than the one which was seen at Bollington Recreation ground on Saturday. It was with the very last ball of the game that the home side ended the Macclesfield innings with two runs to spare.'*

But the disappearance of league cricket did mean that the Macclesfield X1 was now able to play neighbouring teams which had not featured in the Lancashire and Cheshire League. In May 1941 they played Leek, in June Manchester University and Alderley Edge, in July Buxton, in August Cheadle Hulme, and in September Leek again. Other Macclesfield local sides were Langley, the Maxonians, Parkside Hospital, the silk firm Langley BWA (Brocklehurst-Whiston Amalgamated), and Belmonts, the textiles firm which had been evacuated from London to Macclesfield.

Meanwhile teams from the Forces, the Home Guard, the Police, and the National Fire Service, began to feature in Sports reports. In 1943 the Macclesfield Cricket Club's fixture list included the King's School, Bollington, Didsbury, the Royal Artillery, Fairey Aviation Works, Manchester University, Heaton Mersey, an RAF team, a Royal Artillery team and 'Cheshire Wayfarers'. Bollington was the only match which had been a normal peacetime fixture. Significantly, in May 1944 however, Macclesfield played Levenshulme, Cheadle Hulme and Bollington, all previous members of the Lancashire and Cheshire League. It was as if one could now see beyond the War to renewed peace.

The practice of Cricket seems to have survived in Macclesfield far better than any other team sport. Golf, dependent on older men perhaps, survived well and even competitive angling had its moments - in July 1942 both the Lord Desborough and the Victoria Angling Societies enjoyed competitions. But football fell away at many levels.

So far as the schools were concerned the King's School was pre-eminent, not only in cricket (in which sport it supplied numerous players to the stronger local clubs), but strikingly so in Rugby, and satisfactorily so in Shooting and Fives. The High School continued to give its girls opportunities in Hockey and Netball. But the wonderful system of Inter Elementary Schools' Athletics, Football and Cricket which had taken place in the 1930s disappeared - the call-up of young staff, the shock of receiving evacuees in the first two terms of war, and the loss of pitches to wartime needs (air raid shelters in parks and on local authority games' fields, both of which also sustained military training and vehicle maintenance) seem to have been contributory factors.

Clearly then the War damaged the sporting activities of the people of Macclesfield. But cricket flourished, in spite of the tremendous attention which cricket pitches require, to such an extent that one is tempted to think that the very nature of the game was of significance to the people of Macclesfield. Sufficient sport generally was practised throughout the War to enable the town's clubs to return for the most part after the War.

Did people go on holiday during the War? Yes, they did. But wartime produced different needs, different objectives, different principles in this sphere as in so many others. The government encouraged holidays at home to lessen wear and tear on railway rolling stock (the requirements for the moving of servicemen and war material by rail were enormous) and to stimulate savings. Local councils took upon themselves the responsibility for organising holidays at home. In 1942, for example, the Macclesfield Borough Council discussed on Wednesday 3rd June a 'stay-at-home Barnaby'. Yet another opportunity was thereby given to make full use of the parks of the town. The West Park would host dancing round the bandstand on the first Saturday, a concert on Sunday, and, on the Thursday afternoon a Children's Concert, a Punch and Judy Show, and a Talent Competition. In the evening a display was to be given by the Home Guard (now two years old), with music by the Air Training Corps band. On the second Saturday evening there was to be an All Star Variety Concert, supported by the new Macclesfield Augmented Orchestra, which was to play again the next day in the evening.

A week later, at the end of the holiday fortnight, the famous Foden Motor Works Band would play to complete the holiday activities in the West Park. The South Park had a similar programme with dancing, music, a cabaret and a Civil Defence display, but in addition the venue was to be used for a rejuvenated Inter Schools Sports Competition lasting two days. There was also to be a 'Victory Parade' with a cavalcade, professional artists and an augmented orchestra.

The urge for community activities spilled over into the next few weeks and months and, indeed, became a feature of wartime living. For example, in July 1942, inspired by councillors of the Entertainment and Sports Committee, a very successful Field Day took place at Langley on the BWA Print Works' Cricket ground. There were games, competitions and side shows and the entries for the sports numbered 300.

Although similar arrangements were made in 1943 there was a lesser inclination on the part of the population to stay at home. Indeed *the Macclesfield Courier and Herald* reported as follows: *'Macclesfield people did not respond well to the government's appeals of "Is your journey really necessary?"* There were long queues at the two stations on the Saturday morning (20th June), those for the Central Station stretching to the bottom of Sunderland Street. *The trains were crowded and most people had much luggage, in many cases packed with food.* 2700 people (700 more than in 1942) went to Blackpool, and 700 to Llandudno. Some 1500 others travelled to Manchester on Monday 22nd June, some to spend the day there, others to go to places beyond Manchester.

By Barnaby 1944 the situation had changed. The opening of the 'Second Front' - the Normandy landings by Allied troops on 6th June - probably gave people the feeling that they would be helping the Allied troops more by staying at home. In any case three holiday trains were cancelled at the last moment. Nevertheless 2000 people went off to Blackpool and even more to North Wales, while each day some 1000 travelled as far as Manchester, mainly on day trips.

But the local authorities had made adequate provision for those who wanted to stay at home. Planning for the Holiday at Home had begun on 7th March 1944 and a special council sub-committee was set up to deal with the first week of the Barnaby Holidays. Arrangements were confirmed on 13th June 1944. The programme included concerts in the West Park on Wednesday 28th June by the Fairey Aviation Works Band - at a cost of £30 to the council - and in the Victoria and West Parks on Saturday afternoon and evening respectively (1 July) by the Foden Motor Works' Band - at a total cost of £45. Other events were a Schools Swimming Gala on Tuesday 27th June in the Swimming Baths in Davenport Street, open Bowling competitions, and evening cricket matches between the Home Guard and Civil Defence.

When the Borough's Cemetery and Parks Committee met on 13th March 1945, the American troops had already crossed the Rhine (at Remagen on 7th March). There seemed no need to arrange Barnaby Holidays at home for that year - and no plans were therefore made.

It is perhaps no exaggeration to say that the parks of Macclesfield had never been used so much or so purposefully as they were during the Second World War. It was not just the result of Holidays at Home, but rather of all the opportunities for parades, gatherings and common activities provided by the many Charity weeks together with military, Home Guard and Civil Defence demonstrations. These wartime phenomena did not lead to any developments after the War, as did so many other features of wartime living connected to industry, schools and hospitals. But they did help to give people a sense of common purpose.

The halls and church halls and clubs which had provided such competition in the evenings for the cinemas of the town before the War continued to flourish during the War in spite of the black-out. From April to early August 1942 the following featured amongst the events advertised in the Macclesfield Times. On Friday 31 April 1942 there was a 'big musical event' in the Morton Hall, where in May the Hovis (amateur) Players gave a performance of J.B. Priestley's *When we are married*. The Bancroft (professional) Players put on G.B. Shaw's *Candida* in the week ending 16 May and *Addresses will Happen* by Walter Ellis two weeks later. A series of whist drives were organised for charities by Mrs W.E. Poole of Victoria Road, raising over £100. In August the Bancroft Players performed J.B. Priestley's *Laburnum Grove*. During this period of three or four months something like a dozen 'social evenings', 'choir concerts' or other concerts had taken place at the 50 or so church buildings in the town; amateur groups like the 'Young Rascals' based on Townley Street Sunday School, or the Central School Old Boys, had produced variety evenings or plays; schools had enjoyed their own plays or concerts; and the Town Hall, Stanley Hall, Morton Hall, Beehive Café and the Dancing Schools had held many dances, especially on Saturday evenings. The hundreds of public houses, large and small, had been well patronised, not least by the American 9th Armoured Division now moving into the town. Hence there was no shortage of evening entertainment in Macclesfield quite apart from the cinemas. And at home a main source of information and entertainment was the wireless and the enormously successful BBC programmes.

In the winter of 1943-1944 my brother Norman and I were given two tickets for an evening of entertainment at the Beehive Café in Sunderland Street. We groped our way through the black-out and mounted the stairs to the room above the Co-op's Furniture Department. Various local amateur entertainers sang, cracked jokes or performed musical items. There was an interval when small sandwiches and cakes and cups of tea were consumed. The whole atmosphere was pleasant, indeed jolly. It was a very civilised evening.

The popularity of country walks probably increased in Macclesfield during the War. Certainly it was during this time that I developed a love, which I have never lost, for the countryside surrounding the town. My eagerness to walk to Wildboarclough was also inspired by the fact that, in spite of wartime rationing, it was possible to enjoy a cheap and reasonably substantial meal at the Stanley Arms at the eastern end of the valley. More often than not I would go with my brother or school friends. Our intention was to create an appetite by brisk walking and then finish up at the Stanley Arms. We would walk to Langley (or occasionally take a bus there), whatever the weather or season, make our way through the village, walk between Tegg's Nose reservoir and Bottoms reservoir and eventually enter into those dense areas of trees which we called The Plantations. After about an hour of semi-darkness in the trees we emerged onto a path which overlooked the Stanley Arms, and we observed the comforting curls of smoke from the building's chimneys.

The name Stanley was associated with Lord Derby, traditional owner of much land in this as in other areas of the country. But it was a very appropriate name, for the main provider of meals was a man called Stanley. Stanley was a strange person who seemed to be permanently middle-aged. Pleasant and courteous, he was nevertheless a little remote, unwilling to lengthen a conversation and seldom hasarding a smile. He was slightly effeminate in manner and seemed to spend most of his time preparing and serving meals in a wooden hut which had been erected at the side of the public house. Much of the width of the hut was filled with some five or six trestle tables, neatly covered with white tea cloths. Whatever time of the day you always received the same meal. This consisted of a thin slice of meat in the middle of a small plate, a container of pickled onions, a large plate of bread and margarine, pieces of home-made cake, some home-made jam, and a large tea-pot with a jug of milk. (Wartime rationing did make certain allowances to cafés, restaurants and other eating places).

We made this meal last for hours, asking for frequent refills of hot water, no matter how weak the resultant tea was. If we were bold, as we sometimes were, we also asked for more bread and margarine, hoping that we would not be reprimanded in some way for our cheek. Stanley however always complied with our wishes without a hint of reproach. There was an oil lamp in the hut and a weak gas light attached to the ceiling. We paid one shilling and nine pence for this tea and had no complaints. Whether Stanley made any profit out of us is questionable.

Invariably during the War at Easter time we would go into the country, especially into the hills, in an endeavour to acquire a sense of freedom and peace and joyfulness. One Good Friday we were walking in Wildboarclough when we were passed by a Royal Marine Commando in full regalia, including his clanging regulation boots. He seemed a little out of place. He was extremely smart, proud in the nicest possible way, healthy, strong, vigorous, walking as if he were marching in a platoon. He glanced at us totally unembarrassed and strode on. Some time later he passed us going in the opposite direction. Everything about him was the same, except that this time he was smoking a cigarette. We looked at him inquisitively and he stared us out. We realised that he had probably changed direction simply in order to buy cigarettes at the Crag Inn which we had now left behind us. I wondered what he was doing - perhaps just going home on week-end leave, having left a train or bus at some inconvenient place and then deciding to walk the rest of the way? Was he going to survive the War or possibly perish half way up a cliff as he struggled to engage the defending enemy soldiers?

BRITISH RESTAURANT.

PARK GREEN RESTAURANT

WILL BE OPENED ON

WEDNESDAY, 4th MARCH, 1942, at 11-30 a.m.

Mid-day meal will be served each week-day between 11-45 a.m. and 2-0 p.m. at the following prices, namely:—

Soup	2d.
Meat and Vegetables	7d.
(Children under 7 years 4d.)	
Pudding or other Sweet	2d.
Cup of Tea	1d.
Cup of Coffee	2d.

Park Green Restaurant

FIRST DAY SUCCESS

MACCLESFIELD'S British Restaurant, on Park Green, was officially opened on Wednesday by Alderman Edmund Lomas, Chairman of the Feeding Centres Committee.

Among those present were members of the Council, the Food Control Committee, the Feeding Centres Committee, the Silk Trade Employers' Association, the National Silk Workers' Association, and the W.V.S.

The Mayor (Alderman C. W. Kirk) who presided, congratulated Alderman Lomas and the Borough Architect (Mr. M. B. Tetlow) on the successful transformation they had effected in the old Park Green School. He stressed that British Restaurants were open to every section of the public. If workers had a good mid-day meal they would work ever so much better, and he hoped it would be patronised by them.

Alderman Lomas, in officially opening the Restaurant, said he expected there would be snags to commence with, but these would soon be rectified.

A vote of thanks to the Chairman was proposed by the Deputy Mayor (Coun. F. Baron), and seconded by Mr. Edward Lomas, K.S.G., J.P.

The representatives were entertained to lunch as guests of the Chairman.

DESCRIPTION

The interior of the restaurant is beautifully clean, fresh and inviting. The walls have been painted cream, with the lower portion orange colour, and the floor is covered with blue linoleum with furniture to tone.

The dining room used to be the main hall of the Sunday School, and the floor space has been enlarged by taking away smaller rooms which were formerly partitioned from it. Diners will sit at small tables, some accommodating four people, others eight. One hundred and thirty persons can thus be catered for at one time. These numbers can be increased to 180 as and when the demand arises. The restaurant chairs have not arrived yet and those at present in use are from the Town Hall.

The restaurant is being run on the cafeteria system. Diners buy their tickets at the cashier's desk, after which they pick up the cutlery they need. Then they pass along the counter, purchasing the various items for which they have tickets, and proceed with their meals to the tables. They can get the complete meal at once, or collect the courses separately. In the former case a system of heated plate rings helps to keep the food warm. The counter is equipped with hot plates for the same purpose.

PRAISE FOR BRITISH RESTAURANT

At a meeting of the Feeding Centres Committee held recently, it was revealed that the number of meals served in September was a record, the figures being 12,210, a daily average of 556. A letter was received from the Divisional Inspector of the Ministry of Food following her recent visit, in which she reported on the excellent work being done at the Restaurant. The Inspector said she was well pleased with the general conduct.

CHILDREN CROWD BRITISH RESTAURANT

SO many children are attending the British Restaurant that unless they are accompanied by a parent it is possible they may be excluded.

At the Education Committee on Friday Ald. E. Lomas stated that children were interfering with the service to the workers, which was the main essential of the Restaurant.

Mr. E. R. Clark said some Lancashire towns were refusing admission to school children.

Head teachers are to ask the children to go to the School Feeding Centre for their dinner, and if this does not bring about the desired result, then it is possible that children will be excluded.

THE GEORGE
SANGER CIRCUS

4-30 ———— Twice Daily ———— 7-30

WILL VISIT

ROBINHOOD FARM
LONDON ROAD, Macclesfield.
MONDAY NEXT, JULY 13th

THE WONDER SHOW OF 1942

| U Must C The Great | **PIMPO** | BRITISH CLOWN |

Little Sylvia
Charming Lady Rider — **Ella Hannaford**
In a Novel Speciality Wire Act

George Sanger's Greatest Comedy Animals · **Dogs, Ponies, Monkeys**

Mysteries of the Nile; Baffling Illusions in the Circus Ring

THE GREAT HILLARDS
POPPETT GINNETT'S PONIES
VICTORIA GEORGE and her Wonderful Coloured Pigeons

The Rio Grande Troup of Bareback Riders

ELENORA
In her Death Defying Sensation "On The Sliding Rope"

THIS IS A SANGER SHOW

ADMISSION (inc tax) 3/6   2/6   1/9   1/3
CHILDREN (under 12) : 1/9   1/2   1/-   7d.

Stay at Home Holidays

Barnaby Programme Success

Mayor's Tribute To Organiser

THE MAYOR and Mayoress (Ald. C. W. and Mrs. Kirk), took a spirited part in the Barnaby " Stay-at-Home " activities on Saturday evening at the South Park, when along with an enthusiastic crowd, they danced the Valeta. The action of the Mayor and Mayoress was greatly appreciated, not only by the dancers, but also by the spectators, who heartily applauded the part played by their Worships in the activities.

W.V.S. CANTEEN
One Year of Fine Work

AMONG the manifold activities of the W.V.S., there is none which, locally, has proved more successful than the Home Guard and Forces' Canteen in Mill Street.

Almost two thousand meals each week are served, chiefly to members of the Forces, who also make free use of the facilities provided for reading, writing, billiards, etc. It is used, in fact, as a social club, and as they are away from home, they might otherwise find it difficult to dispose of their spare time in so satisfactory a manner. They are not slow to express their appreciation, and more than once the remark has been made that it is the best canteen they have met with in a wide experience of them in the various towns in which they have been quartered.

UNION JACK CLUB TRIBUTE

Dear Sir.—Does the average soldier fully appreciate all that is being done for his comfort and enjoyment during his spare time? It would be interesting to have the opinion of your readers.

Here in Macclesfield we have the Union Jack Club, run by the Ladies' Voluntary Workers. This is one spot in Cheshire where a serving member of H.M. Forces is sure of a welcome—a good meal, free billiards and snooker, writing and reading rooms, and, above all, the only canteen open on Sundays, and always a friendly smile.

May I, at any rate, say "Thank you, L.V.W. You are doing a grand job."

(Signed), **CORPORAL B.**

6, Beech Lane

CONCERTS FOR THE TROOPS

LAST Thursday evening the first of a series of concerts for the troops, organised by Margaret Burgess, the well-known soprano, was given at a north-west R.R.F. camp and was a great success.

The party, which consisted of many of Macclesfield's own popular artists, was in excellent form. It would be unfair to say which individual artist received the most applause, as each of them contributed to a wonderful performance.

The grace and beauty of the dancing of Beryl Battersby, the "Adagios" and Little Betty, combined with the accomplished singing of Margaret Burgess (soprano) and James Oliver (tenor) in duets, operatic arias and ballads, and the professional playing of Alice Swindells (accordionist) and Harold Swindells (saxophonist), was very much appreciated by the large audience.

Will Coogan proved himself to be an ideal compere and versatile comedian, while Alice Slater at the piano accompanied in an able way.

Entertains the Tars

IN JUNE, Gordon Spencer, 20-years-old son of Mr. and Mrs. T. H. Spencer, 11 Brown Street, joined the Royal Navy. He was posted to H.M.S. Raleigh, where a number of other local men are receiving

their training, and has become one of the most popular members of his College. The reason is that he can play the piano accordion extremely well, and very often he is called upon to oblige for impromptu jigs that are arranged. Educated at Athey Street School, he was employed by Whitmore's, cork manufacturers, Crompton Road. He attended the Large Sunday School.

KILLED IN TANK ACTION
Trooper T. Shufflebotham

AFTER having the tank he was driving wrecked on two occasions, and being wounded in the leg in recent tank battles, Trooper T. Shufflebotham, R.T.C., 2, Gunco Lane, has been reported killed in action following the fall of Tobruk.

The letter conveying the information to his father from the War Office was received on July 16th, and it stated that Tr. Shufflebotham had been reported killed on June 26, 1942, whilst serving with His Majesty's forces in the Middle East.

He volunteered for service in H.M. Forces at the beginning of June, 1940, served in England until October, 1941, and then went to the Middle East. He had been in numerous tank conflicts (being a driver), and, as already mentioned, he was wounded in the leg. This was two months ago, but he soon recovered, rejoined his unit and then again went into battle, fighting until he was killed in the vicinity of Tobruk.

Reported Missing

"Courier" Employee

LAST THURSDAY Mr. and Mrs. Frank Merriman, of 10 Grange Road, were officially notified that their elder son, Fusilier Frank (Vic) Merriman, had been classified as "missing" after Singapore.

Fus. Merriman is the second member of the "Courier" staff to be reported missing in the Malayan campaign, for a few weeks ago C.Q.M.S. D. S. Heaps was similarly classified. Fus. Merriman, who is 23 years of age, was employed in the "Courier" printing department, where he was one of the most popular members, and a most capable workman. His father is a Corporation gas collector.

All members of the "Courier" staff, together with the many friends of Mr. and Mrs. Merriman, join in extending to them sympathy in their anxiety, and the fervent hope that the near future will bring much more re-assuring news.

Wife's Anxiety Relieved

Local Seaman on Bombed Destroyer

A MACCLESFIELD WIFE who was listening-in to the wireless on Friday evening, heard a B.B.C. announcer say that H.M.S. Wild Swan, the destroyer on which her husband was serving, had been sunk after an attack by twelve German bombers. After two days of anxiety she learnt, however, that along with many others, her husband was safe, and he is now home on survivors' leave, having been picked up after 13 hours on a raft.

The local seaman on board this ship is Telegraphist Donald Lingard, and his wife lives at 5 Delamere Drive.

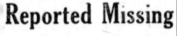

The official communiqué states: "On the evening of Wednesday, June 17, a force of German bombers attacked H.M.S. Wild Swan (Lieut. Commander C. E. L. Slater, R.N.) in the Atlantic, 100 miles West of the French coast, and also turned their attention to a Spanish trawler fleet which was fishing in the vicinity.

Killed At Sea

NEWS has been received that Gunner Frank Harrison, of 4 Blackshaw Street, has been killed in action at sea while serving on a merchant ship. He was 27 years of age and leaves a widow and two young daughters. Before joining up 18 months ago he was employed at Macclesfield Dyers Ltd. He attended St. John's Church.

Prisoner In Libya

SIG. J. K. HUTCHINSON

FROM an enemy source, it has been learned that Signaller J. K. Hutchinson, elder son of the Rev. J. J. and Mrs. Hutchinson, of 284, Park Lane, has been captured in the Western Desert, and is now a prisoner of war.

A former local journalist, Sig. Hutchinson was on the Macclesfield staff of the Stockport Advertiser, and is well-known in the town and district. He was very popular with his professional colleagues, being of a cheery and amiable disposition.

Twenty-two years of age, he joined the Royal Corps of Signals in May, 1940, and went overseas in December, 1941. The last letter received from him was dated May 18th.

An entertainer of outstanding ability, he was a member of "The Gay Revellers" Concert Party, which was associated with Park Street Methodist Church.

The sympathy of a wide circle of friends will be extended to the Rev. and Mrs. Hutchinson in these dark days of anxiety.

Reported Missing

NEWS has been received by Mrs. F. E. Cadman, of 9 Brown St., that her son, Sergt. James Wilfred Cadman, of the R.A.F., is missing. He was to have been married shortly.

Mrs. Cadman has received the following message from the Air Ministry: "Regret to inform you that your son, Sergeant James Wilfred Cadman, is missing as the result of an operation on the night of January 4th."

He was a wireless operator in the R.A.F., which Service he joined in October, 1940. He was 28 years of age, and was shortly to have married Miss Joan Gorton, of Bank St. Before joining up he was employed by Messrs. D. Whitfield and Co., and received his education at Mill St., Central, and King's School.

Peover Hall, near Knutsford, in 1997. This was the headquarters of the US 9th Armoured Division under General George S. Patton. The Division's troops were spread all over Cheshire, and Macclesfield had its fair share of both men and equipment.

Left and below, General Patton is seen talking at the Ruskin Rooms in Knutsford, and with locals at Over Peover church.

Even before General George S. Patton ("Old Blood and Guts" to his troops) came to the area early in 1944, he had achieved fame, and some notoriety, as a result of his leadership in North Africa and Sicily.

CHAPTER 6
The Impact of the Americans in Macclesfield between 1942 and 1945

The United States of America entered the War on 7 December 1941 when Japanese forces destroyed the American fleet in Pearl Harbor. Until that moment American opinion had been against a decision to join the War on the Allies' side, even though the United States had been giving material, technical and moral help to Britain since May 1940. In July 1941, for example, US troops landed in Iceland to release British troops for service elsewhere; and on 30 June 1941, 400 American civilian technicians arrived in Northern Ireland.

After Pearl Harbor there were hurried conferences in Washington throughout December concerning the implications of the Japanese attack. One of the decisions made as a result of those conferences was that American troops should be sent to the British Isles. The first GIs to arrive sailed on the transport ships the Straithaird and the Chateau Thierry and they entered Belfast Docks on 26 January 1942. The name given to the subsequent schemes for this transportation of troops was BOLERO, after Ravel's music - the American planners intended to increase the number of GIs sent to Britain building up progressively to a climax .

On 31 May 1942 the first BOLERO plan stated that Britain would receive 1,049,000 men, of whom 240,000 would be from the U.S. Army Air Force. The climax of the scheme, in May 1944, marked the presence in the United Kingdom of 1,526,965 men, although it is probable that the total number of those who passed through the country en route for North Africa or France was in the region of two millions.

There is a temptation to think that units of American troops spent a long time in specific parts of the country and hence had time to get to know their hosts intimately. Doubtless this is what happened in a certain number of cases. The troops who stayed in Macclesfield between 1942 and D-Day 1944 mainly belonged to the U.S. 9th Armoured Division, based on Knutsford and spread over Cheshire. They brought their tanks with them; they possessed hundreds of vehicles which they spent much time in repairing, maintaining and driving in and around the town. So far as the inhabitants of Macclesfield were concerned they became familiar faces, anonymous, but because they were so extrovert and cheerful and noisy, they were individuals too. There may have been many changes of units but they remained undetected by the people of Macclesfield. The GIs were like the sea - ever changing and yet ever the same. But - especially after the approach to D-Day and in the later stages of the European campaign - American troops spent an increasingly smaller amount of time in the United Kingdom before departing for continental battles. Indeed the majority of the U.S. soldiers who came in the autumn of 1944 scarcely had more than a week or two in Britain before being packed off to France, Belgium and Holland to pave the way for entry into Germany. The larger part of the GIs who spent time in Macclesfield in November 1944 came into this category. The usual pattern was to dock in Liverpool on a dull dark day, be transported to Macclesfield, be employed in the organisation of material, equipment and weapons for two weeks and then to be sent to the frontiers between Luxembourg, Belgium and Germany where they began to 'dig in'.

Almost all who went through this process found themselves engaged in the Ardennes in the bitter Battle of the Bulge (16 December 1944-13 January 1945) and almost all were in the

U.S. 87th Infantry Division, the Golden Acorn Division, which was based at Peover Hall, near Knutsford, a Hall made famous as General Patton's Headquarters from January 1944 until July 1944. Colonel Charles Connor, for example, arrived in Liverpool on the Louis Pasteur on 13 November 1944, just after a bombing raid which had sunk several docked ships. Leaving the Louis Pasteur at 04.15 he and his colleagues marched up cobbled streets and caught a train to Macclesfield, arriving at 8 am. They were then marched to Tytherington Hall, half a mile outside the northern boundary of the town, and to its adjoining Nissen huts (called Quonset huts - to which they were similar - by the Americans).

Charles Connor recalls some of his time in Macclesfield in the following way: *Here we learned to drive on the left side of the road...... the streets were blacked out except for dim street lamps directed towards their bases..... every frosted window, behind which one could vaguely detect a pale orange glow, was a pub..... The English girls, hatless, bare-legged, had broad smiles, characteristic accents and warm notions.... One could hear their soft laughter and American wisecracks in all pubs.* He only spent 13 days at Tytherington Hall, during which time he made two trips to Scotland to pick up vehicles. He was in the 335th Field Artillery of the 87th Infantry Division and was involved in the Battle of the 'Bulge' hardly three weeks after leaving Macclesfield.

His immediate Commanding Officer (335th Field Artillery), Colonel Carrol W. Bailey, went through similar but not identical experiences. He left the United States on 1 October 1944 as part of an Advance Party and went first to Peover Hall, arriving at Tytherington Hall on 17 October. He too was one of those men who left Metz to go north to Bastogne in the Ardennes Battle just before Christmas 1944 to help in the relief of that beleaguered town.

An 'other ranks' soldier in the same unit was Sanford Ziegler. He was billeted in one of the Quonset huts in the grounds of Tytherington Hall and, unsurprisingly, found the snowy December in the Ardennes less cold than the raw dampness of Macclesfield in November.

Another American soldier transported to the United Kingdom by the Louis Pasteur was Rex O'Meara, who has written a book about his experiences, and who was billeted briefly in Lord Street Sunday School. Another temporary resident in Macclesfield - he was billeted in the Parochial Church Hall, Roe Street - who also took part in the Battle of the Bulge, was Bill Koranda, a member of Battery B, 912 Field Artillery Battalion.

Mr Derek Way has described the arrival of the Americans in Macclesfield: *'They arrived in Roe Street late one dark night. The whole street was dominated by their astonishingly large army trucks, all possible sounds were obliterated by brash young voices with a strange twang, and there seemed to be a complete but totally inoffensive disregard for all blackout regulations.'* A new kind of soldier had arrived. The mainly quiet discipline, smart demeanour, stoic obedience and undemanding presence of the previous military occupants of the town - of course there had been exceptions - had disappeared for good. Such new soldiers were bound to have a striking effect on Macclesfield, as indeed they were to have on every area of the United Kingdom where they stayed. They sounded like the confident people we had seen in American films; they had a lot of money; they were brash and kind at the same time; they picked up girls easily; they treated them well and talked extravagantly, showering nylon stockings and other gifts upon them, not being afraid to exaggerate the beauty and general qualities of the young ladies. Girls fell for them in a way which astonished even the girls.

What happened in the United Kingdom in general certainly happened in Macclesfield.

Little wonder, then, that the evening life of the town became even more boisterous than it had been when the more restrained British troops had been present. Sanford Ziegler, the GI previously mentioned, describes how a circle of individual guards was, in accordance with custom, placed around the Nissen (Quonset) huts in the grounds of Tytherington Hall. Then it was discovered that a large number of these guards were disappearing regularly, enticed into the nearby woods by girls from the town. So the Commanding Officer ordered the guards to act in pairs, each individual being responsible (on pain of severe punishment) for the good behaviour of his companion. That particular sort of 'fraternisation', as the Americans called it, ceased immediately.

But the town itself, filled in the evenings by GIs on short leave, did not lend itself to such close control. The cinemas were full, and alley-ways were often occupied. In December 1942 the local police raided a brothel in Bridge Street where American soldiers were present. The lady of the house explained that they had brought candy for the children and that she herself had simply been making the GIs welcome. The same week a girl and an American soldier were before the magistrates for indecency, having been discovered by *'a Police flash-light patrol'*. The magistrates ruled that the American was not subject to this country's jurisdiction and would be dealt with by the American military authorities.

In December 1943 a 13 year-old Macclesfield girl was in court for committing an act of indecency in the Market Place car park with an American soldier. She was ordered to be at home every evening by 6-30 pm and to visit the cinema only once a week and not to associate with another girl mentioned in court. On 2 June 1944 two Macclesfield twin sisters of 13 trespassed on a U.S. Army Camp, in search of 'a good time'. In July 1944 an American soldier was brought before the court for an act of indecency in a cul-de-sac off Charlotte Street *'to the annoyance of passers-by'*. In September 1944 a 12 year-old boy was sent to a remand home because he *'had undesirable connections with American soldiers'*. In May 1945 two other Macclesfield women were charged with trespassing on a US Army Camp. Charges had already been laid against one for running a brothel.

All these stories were reported in the Macclesfield local newspapers. Although such reports cumulatively give an impression of poor behaviour, the presence of the Americans in the town produced a most welcome joie-de-vivre. Enormous efforts were made in Cheshire, not least in Altrincham, Congleton and Macclesfield to receive the Americans in a most hospitable and friendly way. Altrincham had a very active Forces Welfare Committee, which met regularly and fruitfully. The Mayor of Congleton, G. Rowell, wrote an open letter to *the Macclesfield Courier and Herald* of 12 January 1944, stating that new groups of Americans would soon be arriving and that questions of entertainment and hospitality needed to be dealt with. There would be a meeting of all interested on 24 January 1944. As early as November 1942 a Macclesfield clerical worker had written to *Mass Observation* (a national organisation set up before the War by Tom Harrisson to record the experiences of the man in the street) as follows: *'There will be no turkey this year, although we hope to do better than last year as regards one or two fowls, as we are expecting to make up a party for a few American troops. One has only to make such a suggestion to receive offers of all sorts of things.'*

Mr P. Clegg (Borough Electricity Engineer) and Mr J. Lomas (Secretary of the Rotary Club) organised a series of dances on behalf of the American forces stationed in the district and were thanked profusely in a letter to the local paper by representatives of American servicemen.

There were clearly some very happy relationships between Macclesfield people and the GIs. Mrs J. Barber of 26, Hawthorn Way, Macclesfield, lived with her grandmother who, like many people throughout the country, regarded the girl friends of GIs as being over-adventurous if not immoral. One day both the girl and her grandmother were dumbfounded to find a whole unit of GIs halted in front of her house. Their N.C.O. knocked at her door to remind the young girl - to the alarm of her grandmother - of the date she had that evening with one of his friends. She was sixteen at the time and found the mixture of pleasure and misgiving she experienced difficult to digest. Altogether she came to know three Americans, one living in a tent at Mottram St Andrew (some 5 miles north west of Macclesfield), two also in tents in the grounds of Beech Hall School, Beech Lane, Macclesfield. The first was known to Mrs Barber only as 'Red'. The other two, Gus Rogers and Joe Powers, had met on the ship bringing them from the USA but had come from opposite ends of the States, Gus from a farm in Buffalo, Wyoming, Joe from a tenement in New York.

Gus, a worrier by nature, wide-eyed at what he saw in his travels to the United Kingdom, and overwhelmed by the amount of pay he received, was thrilled to visit the Macclesfield May Fair a month before D-Day. He was killed, Mrs Barber receiving the news via a returned letter. Joe had one leg blown off and the other shattered and Red wrote to Mrs Barber that Joe had died of his wounds. Red's mother later informed Mrs Barber that Red too had been killed.

Mrs Barber hence has disturbing memories of this period of her life. Clearly her experiences were far different from those conjured up by the local newspaper reports mentioned above and were totally innocent and wholesome. So too were those of Rex O'Meara as recorded in his autobiography. Having arrived at Liverpool in a heavy fog in November 1944 on the Louis Pasteur, his unit was put onto a train for Macclesfield. The troops, exhausted, arrived in the dark and were marched from the railway station to Lord Street Sunday School. The next evening he was given leave of absence and with a friend felt his way, in the blackout ('*the blackest night I've ever seen*') down to the Sun Inn. After drinking unfamiliar beer the two companions and a pianist colleague brought the place alive but at 9-30 pm the landlady announced that it was now closing time. '*They close the pubs here when they run out of beer*', they were informed, '*you chaps have drunk the place dry*'.

The atmosphere of friendship was extremely evident and Rex and his companion were invited by a couple they met in the pub, who lived in Lord Street, to come home for supper. While supper was being prepared by the couple in the kitchen, the two GIs, anxious to be helpful, emptied the contents of the coal scuttle onto the fire and made the room gloriously warm and cheerful. Although they all had a wonderful evening, the Americans were puzzled by the reaction of the English couple to the blazing fire in the living room. The next morning, during a lecture on British ways of life, they looked at each other as they simultaneously realised that they had probably used up the remaining coal ration of the couple. Their consequent dragging of American fuel supplies through guards and sentries caused even more embarrassment to the English couple who only eventually accepted the gesture after the most outrageously mendacious reassurances of the GIs.

One of the features of American attitudes which came over very clearly not only to the people of Macclesfield but to the whole of the United Kingdom was racial segregation. The historian Angus Calder wrote in his book *The People's War*: '*When the WVS in Bristol opened two canteens for the GIs, one was for whites and one was for negros. Yet a poll taken in 1943 suggested that the British people were overwhelmingly opposed to racial discrimination'.* Graham Smith wrote in his book on black American troops in World War ll *When Jim Crow met John Bull: 'General Eisenhower told Merle Oberon, the Hollywood Movie Star, who came to Britain in 1942, that he was worried about the black troops because they were running off with English girls.'* Graham Smith went on: *'At the end of 1943 Brigadier General Oliver Haines, making an inspection tour, discovered that there were some 5,000 black troops in and around Liverpool at Maghull, Aintree and Huyton, and others in Manchester. There were about 2500 whites in the same area and another 3500 at the large air depot at Burtonwood near Warrington. Both races used Liverpool, and relations there were said to be satisfactory, in part because both cities had separate Red Cross Clubs for blacks and whites.'*

In another part of Cheshire - by April 1944 there were over 50,000 American troops in the county - a similar compromise seems to have been made. This was near Northwich, at Marbury Hall, where black and white troops were close to each other, with another 600 whites 6 miles away at Delamere. The careful organisation of passes ensured that Northwich became *'the black town'* while Chester, 15 miles away, became *'the white town'*, according to Graham Smith. Evidently the prejudice against negroes was strong in both USA citizens and the members of the armed forces, particularly among Southerners. Indeed the American Army refused to use negroes as fighting troops until the Battle of the Bulge in December 1944. David Reynolds, author of the book *Rich Relations, the American Occupation of Britain, 1942-1945*, writes of the occasion when the GOC of the Western Command of the British Army complained to the city of Chester that black GIs stationed nearby had been seen walking around with white women and that *'this sort of thing is not customary in America and we do not wish to infringe American customs'*. The Lord Mayor of Chester, taken aback, replied that Indians and West Indians, who happened to be British subjects, could also be described as coloured. What, he asked the GOC, did he propose to do about them?

The people of Macclesfield were likewise shocked to discover the existence of this racial segregation. One area of the town not previously mentioned, Chester Road, on the way to Broken Cross, received a large number of troops, both black and white, in the grounds of the Parkside Mental Hospital, where they lived in tents while their officers lived in the old St Michael's Vicarage nearby. American officers visited all shops and pubs in the area and asked their proprietors to place notices in their windows if they did not wish black GIs to use their premises. The inhabitants were astounded by this request and raised no objections to the presence of black troops. Indeed there was genuine affection for them. Mrs Jacqueline Potter was, during the War, the only child of a couple who owned a fish and chip shop (still in existence) at the corner of Chester Road and West Street. Her father worked as a silk loom weaver making parachutes at Smales Mill off Sunderland Street, a reserved occupation, which meant that he could not join the forces. Instead he became a part-time Auxiliary Fireman. One evening, returning from fire duty in Liverpool and discovering that his daughter was not at home, he went in search of her in the grounds of Parkside Hospital. He found her sitting happily on the shoulders of a negro soldier, watching black Americans playing dice. Many children of the district remember being asked to kiss the dice to give them luck.

Mrs Potter looks back on that time as a very happy one. Her parents welcomed the Americans both black and white into their fish and chip shop, her mother showing American chefs how to make 'real' batter, her father taking troops of all kinds to the nearby Talbot

Public House and introducing them to skittles, darts and dominoes. For a period her mother was ill and it was the American black chefs who kept the business going and looked after the young daughter when her father was away at work or on firefighting duties.

Mrs J. Barber, friend of GIs Red, Gus and Joe previously mentioned, was sitting in the Black's Head at the corner of Mill Street and Castle Street with two American acquaintances when a black GI came in. One of her companions asked with some indignation: *'They aren't going to serve that Goddam Black, are they?'* The girl thought that he was joking; that he must know the black GI and was pulling his leg. She was shocked to be told that the white soldier did not know him, and that, in his part of the world, a negro would not be served.

In his book David Reynolds puts things into perspective from an American point of view when he writes: *'In many units the Civil War was fought and refought, its passions doubtless rekindled by the movie Gone with the Wind, which premiered in December 1939.'* He quotes a marine from New York who was sharing a tent on Parris Island, South Carolina with some troops from the South and who commented: *'Back in the Bronx we just didn't look at people as either Rebels or Yanks..... but those southern boys sure did.'* Reynolds, pointing out that most new training camps were in the old confederacy, where there were large cheap tracts of land, continues: *'In handling blacks the Army way was the southern way, which to northerners was a rude shock.'* The northern blacks, it seems, found that they were physically segregated on all forms of transport, were forced to do menial jobs, in all-black units, were banned from cinemas, and were abused by white non-combatant soldiers. They suddenly discovered that they were now being treated differently - as *'niggers'* in fact - and their response was resentment.

The generosity of the American troops to the people, not least the children, of Macclesfield was noteworthy. Mrs V. Kent remembers attending a Children's Party given near the old St Michael's Vicarage and amongst the Quonset huts at the top of Nixon Street, off Chester Road, receiving astonishing food and being entertained by the GIs. When the Americans left this part of town they presented a cellar full of mainly tinned but mouth-watering food of all kinds to the civilians of the area. The mother of little Jacqueline Potter was given the responsibility of distributing the food to whomsoever she wished.

There was one aspect of American occupation of the town which was physical and almost indelible. The arrival of the US Armoured units from 1943 onwards, units which were to form the spearhead of General Patton's 3rd US Army in their dash across Europe in the summer and autumn of 1944, did an enormous amount of damage to roads, footpaths, kerbs and walls. Tanks and tracked vehicles were driven from the Hibel Road Station Coal Wharf to Crompton Road Barracks, the Cottage Street Playing Fields and the Windmill Street Playing Fields, where they were fitted out with extra armour and equipment, an operation which went on night and day under canvas in some appalling weather of the 1943-1944 winter.

The drivers were fresh from training and the narrow streets of Macclesfield were dissimilar to the routes they had been trained to negotiate. All the costs of repair to roads and streets were met by a department of the US Corps of Engineers.

Two local companies benefited enormously from the presence of vast American forces in and around Cheshire. The first, Ashton and Holmes, experts in quarrying in the Tegsnose area, sold thousands of tons of stone to build the foundations of the runways as well as the numerous hangars and accommodation blocks at the huge US Air Base at Burtonwood, near Warrington. They were also the suppliers of stone for the foundations of many of the US camps in the Knutsford and Northwich districts which received large numbers of the troops landing at Liverpool. The second, Brotomac, were suppliers and layers of tarmac paths in these camps, and their business likewise flourished.

Macclesfield, much more than most localities in the United Kingdom, had a very clear and traditional connection with the United States. During one of the periodic slumps in the silk trade in the nineteenth century John Ryle, the superintendent of a Macclesfield throwing mill, left Macclesfield for Paterson, New Jersey, in 1839 and there, in 1845, established the first factory dealing with spooled sewing silk which the States had known. A year later he started the weaving of silk with a colleague. Another silk finishing business was established in the same town by two other Macclesfield men, Alfred Crewe and Thomas Henshall. By 1900 these two firms had attracted 3000 Macclesfield people to emigrate and work with them. Many people in Macclesfield have heard from parents and grandparents of this necessary but emotional upheaval which brought prosperity but separation, sadness and nostalgia to many of the townsfolk's ancestors.

In 1943 a Macclesfield Merchant Navy man found himself near Paterson in New Jersey and expressed a wish to help cement the bonds of friendship between the British and the Americans. In addition an American woman wrote to *the Macclesfield Courier* proclaiming her admiration for 'the English' - and as it happened both events merged into one when reported in the local *Courier and Herald* of 27 August 1943. Moreover a Paterson newspaper carried a letter sent by an American soldier to his family praising Macclesfield's hospitality.

In July 1943 the local police played the Americans on the Moss Rose Football Ground at both soccer and baseball. The Americans won both matches. In February 1944 the town's authorities made strenuous efforts to enhance the attractiveness of the numerous dances being organised for the Americans (not least at the Stanley Hall and Town Hall) by persuading catering establishments (particularly pubs and the British Restaurant) to stay open later.

In March 1944 the Merchant Navy Campaign Week included a non-stop All American Dance (*'Ladies, meet the Doughboys!'* proclaimed the advertisement). In May 1944 (only three weeks before D-Day) there were again matches between the local police and the US Forces on the King's School grounds in Westminster Road. The infirmary benefited from the charges for admission. In the *Macclesfield Courier and Herald* edition of 2 June 1944 American officers stationed in the district wrote to thank Macclesfield for the organisation of dances. In July 1944 there were baseball and cricket matches. In September 1944 the local Anglo-American Friendship Society organised a dinner-dance in the Stanley Hall.

In November 1944 an American Evening was organised on Thanksgiving Day, when a US army chaplain gave a talk on the Mayflower and negro spiritual songs were sung. In January 1945 a dance in the Stanley Hall, organised by the Macclesfield National Fire Service, was graced with the presence of Sergeant Eardley, VC, a native of Congleton, who was *'loud in his praise of American troops'*, to the delight of all who were present. In April 1945 an official Anglo-American darts match took place in the Yates Mill Street Wine Vaults.

On VE Day (8 May 1945) American soldiers participated in the celebrations. A justifiable conclusion from all this is that in Macclesfield there was an enormous amount of good will, mutual respect and sincere friendship between local inhabitants and American billetees.

Retirement From West Park

PRESENTATION TO MR. & MRS. MARTIN

ON the occasion of their retirement on Tuesday, Mr. and Mrs. H. J. Martin, the Clerk and Steward and the Matron of West Park County General Hospital, were presented with a cheque and a pair of candlesticks carved from timber out of the old clock tower. The gifts were handed to them by Alderman H. Hodkinson, Chairman of the Management Committee, at a ceremony held in the dining room in the presence of the staff of the institution.

Mr. and Mrs. Martin have been at West Park Hospital 10 years, prior to which they were Master and Matron of Tarvin Hospital for 13 years. In 1939 Mrs. Martin was honoured by the King when the O.B.E. was conferred upon her for her service to hospitals in Cheshire. Mr. Martin is the immediate Past President of the National Association of Administrators of Local Government Establishments, which office was the highest honour his colleagues could pay him.

Nearly £10,500 For Infirmary

Bollington Committee's Fine Work

£1,000 FOR INFIRMARY

THE Farmers' and Country Effort on behalf of the Infirmary has this week reached the record figure of £1,000.

The Mayor (Ald. C. W. Kirk), who is Chairman of the effort, is a proud man, because he had, all along, been hoping that this year's effort would be a bumper one. The final figure will be over the £1,000 mark, and the presentation of the cheque to the Infirmary Governors will take place in the near future.

Gifts For Infirmary

ON behalf of the Governors of the General Infirmary the Secretary-Superintendent (Mr. H. K. Gwilliam) has pleasure in acknowledging receipt of the following gifts in cash and kind received within recent weeks:—

Donations.—Bernhard Baron Charitable Trust £50; The King's School £30 18s.; Macclesfield High School for Girls £10 6s. 3d.; Cheshire Cheese "Swing-round Club," £6 3s. 6d.; The Brewers Arms Comforts Fund, £5; Mr. J. Schofield, M.A., £5 (a thankoffering); Marks and Spencer Ltd., £2 12s.; Mr. J. Cantrell, proceeds of Hymn Festival £1 9s.; The King's School, proceeds of dance, £4 10s.; Order of Rechabites Approved Society, £2; Lucas Warburton Memorial Fund interest, £6 7s.;

Hospital Sunday Collections.

St. Michael's Church, Mayor's Sunday Service, £33 10s. 7d.; Macclesfield Congregational Church, £4 4s. 5d.; St. Saviour's Church, Wildboarclough, £2 12s.; Brunswick Methodist Church (Civil Defence Service) £2. 2s.

Workers' Ambition Achieved

£4,000 FOR INFIRMARY

WHEN the annual meeting of the Workers' Infirmary Fund Committee is held next month, it will be reported that during 1941 the workers of Macclesfield raised by their weekly contributions the sum of over £4,000 for the Institution.

This is a record in the history of the Fund and a great achievement in such difficult days when so many of the men of the town are on active service.

A fortnight ago the fund was £80 short of the £4,000 mark and an appeal was made to those firms who had not paid over the whole of their 1941 collections to do so. There was an immediate response and the final figure for the year has now been declared by the Secretary (Mr. H. K. Gwilliam) to be £4,007—an increase of over £250 over 1940.

It is interesting to note that ten years ago—1931—the total for the year was £1,780, so that in that period it has more than doubled. This fine figure for the past year is a great encouragement for the officials—Mr. G F. Barlow (Chairman), Mr. F. Williams (Vice-Chairman) and Mr. Gwilliam (Secretary), and also to the committee, and now the aim will be £5,000. Will it be achieved in 1942? With whole-hearted co-operation and a one hundred per cent membership of the Fund there is no reason why it should not be an accomplished fact twelve months hence.

CHAPTER 7
Macclesfield's Hospitals during the Second World War
The development of the West Park Hospital

There were four hospitals in Macclesfield during the Second World War, the General Infirmary in Westminster Road/Cumberland St (where Sainsbury's is now), the Isolation Hospital in Moss Lane, the West Park in Prestbury Road and Parkside Hospital in Victoria Road.

Although the General Infirmary and the Isolation Hospital were to continue for some years to serve the community, Macclesfield's long-term future hospital care would be based at the West Park and the Parkside. What happened during the Second World War was therefore of immense importance to the people of Macclesfield.

Parkside, erected in 1868-1871 as a 'County Lunatic Asylum', had 1315 patients, 553 males and 762 females in December 1939. There were 146 private patients, including 51 patients from the armed services and 2 ex-Service patients. The Ministry of Health had decided (through its EMS - Emergency Medical Services) to regard, what was still known in common parlance as the 'Parkside Lunatic Asylum', as an emergency military hospital. Patients who had been housed in an area called the 'annexe' were to be transferred to the main building to make way for the expected sudden inflow of war-wounded. The first convoy arrived on 8 June 1940, as a result of the fighting in France and the evacuation from Dunkirk.

Parkside Hospital

The EMS Parkside Hospital dealt with a total of 8950 patients between 1940 and 1946, with as many as 6344 members of the British forces, 279 prisoners of war, 95 air raid casualties and 1581 civilians. Only 56 deaths occurred in those patients during that time.

Christmas 1940 was a particularly busy time. Military patients had to be temporarily transferred to other hospitals while Blitz casualties were arriving from Manchester. The demands for meals were considerable. The problems were increased by the number of Air Raid warnings - 15 in the latter part of 1940 were followed by 42 in 1941.

Parkside, while still carrying out, at least partially, its obligations to civilians, performed a huge task as a wartime military hospital. After the War it resumed its role as a mental hospital, but when the National Health Service started on 5 July 1946 - it came into force two years later, 5 July 1948 - Parkside, unlike West Park, did not become part of the Macclesfield and District Group. The policy of the Ministry of Health was to avoid the amalgamation of

Psychiatric Hospitals with others and Parkside, like all such establishments, remained a single unit. Indeed it was not until 1970 that the Parkside Hospital joined the Macclesfield and District Group to form the East Cheshire Hospitals.

In 1939 the West Park Hospital was still only a 'workhouse', although by now also called a Public Assistance Hospital, still a home for the poor and homeless, and known familiarly as 'the grubber'. Hence it continued to be administered by the Public Assistance Committee until June 1940. The future of the eventual West Park Hospital depended upon two different visions, one pessimistic, the other optimistic. The first belonged to the Ministry of Health, working through EMS, who had foreseen the need for many more beds to deal with the victims of a probable European conflict. The second was the vision of the Cheshire County Council which was anxious to increase general hospital amenities in the County. The two visions were to fuse to create a hospital for the post-war medical needs of Macclesfield.

West Park Hospital

But only in June 1940 was the term 'workhouse' finally officially abolished in favour of the 'West Park County General Hospital', with 375 beds under the control of the County's Public Health Committee. The new name became established when the first Medical Superintendent, A. Norman Jones FRCS, took up his position in July 1940.

There was an acute shortage of manpower, materials and money but, with the backing of the EMS, enormous changes were made to the original workhouse buildings throughout the whole period of the War. The Workhouse inmates were transferred, as were the patients from the General Infirmary and Parkside, to other institutions such as Arclid at Sandbach and the Barony at Nantwich.

The old Workhouse Master and Matron, Mr and Mrs W.J. Martin, continued to be employed, the Master as Clerk and Steward and the Matron remaining in charge of nursing, domestic, laundry and catering staffs. G.P. Siggins joined the staff in 1939 and shared an office with Miss Marion Reddish, the first Almoner (social worker). Mr Siggins' task was to look after salaries, wages and general staff matters, and he soon became, to all intents and purposes, the administrator.

A small number of able-bodied inmates were offered paid jobs on the staff, and the complex nature of the staffing demands together with the call-up of established staff resulted in some peculiar appointments. The official joiner had been previously employed solely in making coffins; the 'tramp major', whose principal responsibility had been to supervise and delouse the tramps, became a porter, while the lady who had made shrouds now proudly bore the title of seamstress.

The buildings were not beautiful and all the walls had iron railings with fearsome spikes on top. Fortunately these were taken away for the war effort as were so many other railings in the town. The crumbling stone steps which had been tolerated by the workhouse needed to be strengthened and retreaded now. There were no covered ways; lifts did not exist on the site; the state of decoration was said to be 'depressing'. The very cumbersome windows had to be replaced while the sanitation to the original wards either did not exist or was of very poor quality. The sort of clinical rooms and facilities that the subscribed 'voluntary' hospitals demanded in the 1930s were unknown to West Park in 1939/1940. The wards which had served the workhouse were too narrow for a hospital, so much so that the measurement regulations laid down by the Ministry of Health just had to be ignored.

There were 28 nurses living in the Nurses' Home and a special recreation room was constructed for them in 1939. Their training consisted of two years in the West Park and two at Clatterbridge, a hospital on the west side of Cheshire in the Wirral. But the Macclesfield Infirmary which was at that time a voluntary hospital, was a well-established training school for nurses who were given a 3-year course. The comparison between the living and working conditions and opportunities of the two sets of nurses was such that, in any recruitment drive, the West Park was bound to be much less successful than the Infirmary. In their first year the nurses received £30 per annum; and this went up to £32-10s in their second year. In their third year the nurses received £35. They were deemed to be receiving in addition, in each year, £52 worth of benefits in the shape of boarding, lodging, uniform and laundry. Student nurses received 3 weeks' annual holiday which included the 6 statutory bank holidays. They were entitled to one day off each week but often, on their free day, they had to attend lectures. Staff nurses received £65 per annum and Ward Sisters £75, in each case benefits being assessed as worth £70 a year. The 48 hours per week of all nurses was often exceeded, while the ancillary staff worked 56 hours over six working days.

A balance had to be made between the number of civilian patients and the number of military patients. A flourishing Maternity Section started once expectant mothers overcame their prejudice against the former workhouse status of the institution - and the mothers paid willingly for their statutory 14 days confinement period in hospital. But the possibility of looking after military personnel, as well as civilian victims of air raids, remained paramount in the thinking of the EMS, and military staff were appointed to both the West Park and Parkside hospitals. In the former there was a military registrar with the rank of Major in charge of 18 NCOs and other ranks.

MATERNITY CHARGES

THE Maternity and Child welf -are Committee has revised its scale of contributions payable by patients towards the cost of their maintenance in West Park Hospital.

The amount payable by the committee is £3 10s. 0d. per week per bed, and the maximum payable by patients is as follows:—

Where the average weekly income of the family per head (after deducting rent and rates) is under £2 10s.: —£4 10s. for two weeks .

Patients in receipt of one maternity benefit, and where the average weekly income of the family per head (after deducting rent and rates is: £2 10s. or over: to pay £6; 9s. or over: to pay £1 10s. and a portion of the remaining £3 in accordance with the scale for home helps; under 9s. but over 7s.: to pay £1 only; 7s. or under, no contribution payable.

Patients in receipt of two maternity benefits, and where the average weekly income of the family per head (after deducting rent and rates) is:—£2 10s. or over: to pay £7; 9s. or over: to pay £3 and a portion of the remaining £1 10s. in accordance with the scale for home helps; under 9s. but over 7s.: to pay £2 only; 7s or under: to pay £1 only.

The combination of the Dunkirk evacuation in the early summer of 1940 and the bombing of London (from 7 September 1940) resulted in a convoy of war patients arriving at the West Park in the second week of September 1940. They actually came in two trains from Brighton, where they had first been sent, but the threat of invasion was causing such concern that patients were diverted to safer areas in the Midlands and the North. The first train was full of civilian women and children. They were due to reach the West Park at 10 pm, but actually arrived at 3 am, the train having sheltered in tunnels during air raids. In the other train were a large number of service personnel, many with amputated limbs, and many with ulcerated feet after forced marches in France.

They were ravenously hungry, having left Brighton at 6-30 am the previous day. Altogether there were in that convoy of two trains 250 patients who had experienced a dreadful journey. (One 'patient', a farm labourer, had gone to Brighton station to see off his sick sister and had left his departure from the train too late! His protests had been vociferous and continued to be so). The patients had been wrapped in blankets marked 'Southmeads, Brighton'. A few years later, after furious enquiries, they were discovered at the West Park where 'W.P, Macclesfield' had been stamped over the original marking.

Soon a further convoy of another 100 patients arrived, mainly elderly people from East London. As had happened at the Infirmary and at Parkside, similar elderly Macclesfield patients had to be transferred to Arclid, Sandbach, and to the Barony, Nantwich. They did not return until late in the War or even after the War.

Just before the Germans occupied the Channel Islands in July 1940, a school run by an educational order of nuns was evacuated from Guernsey to Macclesfield. Sister St Adolphe became a patient at the West Park as did several pupils at the school. And a party of 'impressive' Dutch NCOs from the Princess Irene Brigade (part of Queen Wilhelmina's personal bodyguard) and now billeted in Congleton, were at the West Park for a time guarding a Dutch soldier with a self-inflicted gunshot wound to his foot.

But the Cheshire County Council was anxious to develop the West Park Hospital for its own patients for when the War was over and a real start was made in this direction in January 1941. The hospital was now improving many of its facilities. A large number of wounded military and other services were, whenever possible, transferred to Parkside Hospital. Both hospitals, being virtually on the same site, were excellent premises from the point of view of the Emergency Medical Services. At the main (and only) entrance to the West Park in Prestbury Road there was an Out-Patients Department, with a waiting room and the normal ancillary rooms. The building which had formerly contained the cells for tramps, together with the 'delousing chamber', were converted to become the telephone exchange. A venereal disease clinic was also started in what had been one part of one of the tramps' wards. Three wards, A, B and C, on the left of the main entrance, had sufficient space to conform to the regulations required for beds placed on both sides. The upper floor became the midwifery section with a nursery in the end ward.

This process of getting on with its wartime military requirements as well as looking to its future development as a civilian peacetime hospital, pursued by the Cheshire County Council throughout the War, was impressively undertaken. The maternity section continued to be developed and a 4-bedded Special Care Baby Unit, with its own milk kitchen, was set up in the nursery. The maternity department increased in stature and reputation, reaching a peak of 125 cases every 3 months. C ward on the ground floor became a lying-in ward for the maternity department, while A and B wards specialised as female medical wards.

One problem was that K Block, which contained the operating theatre, was designated as the male surgical block, and this meant that when female patients had emergency operations during the night they had to be wheeled back to wards A and B on a trolley in complete blackout darkness - covered ways had not yet been built. One wet and dark night those in charge were persuaded to keep their female patient behind a screen in a male ward, a practice which eventually led to the idea of mixed wards.

The House Block M became the Nurses' Training School, while F Block became the Paediatric Department, installed in what, in workhouse days, had been a punishment cell - offenders had been thrust into this cell naked so that they could be sprayed with cold water from a sprinkler in the ceiling.

So the hospital was constantly undergoing transformation and the original purpose laid down by the Emergency Medical Service - that the West Park Hospital should be able to look after wounded and injured servicemen and civilians - became blurred. Nevertheless service personnel continued to receive treatment at the West Park. In 1943 and 1944 an astonishing number of British soldiers were admitted with broken bones of all kinds, but especially of ankles and legs. The West Park authorities were told that these injuries were sports injuries but no one doubted that the explanation was much simpler. They were the result of paratroops being trained to jump from aircraft for D-Day and beyond. The booklet Wartime Cheshire, 1939-1945, does not mention parachute casualties but sets the scene well:

"Barrage balloons were used over Tatton Park during that time and one - known as 'Bessie' - was equipped with a cage suspended underneath from which trainee parachutists made their intermediate jumps after basic training in the hangar at Ringway. The jump from the cage was thought by many to be even more terrifying than a jump out of a moving aircraft at high altitude.

By 1943 and 1944 more civilian patients than service personnel were being admitted to West Park. The hospital gradually acquired a list of visiting specialists, while the names of resident medical staff, which included a Czech, an American, a Pole and an Irishman, revealed its international character. All these appointments had been made over a period of the early war years by A. Norman Jones, the Medical Supervisor. The transformation had been rapid - as a workhouse the only medical care to the institution had been part-time by a local G.P.

Many difficulties had to be surmounted. Clothing and bed linen were in short supply, as indeed was food, although spam and tinned chicken from Canada and the USA relieved the acuteness of the shortage. One child with coeliac disease was in great danger until some bananas were obtained from a source in the north of England. Radium, used by Manchester specialist hospitals in the treatment of cancer, had to be moved from that city because of the likely frequency of air raids. It was stored in an air raid shelter near F Block in the West Park Hospital, where not a few Manchester patients were housed and to which their specialists came from Manchester to treat them.

Because of the large number of maternity cases, fresh milk had been made available for mothers and prospective mothers by employing a farm bailiff who looked after 16 cows on the land between the hospital and the Victoria Road cricket ground. Unfortunately a gynaecological patient who had been treated with radium died as the result of 'gas gangrene', and it seemed likely that the death had resulted from infection introduced by airborne spores from the cattle dung. The cattle were duly sold and farming ceased completely.

By the time war ended, West Park Hospital was so well organised in its nursing arrangements that the General Nursing Council recognised it as a complete training school for nurses. Moreover the Central Midwives' Board recognised its fitness as a Part II Training School for Midwives. In addition several junior medical posts received authorization from the Royal Colleges as training posts. After the War Austrian nurses were trained at the West Park.

The National Health Service started on 5 July 1946 and, two years later to the day, West Park became part of the Macclesfield and District (later in 1970 the East Cheshire) Group, which included the Infirmary, Moss Lane Hospital and five hospitals in Congleton, Prestbury and Alderley Edge. It was the Number 19 Group Hospital Management Committee of the Manchester Regional Hospital Board. In 1974 the West Park Hospital was transferred to the Cheshire Area Health Authority and in 1982 to the Macclesfield and District Health Authority. It is now designated the West Park Branch of Macclesfield and District General Hospital.

Parkside remained a separate psychiatric hospital until 1970 when it became attached, like the West Park, to the Macclesfield and District Group, to form the East Cheshire Group and thereafter was directed by the same authorities.

Dr A. Norman Jones who, together with G.P. Siggins, had done so much to guide the West Park Hospital through the War into the acknowledged status of a general hospital from its pre-war workhouse status, left in February 1946 to join the staff at Whipps Cross Hospital, Leytonstone, London.

Much of the above was written with the help of G.P. Siggins' *History of West Park Hospital, Macclesfield, 1939-1949,* Arthur W. Clowes Ltd, 1989. The illustrations are from *A History of Parkside Hospital, 1871-1996, A Sense of Perspective* by David A. Broadhurst. Churnet Valley rep. 2000.

The main entrance to the Admission Hospital annexe at Parkside Hospital, which also contained the laboratory services for Macclesfield from 1920-1950.

CHAPTER 8
Warlike Activities in and around Macclesfield, 1939-1945

Macclesfield, for most of the War, looked war-like. Its streets and open spaces were filled with troops, military vehicles, rifles, guns, tanks (not least when the Americans arrived), men in Home Guard uniform, men in Special Constable uniform, men and women in Civil Defence uniform, and boys in Army Cadet or Air Training Corps uniform. On many street corners were emergency phone posts at which the Special Constables regularly reported their position as well as the state of affairs if an Air Raid Warning had been given. For a time the police station was plagued by a host of false calls from naughty boys who simply had to pull open the little door at the top of the contraption to get immediate attention.

Church stained-glass windows had disappeared and many other windows all over the town were criss-crossed by sticky material to protect them from bomb-blast. Many air raid shelters, and notices pointing towards them, were in open spaces, streets and parks. Prominent buildings and the sides of their doorways were guarded by walls of sandbags. In the early years there was a constant succession of whining air raid warnings, mainly at night. Most of the kerbstones were painted white to provide greater security for vehicles and pedestrians in the black-out. It was nevertheless dangerous to walk around in the black-out for the hazards were plentiful, unseeable and treacherous.

It is true that not a single bomb was dropped on Macclesfield itself during the Second World War, but the townsfolk were well aware that air raids were going on further north and further west, especially on Manchester and Liverpool. They knew that a vast number of other towns and cities were the targets of the Luftwaffe, Marshal Goering's German Air Force; and they listened with dread as Dornier, Heinkel and Junkers, heavy and medium bombers, droned, chugged and throbbed overhead. The term which everybody used to describe the air bombardments of British towns and cities was 'The Blitz'. Indeed this noun also became a verb - *'Liverpool was blitzed last night'*. The word 'Blitz' is an abbreviated form of the German word 'Blitzkrieg' - 'lightning war' - and, like many such words, does not in itself represent a logical translation of the original phenomenon it is describing. The short harsh sound of the word and the association of frightful bombing raids (on Warsaw in September 1939 and Rotterdam in May 1940, for example), with the beginning of invasion by the German army, both played a part in the use of this generic term for the whole series of German air raids on British towns and cities throughout the Second World War. Historians, however, tend to limit the 'Blitz' to the period between the attack on London on 7th September 1940 and on Birmingham on 16th July 1941, the period that began when Hitler had apparently given up the idea of invading Great Britain in the summer and autumn of 1940. It continued until Hitler launched his massive assault on the Soviet Union, the operation named 'Barbarossa'.

Manchester had three heavy raids over the Christmas period of 1940-1941. On 22nd December 270 German aircraft dropped 272 tons of high explosive and 632 incendiary canisters on the city. The very next night (23 December) 171 aircraft dropped 195 tons of high explosive and 893 incendiary canisters. On 8th January 1941 143 bombers dropped 110 tons of high explosive and 735 incendiary canisters. (From Basil Collier's *The Defence of the*

The shrine to the 5 members of the crew of the Flying Fortress 43-38944 which came down on Birchenough Hill 2nd January 1945. Top: The memorial.
Middle, in 1997.
And below, rebuilt in 2002 by Kevin Whittaker, Roland Griffith and Mark Sheldon.

A Civil Defence parade in Park Lane in the War.

United Kingdom, HMSO 1957, p. 503). The objective was not simply to destroy Manchester but to terrify its inhabitants. The people of Macclesfield observed the crimson smoky sky 18 miles north of them. They heard the engines of the aircraft as they came over and circled and departed, and the noise of anti-aircraft fire was clearly audible, while dull distant thuds made the ground tremble.

Macclesfield citizens, while fervently and compassionately thinking of the people of Manchester, hoped that a German plane going to that city or returning from it, would not by chance release one of its bombs on their town. But nothing fell during any of these raids except an anti-aircraft shell which pierced a bedroom window in Riseley Street and killed a sleeping woman. The raids of 22nd and 23rd December 1940 in the Manchester, Salford and Stockport areas cost 596 lives. A further 2,320 people were injured, 719 of them seriously. Police, Fire Fighters and Civil Defence casualties for the two nights were 64 killed and 250 injured. The raids of December 1940 were followed by other raids in 1941, in addition to the one on 8th January 1941. *The Times* of 3rd June 1941, in an article entitled *'Heavy attack on Manchester'*, referred to *'thousands of incendiary bombs and many tons of high explosive'* being dropped indiscriminately. Astonishingly, fatal casualties were not particularly heavy, but churches, hospitals and ordinary homes suffered badly.

The 'Blitz' in its general sense was to continue almost until the last few months of the War. A significant period of bombardment of English cities by German aircraft took place in the spring of 1942. This series of attacks was called the Baedeker raids or Baedeker Blitz because the cities involved were mainly those which appeared in Baedeker tourist guides as places of beauty and cultural interest. It appears that these raids were in retaliation for a British raid on the German Baltic Sea port of Lubeck on the night of 28-29th March 1942. Exeter sustained 4 raids between 23rd April and 4th May and suffered over 200 deaths, many casualties and severe damage, especially by fire. Bath was attacked on 2 successive nights,

Rolls-Royce at Crewe.

25-27th April, and some 300 people lost their lives. High explosives characterised the first night and incendiaries the second. Four attacks were launched against Norwich between 27th April and 27th June. There were approximately 80 deaths. York was the target on the night of 28-29th April. Canterbury had three raids between 31st May and 7th June, 48 people losing their lives and a considerable amount of damage being done through fire to the centre of the city.

Although Germany was now engaged in a most ruthless war against Russia, a war which was absorbing more and more of its resources, the 'Blitz' against other British cities and towns and ports continued, perhaps not so severely as in 1940 and 1941. Liverpool and Manchester continued to be targets. Doubtless some of the many raiders were shot down on their way back either by anti-aircraft fire or by British fighters. Only one German bomber - and this was after a bombardment of Liverpool on 8 May 1941 - crashed in the Macclesfield area. It was a Junkers 88 medium bomber. These very efficient planes had a crew of four, two engines, nine machine guns and could carry a bomb load of 4400 lbs. This particular aircraft came down at Black Brook, Gradbach, on a piece of land which is now very well known as a scout camp site in a beauty spot next to the River Dane. It must have swooped over the area known as the Lud Church before it crashed, scattering many pieces of molten metal as it exploded and burned fiercely. Its crew of four were

The Royal Exchange, Manchester.

killed instantly. The dead airmen were buried first in a cemetery in Leek and later removed to a cemetery in the Midlands after which they were taken back to Germany. Very little was left of the Junkers 88 that was recognisable except the tail which seemed to be full of bullet holes, indicating that a fighter plane rather than anti-aircraft fire had been responsible for its destruction.

But most crashes concerned Allied planes. One particular crash remains in the mind as exemplifying all the ramifications and implications of the coming-down of a warplane. This occurred at 5.25 pm on 2 January 1945, when the Allies were moving towards complete victory in Europe. This aircraft was a Boeing B-17 G Flying Fortress, number 43-38944. These U.S.A heavy bombers were a source of enormous comfort to the British people who were relieved and delighted by the vast American contribution to the war against Germany. They epitomised the turning of the tables on Hitler for his onslaughts of the early part of the war. They proclaimed that the trials and sufferings imposed by the Blitz on the British people had now lessened and that the enemy who had imposed them was now receiving fully justified reprisals. They were terrifying sights. They were huge and their four engines emphasised their size. A dozen machine guns bristled from all parts of the plane. Their normal bomb load for long range missions was 4000 lbs but their maximum load could be as much as 9600 lbs. Without a load their maximum range was 3400 miles. When fully operational they carried a crew of ten.

Between 1943 and 1945 they were being turned out at the factories at a rate of about 330 a month. In the last few months of the War this figure was more than 500. Boeing B-17 G Flying Fortress number 43-38944 crashed on to the very top of Birchenough Hill, Wincle, in January 1945. It was flying from Burtonwood to the 398 Bomb Group, 603 Squadron, Nuthampstead, Cambridge. The disaster was ascribed at the time to instrument failure. No bombs were being carried so that the crew on that journey numbered only five, all of whom were killed. They apparently emerged from low cloud and cannot have known anything of the sudden impact with the hill.

In late June 1994 Kevin Whittaker, who was then secretary of the Macclesfield Historical Aviation Society (and who has supplied many of the details of Second World War aircraft crashes dealt with in these pages) organised a visit to the site above Wildboarclough by more than 30 wartime American airmen and their families. There was first of all a moving service at St Saviour's Church and as the visitors came out of the church the 236th Army Training Corps, based at Bollington, formed a guard of honour of more than 28 young people aged between 12 and 18. All now walked up to Birchenough Hill and to the site of the crash marked clearly by a memorial plaque. (See page 108)

Jim Hooley, who was living at a nearby farm in 1945, recalling what he had experienced nearly fifty years previously, explained that he had heard the aeroplane pass overhead and was almost deafened by an immediate explosion. He ran out of the house into the farmyard and, looking up Birchenough Hill, saw a flame-filled sky. Both he and his brother Frank, together with a neighbour Norman Belfield, rushed breathlessly up to and across the road, and scrambled over the wall. They hurried up the grassy slope for three or four hundred yards and were horrified at the devastation they saw on the flat top of this remote hill. They were sick with shock to see one member of the crew, alive a few minutes beforehand, now lying dead on the grass.

Most of the airmen who had come over from the U.S.A. in 1994 to attend the memorial service were in their eighties. One of them, Oral Birch from Utah, eighty-two years old, had been a navigator and a friend and colleague of those who died. Indeed he might well have been on the flight but he had been captured a few weeks previously and in January 1945 was a prisoner in a German camp. He spoke to a reporter and said, *'I'm here today to remember my buddies who died on that day. I don't know if it was fate that I'm still here, but I felt that I had to make the trip over to say a final good-bye to them'*. Another colleague there was Oliver Bradford, also aged 82, who also might well have been on the flight but had been struck down by flu. He said, *'I remember news coming through to the base at Nuthampstead that they'd crashed and that there were no survivors. I felt numb and after that I felt terribly sad. I can't ever remember feeling relieved that I wasn't on the plane. That crew were like a family, you know, and being so far from home, we relied on each other'*. John Borquin, a former pilot who completed 35 bombing raids over Germany, had come to the service accompanied by his two daughters. Speaking of the pilot of the plane, Donald J. Decleene, he said, *'It could have been me. I don't know what happened that night but I still miss those guys'*.

The American veterans presented Kevin Whittaker with a plaque to mark their gratitude for the opportunity which he, together with his American counterpart, William Comstock, had given them to commemorate the deaths of their former colleagues and friends. If you wish to visit the site, simply walk straight up from St Saviour's Church, cross the A54 and climb over the stile. Follow the path upwards for half a mile to where it levels off. Before the path begins to descend there is a mound to the left. Climb this mound and you will see the hollow made by the crashing Flying Fortress, and the memorial is inside this hollow. Propped up against the base of the wall of the memorial is a pale wooden plaque a yard long and 8 inches high. On it is carved:

IN MEMORY OF THE CREW OF THE B 17
FLYING FORTRESS THAT CRASHED HERE ON 2-1-1945
LT. D.J. DECLEENE   LT. M. STRAVINSKIF   FO. T. MANOS
T.SGT. H. F. AYERS   T. SGT. F. E. GARRY   U.S.A.A.F

See page 108 for photographs.

Most plane crashes around Macclesfield concerned Allied aircraft, many of them on training flights. An Avro Anson, a twin-engined British plane used for general reconnaissance and armed coastal patrol duties as well as for the training of navigators, wireless operators and air gunners, crashed in Wildboarclough on 14th November 1940. It was carrying out a cross-country navigation exercise and the pilot, L.A.C. M.J.W. Taylor of the RAFVR, part of 21 group Fighter Command, the only occupant of the plane that day, lost his life.

Three days later, on 17th November 1940, a Supermarine Spitfire, a type of single seat fighter developed from the original Spitfire which had covered itself in glory in the Battle of Britain, crashed into the top of the Roches, a rocky escarpment not far from the Leek-Buxton Road. The pilot Flight Sergeant J.B. White was killed and the plane disintegrated into many pieces which were buried on the site.

Of course, Macclesfield is situated at the bottom of the western side of the Pennine Hills which rise quite sharply upwards from the town. The frequency of bad visibility generally as a result of mists and rain increased the likelihood of wartime aircraft, sometimes on training flights, sometimes returning from bombing missions, sometimes through navigational error, coming to grief in the vicinity of Macclesfield, Buxton and Leek. During the War itself information about such disasters, restricted by the need for secrecy, came only through word of mouth and hence was limited to a small number of people. Consequently the inhabitants of these towns and of the surrounding villages never felt that they were at grave risk from crashing aircraft.

Nevertheless the names of high ground landmarks well known to Macclesfield hikers became increasingly associated with air crashes. In 1939 and 1940 the Handley Page Hampden aircraft was a standard British medium bomber. It was used for minelaying, bombing invasion barges in the autumn of 1940 and armed reconnaissance flights. It was also used for the dropping of propaganda leaflets. But it was soon to be replaced by other more successful medium and heavy bombers. On 30th November 1940 such a Handley Page Hampden bomber found itself in difficulties in the western Pennines and informed its base control. But it then flew into a cloud-covered hillside at Black Edge, Dove Holes, just north of Buxton. There was only one survivor from the crew of four.

There were no casualties when a Fairey Battle plane, a single engine three seater light bomber, capable of carrying a 1000 lbs bomb load, had to make a forced landing at Lyme Green, Macclesfield, in August 1941. The front of the aircraft nosed its way into the hedge of a house on Robin Lane occupied by the Surtees family. The officer pilot was invited to stay the night in the spare room whilst the Sergeant Gunner had to put up with the garden shed. Both were nevertheless pleased and relieved not to have been hurt in the crash. The Fairey Battle was dismantled and taken to Ringway aerodrome (now Manchester Airport).

A member of the Surtees family, John, (known as Jack) became an air gunner in Bomber Command. Alas, he lost his life when, on 15 February 1943, his Wellington bomber of 38 Squadron came down in Crete, whilst attacking the German occupiers there. The pilot of the plane survived the crash and was taken prisoner by the Germans. After the War he came to see Mrs Surtees and told her of the circumstances in which her son had died.

A peculiar incident took place on 16 October 1941 when a British Boulton-Paul Defiant aircraft from 96 Squadron made a forced landing, in atrocious weather, on the hill known as Shining Tor near the Cat and Fiddle Inn. This British plane was a two seater fighter, having 4 machine guns in a dorsal turret. The crew were unharmed but caused general consternation when they set fire to their plane. It seems that a navigational error had led them to believe that they were in occupied France!

The Vickers Wellington bomber, which was given the nickname of 'Wimpey' after the American cartoon character J. Wellington Wimpey, was the most important two-engined British bomber in the early part of the War until it became superseded by the huge four-engined bombers like the Lancaster and the Halifax. There were 8 Wellington squadrons available to the RAF in September 1939 and by the winter of 1941-1942 there were 21 home-based British and Commonwealth squadrons. Wellingtons provided half of the first 1000 bomber raid on Cologne at the end of May 1942. One Wellington bomber of 75 Squadron which might have been on that raid had come to grief when returning from an operation on 22 May. It had flown into high ground at Sheldon Farm, Grindon Moor, near the Manifold Valley. The crew of five were killed and buried at Harpur Hill cemetery at Buxton.

On 13th July 1942 a Short Stirling, a British heavy bomber in the early years of the War, soon to be superceded by the Halifax and the Lancaster, came down at Merryton Low, on the eastern side of the Leek-Buxton Road. It seemed to be flying too low and made a desperate effort to gain height but struck high ground between the Mermaid Public House and the Mermaid Pool. All five crew members were killed. Four are buried in the Harpur Hill cemetery.

The entry of the United States of America into the War in December 1941 meant that from 1942 onwards a huge number of American aircraft began to come into Great Britain. The major base for such aircraft in the Macclesfield area was at Burtonwood near Warrington, Cheshire. It was not surprising therefore that not a few of these planes crashed on or near the hills on the eastern side of Macclesfield. One of the first US aircraft to come down near Macclesfield was a Republic P47 Thunderbolt which came down at Grove Bank Farm, Thorncliffe, in the hills above Leek on 2 December 1943. People who witnessed the fall to earth of this plane claimed that it seemed to dive out of low thick cloud into a natural spring in a field. The severed left hand of the pilot was found on a nearby road. There was much wreckage which was buried at the site, as was the shattered body of the pilot. This P47 Thunderbolt came from the 495 Training group at Atcham in Shropshire. These U.S. single seater planes (some versions of them also carried bombs in addition to the normal 8 machine guns in the wings) were amongst the biggest and heaviest single engine fighter planes of the Second World War.

In the same month - 17th December 1943 - another US single seater fighter aircraft, a two-engined Lockheed P 38 Lightning, famous for its twin boom or double fuselage, each fuselage joining its engine at the wing, came down at Cronkton Grange near Buxton. It was on a ferry flight to 20 Fighter Group, King's Cliffe, Northants. As a result of engine failure the pilot, 2nd Lt Guy A. Senasac, abandoned the plane. Five days later, on 22 December 1943, another Lockheed P 38 Lightning, also on a ferry flight to King's Cliffe - and also piloted by 2nd Lt Guy A. Senasac - crashed at Strines Farm, Merryton Low, not far from the Mermaid Public House. This time the pilot had lost radio contact as a result of bad weather and, once more, he abandoned the plane. He was slightly injured.

There were five air crashes close to Macclesfield in 1944. On 27th May a Short Stirling came down at Rudyard Lake. The crew of 8 were on a cross-country training flight. Onlookers gazed anxiously as the plane flew up and down the lake four or five times. Then they saw four parachutes opening, apparently only just in time. The Stirling lost height very quickly and exploded into the west bank of the lake, killing the remaining four of the crew, who had not been able to bale out. The plane had taken off from Wigsley aerodrome in Lincolnshire. Wreckage from this crash was only moved from the site in 1947 so that, by that time, souvenir hunters had already taken their pickings, leaving very little for the official authorities to retrieve. It has been observed that one boat house on the side of the lake sports a roof consisting of fuselage panels from the plane.

Since the Second World War the two planes most appreciated by British people have been the Spitfire fighter and the Lancaster bomber, and the RAF have ensured that on all national occasions which required a fly-past, including the fiftieth anniversaries of both VE (Victory in Europe) and VJ (Victory over Japan) Days in 1995, they have been led by one of each type. The basic Avro Lancaster was a heavy 4-engined bomber with a crew of seven. Its normal maximum bomb load was 41000 lbs and it had 8 machine guns in the nose, dorsal and tail turrets. It was first flown in January 1941 and its mass production began in October 1941. The first time it was used in operations was in March 1942 and it was to become the most important weapon in Bomber Command's exploits for the rest of the War, being used in 61 squadrons. The destruction of the Mohne and Eder dams in May 1943 in the famous operation led by Wing Commander Guy Gibson was carried out by Lancasters.

So far as Macclesfield is concerned the most significant connection the town had with the Lancaster occurred on 11th September 1944. A.V. Roe (AVRO) Test Pilot Syd Gleave and Flight Engineer Harry Barnes were killed when the Lancaster from Woodford aerodrome, which they were testing, crashed at Birtles, 4 miles west of Macclesfield. Every 10th production aircraft had to be power-dived. (See Chapter 7 for Syd Gleave's story)

By this time, of course, the British public had become very well aware of the efforts being made by the American forces towards the winning of the War. This included the might of the US Army Air Force. An increasing number of American planes were now coming to grief in England itself, not least on the eastern side of the Country. But there were several crashes involving US aircraft around Macclesfield. On 30th November 1944 Sgt Sofranko, pilot of a North American Harvard (a two-seater advanced trainer) took off from Turnhill, Shropshire on a cross-country navigational flight. He found himself in low cloud and descended to determine exactly where he was. He was above the Cat and Fiddle and was unable to avoid collision with the hill, Shining Tor (559 metres). He died instantly.

Less than a month later, on 22nd December 1944, a US C47 Douglas Dakota bound for France came down at Dawson's Farm, Sutton Common. The Dakota was a two-engined transport plane, capable of carrying 28 troops and 10,000 lbs of cargo. It was probably the most effective transport aircraft of any country during the Second World War. This particular Dakota (Number 41-38608) was not full of troops but was carrying a crew of 4 with 3 US Air Force passengers and cargo. Only the pilot, Major Theodore A. Rogers, survived, and he was seriously injured.

Reference has already been made to the American Flying Fortress and its crew of 5 which came down on Birchenough Hill on 2 January 1945. The following day - 3rd January 1945 - an Avro Lancaster from 467 Squadron Royal Australian Air Force flew into high ground in very bad visibility not very far away from Wildboarclough and Birchenough Hill. It came down on the Roches (a favourite climbers' and tourists' haunt) near the Leek-Buxton Road. The same day, 3rd January 1945, a US Republic P17 Thunderbolt, piloted by Flying Officer Johnson, got into difficulties near Flash village, which is just off the Leek-Buxton Road. It attempted to land but there are few flat fields in that part of the world and the plane plunged into the ground blowing up and killing the pilot.

The British Airspeed Oxford was an aircrew trainer and light transport plane. The first such aircraft of this type, of wooden construction, flew in June 1937 and had begun its service with the RAF Central Flying School before the end of that year. Over 400 were flying by September 1939 and altogether nearly 9000 Airspeed Oxfords were built. They were excellent as training planes but at least five of them crashed near Macclesfield and this fact indicates that they were often flown by inexperienced airmen. On 16 November 1941 Pilot LAC Dix of the RAFVR lost his way in bad weather and was killed when his Airspeed Oxford crashed into high ground at Fawside Edge near Longnor. Another Airspeed Oxford came down on 12 May 1943 at Axe Edge near Buxton, once more in bad weather, killing all three crew members. On 29th September 1943 another Airspeed Oxford, on a low cross-country exercise, crashed at Henbury, to the west of Macclesfield and a few miles away from the hills.

It hit a tree and exploded on a piece of land which is now the car park at Henbury Church. Both airmen from the Royal Canadian Air Force, Sgt D.J. Munro and Sgt W.R. Donnelly, were killed.

An unusual and tragic event took place on 4th April 1945 when an Airspeed Oxford flew into the hill known as Shining Tor near Buxton. It seems that three crew members were injured but died from exposure since the remains of their aircraft were not discovered for 5 days. On the very same day another Airspeed Oxford crashed into the popular hill called Shutlingsloe which rises steeply from Trentabank reservoir and then descends into Wildboarclough. This plane was on a cross-country flight and tried to negotiate low cloud with tragic results. The pilot and two crew members were killed. Astonishingly two passengers from the RAF survived.

In the last 18 months of the War, as it became clear that victory for the Allies was becoming more and more likely, the German people heard and therefore talked a great deal about the Fuhrer's so-called 'Wunderwaffen' - miracle weapons - which would turn the tide of success back in favour of Germany. The Allied troops landed in Normandy on 6 June 1944. One week later, on Tuesday 13 June 1944, just as dawn was breaking, a strange small aircraft crossed the coast of England. It seemed to be emitting a red glow behind itself and giving out a rattling sound quite different from that of known aircraft. It pursued a direct north-westward route over Kent and was clearly aiming for London as it chugged alongside the estuary of the River Thames. It was pursued with some consternation as attempts were made to discover exactly what it was. In the event it did not reach London. It came down with a huge explosion near the Kentish village of Swanscombe. It caused no casualties but people had observed that its engine seemed to have given out a few minutes before it crashed.

This was the first 'Wunderwaffe', a pilotless plane which in itself was a large bomb. Its most frightening feature was that it announced the area in which it might fall by turning off its own engine, leaving the people on the ground hoping and praying for some time that its inevitable explosive collision with the ground would not be on top of the building in which they were sheltering. The names given to this new weapon of fear by the British population were varied: 'The Flying Bomb', 'The Buzz Bomb', 'The Doodle-Bug', 'The Pilotless Plane'. Some wags at the time referred to it as 'The Virgin Bomb' - *'Never had a man inside it, you know.'*

These Flying Bombs were despatched from launching pads in France and later from Belgium and Holland. They had certain targets in Southern England such as Portsmouth and Southampton but the major target was London. The attacks continued until March 1945. Over 10,000 were launched, most from special ramps, a proportion of them from aircraft. Two and a half thousand succeeded in reaching London. The defences against them were varied. First there were bombing raids on their launching sites and on the factories which produced them; then there were Allied fighter aircraft which hounded and shot them down - in some cases the Heinkel 111 Bombers which could launch them were also shot down; there were, of course, anti-aircraft guns, especially those moved to the South coast, and these were very successful in destroying many of them; finally there were barrage balloons with their trailing wires which were very helpful in the protection of London.

By late August more than a million Londoners had left the capital voluntarily and had sought refuge in many other parts of the country. Over two hundred thousand mothers and children took advantage of government arrangements for evacuation to safer areas. This period saw the greatest exodus of people from London since the early days of September

1939. Six thousand people were killed by flying bombs and eighteen thousand seriously injured. But Hitler had another 'Wunderwaffe' to give temporary comfort to his own people and to instill further fear into the people of Britain. This was the A-4 rocket developed at Peenemunde on the island of Usedom just off the German Baltic coast. Very soon the British people referred to the Flying Bomb as the V1 and to the A-4 rocket as the V2. The V stood for the German word Vergeltung, meaning 'reprisal', the action taken by Nazi Germany in response to Allied bombing of Hitler's Reich.

By September the allied troops had occupied most of France and much of Belgium and had overrun many V1 sites. But the V2s were being fired from Holland, the first landing in a suburb of Paris on 8 September. The same evening a rocket fell on Chiswick in London, killing three people and causing serious injuries to 10 others. Almost immediately afterwards another V2 landed in a rough uninhabited field near Epping. Londoners felt a little relief for, although the A-4 rockets were huge and their explosion ear-splitting and deadly, they lacked the power to taunt, to threaten, to terrorise which their flying bomb predecessors had possessed. Civilians argued that, if a rocket hit you that was the first and last you knew about it. But a V1 crept up on you slyly, telling you by cutting off its engine that it was now to fall....... and then kept you waiting on shredded nerves while you hoped that its final explosion would be some distance away.

The V2 campaign, which ran in tandem with the continuing V1 onslaught, consisted of 1400 launches, of which over 1100 landed in London or the mainly southern areas of the country. Some 2700 people were killed and over 6,500 seriously injured. These figures were less than those caused by the Flying Bombs.

No rocket fell on or near Manchester or Macclesfield. But Macclesfield was affected in two ways by the operations of the V1 and V2. First the town received a huge number of evacuees in the summer and autumn of 1944. On 7th July, for example, 800 unaccompanied children arrived by train. Half of them were allocated billets with local families and the other half were given accommodation in rural areas surrounding Macclesfield. All were distributed to schools in the town or outlying areas. In Macclesfield, Athey Street School (an 'elementary school' for children aged 5-14) had to be used as a rest centre for adults and families who had arrived from the south and hence was only able to take its share of evacuee scholars in late July when its temporary occupants had found accommodation in the town. Four teachers from Ilford in Essex were helping to alleviate problems caused by the sudden influx of new pupils.

Apart from Athey Street, the schools chosen to receive the bulk of these evacuees were St Paul's, Byron Street, Ash Grove and the Central School for Boys and the Central School for Girls. The old mill in Longacre Street, which had been used in 1939-1940 to provide midday meals for evacuees, was reopened after a massive effort to re-equip the building as a refectory. The Pierce Street medical and dental premises for the Town's schoolchildren were fitted up not only as a dining hall but also as a kitchen which produced the meals for the Longacre Street establishment. Soon the Borough was producing 1750 lunches for evacuated schoolchildren as well as for those local boys and girls who, for various reasons, were unable to get home for a meal. School buildings often had to organise makeshift dining rooms and these were supplemented by prefabricated huts on sites in, for example, the South Park and High Street.

On 1st September 1944 the Secretary of the Borough's Schools' Management Committee

Aircraft Accident

SERGEANT KILLED

MRS. Mullins, of 19, Garden St., has received a telegram from R.A.F. Headquarters, which states: "Deeply regret to inform you that your son, Sergt. Jack Mullins, is missing, believed killed, as the result of an aircraft accident. Letter follows. Please accept our profound sympathy."

Sergt. Mullins, who is twenty-two years of age, is the youngest son of Mrs. and the late Mr. W. Mullins, of 19, Garden Street. Educated at the Central School, he was employed at the County Treasurer's Office, The Castle, Chester, before joining up. Previous to that he was employed by Messrs. May and Wain, solicitors.

He was last on leave five months ago, just after his 'plane had brought down an Axis aircraft. a successful engagement.

His elder brother is serving in the Royal Artillery.

A letter from the Wing Commander of Sergt. Mullins' squadron was received on Tuesday, and in this it was stated that the aircraft was seen to crash into the sea. The letter continued:—"Please let me extend to you the deepest sympathy of myself and his colleagues in your great loss. He was one of our best wireless-operators, no one being keener to get on that he You can be assured the rest of us will do our best to carry on the good work which he started."

He was engaged to Miss Vera Manning, of East Didsbury.

MISSING IN MIDDLE EAST

PTE. J. CLARKE

After having served in the Western Desert since January, Pte. Joseph Clarke (Durham Light Infantry), of 8 Smith's Terrace, has been reported missing. Formerly employed at Messrs. Abrahams' Dyeworks, Pte. Clarke is a son of Mrs. Clarke, of 10 White Street, and the late Mr. Clarke. He was educated at Athey Street School.

PRISONER OF WAR.—Kenneth Neild White, whose father resides at 47, Water Street, is believed to be a prisoner of war. He was reported missing since June 6th, and this intimation was received from the Red Cross by his father. Kenneth, who is 27, is married, his wife residing at Congleton.

Police Amalgamation

A SPECIAL MEETING of the Watch Committee was held on Tuesday, when the Mayor (Alderman C. W. Kirk), and the Town Clerk (Mr. A. Bond), gave a report on the meetings they had attended as members of the Police Committee of the Association of Municipal Corporations and the Executive Committee of the Non-County Boroughs Association concerning the question of police amalgamation.

They reported on the steps being taken to oppose in Parliament the Home Office proposals.

It was resolved to place on record a strong protest against the proposed amalgamation, as it does not appear in the national interest.

Copies of resolutions passed by the Macclesfield Joint Branch Board of the Police Federation protesting against the proposals were submitted and the Committee agreed with the views expressed in the resolutions.

RAILWAY GUARD FATALLY INJURED

THE DEATH occurred in the Macclesfield Infirmary late on Tuesday night of James Henry Lucking, 184 Hurdsfield Road, a goods guard on the L.M.S. Railway, who was found seriously injured on Friday afternoon, lying near the metals on the Gasworks railway bridge.

He was 66 years of age, and would have retired but for the war.

TANKS FOR ATTACK

A GREATER EFFORT is needed in Macclesfield for the "Tanks for Attack" campaign which is being waged on the local Savings Front. The campaign is not progressing as anticipated, and there has only been a 15 per cent. increase in savings as against the desired 20 per cent.

For the first four weeks of the campaign, July 25th to August 15th (inclusive), the total saved is £23,108 against £20,090.

The minimum increase before the town will be allotted Light Tanks is 20 per cent., and it is felt that with a little extra effort it will be realised. The Industrial, Street and Schools Groups are appealed to, to see that Macclesfield shall not fail our boys on the battle fronts of the world.

LOCAL 'BUS STOPS—At a meeting of the Traffic Sub-Committee of the Watch Committee on Tuesday, a letter was considered from the North-Western Road Car Co. stating that the Company were being pressed to economise in the use of fuel, and to reduce the number of bus stopping places on all routes, together with a list of the stopping places the Company proposed to abolish. The Sub-Committee also considered the Chief Constable's report on the proposals, and it was resolved that the report of the modifications be approved and forwarded to the Company.

reported that the Central Schools had been used as a rest centre in August for another party of mothers and children from the south. In Macclesfield's schools there were 572 evacuated children, while approximately the same number had gone to schools in the Borough's rural area.

On 8th September 1944 the Mayor of Ilford and the Chairman of the Ilford Education Committee visited Macclesfield and expressed their gratitude for the way in which their schoolchildren had been accommodated in the town. There was also a large influx of private evacuees, including many adults, especially from the middle classes, who had felt able to afford the cost of leaving London behind for the time being. Macclesfield homes offered rented rooms to these grateful people who were relieved to have escaped the menace of the Flying Bombs and subsequently of the rockets.

But although no bomb was to fall on Macclesfield itself, Christmas Eve 1944 was a dangerous evening and night in the area. Fifty Heinkel 111 bombers from Kampfgeschwader (Battle Squadron) 53 were used to launch Flying Bombs against Manchester, spreading themselves out at points off the east coast between Skegness and Bridlington. Thirty bombs were successfully launched but only one reached Manchester itself. Six bombs came to earth less than 10 miles from the centre of the city. Eleven bombs fell 10 to 15 miles from the city centre. There were over a hundred casualties including 37 deaths. Macclesfield did not quite escape all the excitement. One Flying Bomb landed in a field between Tegsnose and the start of Macclesfield Forest. It made a large sandy hole and blew out the windows of the farmhouse nearby. A considerable number of people from the town walked out to visit the phenomenon.

Although it could never be claimed that Macclesfield was in the forefront of air raids, there was no lack of evidence of action all around the town, justifying the precautions taken inside the town itself.

V1 and V2 bombs.

HMS Royal Oak, pp. 121-124.

The Lancaster bomber of which Sergeant Southern was the navigator, pp. 130-132.

Courtesy of José Price, his daughter

CHAPTER 9

Six Stories of Wartime Macclesfield

Petty Officer Jack

Petty Officer Jack had joined the Royal Navy in the 1920s in order to avoid unemployment. It was the time of the Depression. In Macclesfield there had always been a shortage of jobs for men. The silk mills employed a certain number as managers and engineers and clerks, but what they really wanted was women; women who cleaned and wound the raw silk, or who made it into warps, or who entered the warps into the looms or who then wove the warps into fine cloth. Many women sewed buttons onto the finished products, being paid for the quantity of buttons they successfully attached to blouses or shirts.

The result was that men, on the whole, had to look elsewhere for employment. Jack was the eldest of a large family. He had no training, he could not obtain employment anywhere in the Town, he was an embarrassment to the economic sufficiency of his parents and siblings, and so he joined the Royal Navy. He became a stoker. He worked hard and he enjoyed his new life. Once trained he was drafted to a ship and did a tour overseas and loved it.

He returned to the United Kingdom and was given leave, which he naturally spent in Macclesfield, regaling his family with proud recollections of his career so far in the Royal Navy. Just before his return to Portsmouth, which was his 'port division', he met a girl called Hilda whom he had known at school and he promised to write to her. This he duly did and within a short time their relationship, based mainly on their correspondence, became warm. Just before his next foreign posting Jack suggested that they might consider marriage. Their letters to each other thereafter became regular, a necessity to both of them. But it was two years before Jack returned to cement their relationship. Within six months and during one of his spells of leave they were married.

They managed to rent a small house in the north-eastern part of the town. Soon a child was on the way but before the birth of this, their first son, Jack was already sailing to the Far East. He was part of the ship's company of a veteran battleship which anchored off the island of Singapore. On shore leave one day he spotted, in an unpretentious shop, a five foot high glass cabinet of delicate Japanese porcelain, clearly an item of great beauty. On the various shelves were small condiment jars, milk bowls and dishes; chocolate, tea and coffee cups; tiny white and coloured jugs. There were butter dishes with lids, little porcelain blue and white birds. In all the underglazing and enamelling were immaculate. Jack was no connoisseur but he knew that this piece of furniture and its contents were something special. He was overwhelmed with a desire to take it back to England as a present for Hilda.

Could he afford it? He was now a Leading Seaman and would soon be a Petty Officer. He had saved quite a lot of his pay recently since there had been little opportunity to spend, and his naval allowance to Hilda was adequate for the needs of the small family at home. He took the plunge. He was able to make arrangements through his ship's supply officer for the transfer of the cabinet to the ship and for its subsequent transportation to the UK. Further arrangements were made in Portsmouth on the battleship's return for the sending of the cabinet to Macclesfield.

After not a few difficulties Jack found himself back at home with his wife and son - and the cabinet of delicate and precious porcelain. Hilda was delighted with this lovely piece of furniture and its contents. It held pride of place in their tiny abode. But as the years passed two more children arrived and the house began to bulge. A great concern of Hilda now was the safety of the cabinet. None of the superb crockery was ever taken out of the cabinet and used. But from time to time a noisy and energetic youngster would collide with its glass doors and Hilda's heart beat with alarm. Nevertheless Jack's gift and treasure from the Far East remained intact, a symbol of endeavour and aspiration.

Another child was born, making the house even tinier than it had been. Jack, now a Petty Officer, had to make up his mind whether to leave the Royal Navy after his statutory twelve years or to apply for an extension. He decided that he wanted to be with his family and so he left the service (although he was to remain on the Reserve List) and settled down in Macclesfield. 'Settled down' was hardly the expression for he was unable to obtain employment.

His naval pension was not large and had to be eked out by a small unemployment benefit. The house in which he had to spend most of his days was reasonably quiet when the children were at school but when all members of the family were together there was precious little privacy or sense of space. He began to fidget and found himself having numerous tiffs with Hilda over trivial matters. Hilda was experiencing great difficulty in looking after her family on so little income. She had to create extra money from somewhere. She managed to acquire some sewing work at a nearby silk mill and began to earn thirty shillings a week. But this meant that she had to farm out her youngest child to a child minder at a charge of eight shillings a week.

There was still little possibility of the occasional luxury which many families, even at that time, took for granted. Debts began to accumulate at the nearby grocer's shop and at the clothing club which supplied children's garments so long as its representative continued to receive one shilling each Friday evening when he called - Friday was wages' day in Macclesfield. Hilda needed just a little relaxation of the tight housekeeping budget she had imposed on herself. She eyed the porcelain cabinet. Should she try to sell it? It took up a lot of space and caused her great moments of anguish whenever a child fell against it. Yet it was her pride and joy, a source of self-respect. She hesitated a few more weeks. Then she made up her mind, persuaded Jack that she was doing the right thing and visited a lady of her acquaintance who was known to have some means. Would she like to buy the porcelain cabinet? Would she like to come and see it?

The lady went to see it and found it dazzlingly beautiful. She offered Hilda five pounds, a quite large sum of money in the late thirties. It represented two weeks' wages for any workman in the town who managed to obtain a job demanding a certain level of skill as well as strength. With a little choke of sadness Hilda accepted the five pounds. Jack borrowed a hand cart and was successful in transporting the cabinet and its contents to the lady's house on the other side of the town. It was set up in the lady's front room, opposite the window, a sign of opulence and dignity.

Hilda pined after that cabinet and its contents for several weeks. She then knocked on the lady's door; could she please just sit for a short time looking at the cabinet? Yes, of course. The lady was a little disconcerted. She could return the cabinet free of charge..... and yet, it had become her treasure now, a treasure which she would not be eager to relinquish.......

Jack was called up into the Navy as a reservist in the summer of 1939 when war threatened. He retained his rank of Petty Officer and was relatively well paid. His family began to prosper as a result of the naval allowance received by Hilda. It would be nice to imagine that she now felt able to strike a bargain over the return of the cabinet with its new owner. But time had moved on, Hilda had grown accustomed to feeling unencumbered by the cabinet, and the purchaser was certainly enjoying continued ownership of the lovely piece of furniture. She too never used any of the dainty cups and plates and bowls but would frequently pause in front of her acquisition and smile with satisfaction.

Jack had reported back to Portsmouth. He was shortly drafted to the battleship HMS Royal Oak, which had been commissioned in May 1916 and had fought with the British Grand Fleet at the Battle of Jutland. Within a few weeks the Royal Oak was based near Scapa Flow, a huge natural harbour in the Orkney Islands and graveyard of Germany's First World War fleet, scuttled in 1919.

On the whole Scapa Flow was a well protected anchorage except that doubt had been expressed over the total security of several small entrance channels on the eastern side. These channels linked a series of islands, and blockships had been sunk in them to reduce their susceptibility to hostile penetration. But it was recognised that, under certain conditions, a small vessel could gain surreptitious entry into Scapa Flow. In early October 1939 *The Royal Oak* had been patrolling the sea between Orkney and Shetland. Its task was to prevent the German battlecruiser Gneisenau, based in the Baltic, from reaching the Atlantic and destroying British merchant convoys. The German submarine U-47, under the command of Lieutenant Gunther Prien, left Kiel on 8 October 1939. She intended to seek out any British capital ships in and around Scapa Flow.

Just before midnight on Friday 13 October, this submarine, as the result of great navigational skill, clever timing and a little luck, found herself being swept by the fast incoming tide through the very narrow Kirk Sound, one of several vulnerable eastern channels, and into Scapa Flow. Discovering no ships at the Main Fleet anchorage on the western side of Scapa Flow, Lieutenant Prien turned north-east and, his heart leaping, discovered the Royal Oak. He fired four torpedoes. Only one seemed to hit its target and, eerily, the Royal Oak displayed no reaction. The U-boat, having swept well away in a wide arc for its own safety, returned to close range and discharged three more torpedoes. All hit their target and the battleship, severely holed, burst into flames.

Within half an hour she had sunk, leaving many men in the water and carrying many more to the sea bottom. 786 men lost their lives. One of them was Jack, the Macclesfield Petty Officer. The U-boat sped back to Kirk Sound and succeeded in pushing its way safely through the slim channel against the weakening tide and into the North Sea. A few days later its commander and crew were fêted in Berlin by Hitler and cheering crowds. Later in the War U-17 was sunk with all hands lost.

It is probable that the cabinet of porcelain Jack had brought back from the Far East has passed from one collector to another, gaining in value all the time. It is unlikely that any of its contents were ever placed on a table as receptacles for a dainty meal. But many people must surely have gazed on it with pleasure and admiration.

Jack was one of five Macclesfield men who, between 3rd September and 28th December 1939, lost their lives serving in His Majesty's Forces.

Wing Commander Guy Gibson

The Dambuster Raids had a strong association with the Peak District because of the many hours of practising on the Derwent and Howden Dams. Wing Commander Guy Gibson, who led the raids, also had a substantial connection with Macclesfield towards the end of the War.

An enormous amount of political thinking went on in the United Kingdom throughout the Second World War. It stemmed from the recognition that the War was being fought against a totalitarian government and an increasingly thorough examination of our own democratic system of government was essential. The success of the Soviet Union, a communist state, in throwing back the might of fascist Nazi Germany helped to further a genuinely sympathetic consideration of the claims of Marxism to produce a just society.

The election of a Labour Government in July 1945 (before the Japanese had been eliminated from the War) resulted from the acknowledgement that the huge numbers of people who had fought and won the War deserved, in future, a society based on a fairer distribution of wealth, privileges and amenities.

The political parties, especially the Labour Party, were already preparing for the 'post-war' parliamentary election long before the War was over. The Conservative party in Macclesfield (a constituency which has always returned a Conservative candidate) had not been slow to look ahead. In November 1935 J R Remer, 'National Conservative', who had represented Macclesfield since 1918, received 24,249 votes against G. Darling, Labour, who gained 14,781 votes, and J.L. Poole. Liberal, who achieved 7,151 votes. Hence J.R Remer was the town's MP in 1939, but ill-health forced him to resign in early 1940. He was succeeded by Garfield Weston, Conservative, a Canadian, bearer of a name famous for the production of biscuits. He had founded in Great Britain the Weston Biscuit Company and subsequently the huge food company called Allied Bakeries.

In July 1943 Garfield Weston announced that he did not wish to seek re-election after the War. His intention was to resume his business commitments in Canada. Now Weston had met Wing Commander Guy Gibson VC a short time after the famous Dambusters' Raid in May 1943. He was impressed by this 25 years old leader of the raid - his youth, his ability, the successes he had achieved, and his modesty. He formed the impression that Guy would be the ideal person to succeed him as an MP. He invited Guy and his wife Eve to his large country house at Marlow in Buckinghamshire in February 1944. There the young married pair met the Weston family - Mrs Weston had nine children and most were present that weekend.

Garfield Weston was now quite confident that Guy would be the right man to follow him into the House of Commons. But, of course, it was up to the local Conservative Party to agree to his becoming one of the possibly many who would like to be the Macclesfield Conservative candidate for Parliament. Guy's first obligation was to become acquainted with the local Association, and with the people of Macclesfield.

Garfield Weston had invited Lord and Lady Vansittart to visit the town that same month of February 1944 - Lord Vansittart had spent 8 years as Permanent Under Secretary at the Foreign Office and was now, since 1937, the government's Chief Diplomatic Adviser. He had achieved fame, almost notoriety, for his vigorous verbal attacks on Nazi Germany. Now he was the President of the non-Party 'Win the Peace Movement' and on Thursday 10 February 1944 gave a speech to 500 Civil Defence workers at the Civil Defence Headquarters in

Whiston Street. He asserted challengingly that the Germans/Nazis should never be given the chance to start another war.

By the design of Garfield Weston, Guy and Eve had arrived the previous day, Wednesday 9 February, and, after visiting Woodford Aerodrome, the home of the Avro Lancaster bomber, and the Avro factory at Chadderton, Manchester, returned in time to accompany Lord and Lady Vansittart to the Macclesfield Civil Defence Headquarters. Here Guy gave a speech, without notes, which won the hearts of his audience. By this time, after extensive tours of Canada and the USA he was an accomplished speaker. His political message was that those who had fought this war should not only be treated well afterwards by a grateful nation but should play an important part in running the industry and government of the country.

The fact that the great industrial heritage of Macclesfield was silk production (not least the massive supply of parachute material) was well-known and Guy was anxious to meet some of the workers in the many silk mills of the town. So he and Eve spent two hours at the factory of Edmund Lomas Ltd, situated on Waters Green, talking to the workers, both men and women, and being given explanations of the intricacies of silk manufacturing. This visit too was a great success.

Guy submitted his application for the prospective Conservative candidate and by 10th March a short list of five men had been selected. On 31st March he was chosen as the Macclesfield Conservative Party candidate. The local Labour Party was incensed. Councillor C.T. Douthwaite claimed that if Guy really did wish to represent the needs and aspirations of Britain's fighting men and women, he should have joined the Labour Party.

On 23 August 1944, almost five months later, Guy wrote a letter to the Macclesfield Conservative Association asking to be released from his position as their candidate for the next parliamentary election. He wished to resume his full-time service in the Royal Air Force, which would require all his commitment and concentration. He had no intention of pursuing a political career and would not be seeking (as had been suggested in some newspaper reports) candidature in another constituency. The Association reluctantly accepted Guy's withdrawal and looked forward to his continuing success in the R.A.F. The decision of Wing Commander Gibson came as a shock, not only to the people of Macclesfield but throughout the Country.

Perhaps a look at Guy Gibson's background - and the Dambusters mission - is appropriate here. Guy's father, Alexander Gibson, had been employed in the Forestry Department of the Indian Civil Service. His marriage had been a failure and his wife Leonora had died at the age of 46, in sad circumstances. Guy had a brother and a sister. Joan his sister was sent to a convent school in Belgium. Alick (Alexander) and Guy were first sent to a prep. boarding school in Folkestone and then to St Edward's School in Oxford. Guy did not shine particularly but he tried hard at games with some success. His academic attainments were barely average, the basic School Certificate eluding him at the first attempt, but he developed the ambition to become a test pilot and applied for entry to the Royal Air Force. He was at first rejected on medical grounds, his legs being too short (his height was never more than 5' 6"). But he overcame this 'hurdle' the second time and joined the RAF in November 1936.

He became a Flying Officer in June 1939. He was extremely anxious to shoot down German planes but had the frequent frustration of catching sight of enemy aircraft without getting near enough to open fire. Germany invaded Denmark and Norway on 9th April 1940 and Guy and his crew in their Hampden bomber managed to mine some German coastal areas in the face of fierce anti-aircraft fire. Their return journey was nightmarish, severe weather leading to their being diverted from Scampton in Lincolnshire, where they were based, to Manston in Kent. Most of the time Guy was flying on instruments and it was with relief that, emerging from rain and thick cloud, he and his crew spotted the green lights of Manston beckoning to them.

The German onslaught on Holland, Belgium, Luxembourg and France from 10 May 1940 and the rapid all-conquering advance of their forces left Britain isolated, alone and threatened with invasion. By July 1940 Guy had participated in a considerable number of operations and had been awarded the DFC. Still flying a Hampden bomber he was credited with the destruction of a Dornier plane in August 1940 and on 15 September he took part in 83 Squadron's bombing in Antwerp of German invasion barges waiting for the order (which never came) to set out for English shores.

Meanwhile Guy had met Eve Moore, a dancer and actress living in Brighton. They married in Penarth, Wales, where Eve's parents lived, in November 1940. Although Guy knew how many of his RAF friends had already been killed, he was depressed when his posting in September to an Officer Training Unit prevented him from participating further in the air warfare for which he felt himself best suited. His request for operational duty again was eventually granted and he joined 29 Squadron to take part in night-flying duties as a Flight-Lieutenant. The bad weather of early 1941 restricted the operations of his unit but he was eventually delighted in March when he shot down a Heinkel 111.

As yet there was no suggestion that Guy was anything greater than a competent pilot and reliable airman. Although he had the respect of all aircrews he flew with, he was inclined to be moody and easily upset if things did not go according to plan. He had problems with ground staff personnel for he allowed his own impatience to take charge and this often resulted in his giving offence to aircraftmen of lower rank. In June 1941 he became a Squadron Leader. In July he shot down another Heinkel 111 and in September was awarded a bar to his DFC. His desire was to be part of a bomber squadron, but this seemed to be thwarted when, in December 1941, he was again posted, this time to 51 Officers' Training Unit, Cranfield, in Bedfordshire, as Chief Flying Instructor.

As happened so often with Guy he felt dispirited. Then in March 1942 he received the order to report to the new head of Bomber Command, Air Marshal Arthur Harris, who was clearly aware of Guy's potential. Very soon afterwards Guy was promoted to Acting Wing Commander and, in April 1942, became Commander of 106 Squadron at Coningsby, flying Avro Manchesters, soon to be replaced by Avro Lancasters.

In May he led an attack on the Heinkel factory at Warnemunde, an operation which was successful but, because of the Germans' defence, extremely difficult. On 8 July he led an assault upon Wilhelmshaven with 10 Lancasters. Then came a very long trip to Danzig, the target being the submarine works. On 31 July he led a group of 21 aircraft which bombed Dusseldorf heavily, dropping 63 tons of bombs. By September 1941, in addition to the 99 sorties he had made in fighter aircraft, he had now amassed a total of 56 bomber operations. At a time when the life expectancy of an active airman was short, Guy's ability to stay out of trouble, to be 'lucky', was becoming legendary. In October and November he led flights to Italy, including attacks upon Genoa, Milan and Turin and was awarded the DSO. In March 1943, having completed a year with 106 Squadron, he received a bar to his DSO, the citation for which included the fact that he had now completed 172 sorties.

Guy was due for a rest and was not surprised to be told that a new man was to take over his 106 Squadron. He was asked to write a book for the benefit of future bomber pilots. Guy was astonished and again dismayed. He did not want to write a book - at any rate not yet; he was looking forward to some leave, yes - but he saw his future in continuing the air warfare against Nazi Germany.

He was sent to RAF Grantham and seeing the strain on the faces of the administrative staff who were having to continuously make huge decisions upon which many lives depended, he quietly settled to his writing. But he had hardly been there for two days when he was sent for by Air Vice-Marshal Ralph Cochrane, who asked him if he would like to do 'one more trip'. Guy was intrigued and curious, and somewhat bewildered.

Cochrane summoned him again two days later and introduced him to Air-Commodore Charles Whitworth, who asked him to go away and select aircrews for a new squadron which would need to start training in four days' time. Within an hour Guy had handed in the names of all the pilots he wanted, men he knew, men who were very experienced and had displayed their courage and tenacity. They came from all parts of the world - from Australia, America, Canada, New Zealand and Great Britain. He was relieved to discover that his squadron, to be called 617 Squadron, was to be based at RAF Scampton in Lincolnshire, an airfield he knew well and felt at home. When he was told that he would be leading an attack upon a specific and essential target which would involve low flying over water at night, he immediately surmised that this target would be the powerful and well protected battleship Tirpitz.

He was then asked to visit Mr Barnes Wallis who had invented the bomb which 617 Squadron was to drop. He was taken aback when he realised that this bomb was like an enormous cylinder. Air Vice-Marshal Cochrane informed him that Wallis's new bomb, still to be perfected, was to blow up the dams of the Ruhr, the centre of German industry. His crews had also jumped to the conclusion that their target was the Tirpitz. They continued to think this because Guy, in accordance with instructions, did nothing to undeceive them.

Wallis (known to Guy as Professor Jeff or simply Jeff for security reasons) and his team spent weeks trying to put agonising finishing touches to the cylindrical bomb which was to hit the water, bounce into the air, continue to hit the water and to bounce at decreasing heights until, hopefully, it bumped up against the dam wall. There would be a little pause and then, with a enormous explosion, it would blast the wall into a thousand fragments, releasing tons of water to crush the vital German industries of the Ruhr. Huge technical problems were involved in bringing the bomb casings to the exact strength required. The scientists assessed that the bomb would have to be released when the plane was at a height of 60 feet above the water. From the point of view of the airmen there was also the problem of ascertaining the split second when the bombs were to be released. Air Force boffins came to the rescue by arranging beams of light on the aircraft which would meet at the only possible moment - assuming that the aircraft was being handled appropriately.

Meanwhile the air crews practised low-level flying in the late evenings over Uppingham Lake, Colchester Reservoir, and the Derwent and Howden reservoirs in the Peak District. Nine Lancasters were to attempt to breach the walls of the Mohne and Eder dams, and five more were to attack the Sorpe Dam. The remaining five, a total of nineteen, were to escort the others and be prepared for anything they were called upon to do.

They set out late in the evening of Sunday 16 May 1943. Guy's aircraft dropped the first bomb on the Mohne Dam but he and his crew were disappointed to see that the wall was not breached in spite of the mountain of water and spray which rocketed up. A vast amount of anti-aircraft fire sped up towards them and their comrades, and they all knew how startlingly prominent and vulnerable they were. There were soon many German fighter planes hurtling around, but the lowness of the bombers made them difficult targets from the air. Guy had to wait for ten minutes to allow the frothing water to settle before sending in the following Lancaster. This plane, piloted by Flight Lieutenant J.V. Hopgood, dropped its bomb on the power house beyond the dam, but it was clear that it had been hit by flack and it hovered despairingly as it tried to gain height. It fell apart and exploded into the ground.

It took five bombs to breach the dam, Guy shepherding most of the aircraft in an endeavour to draw the fire power from the ground. Then, hardly able to take their eyes off the gaping dam wall as the water flooded through, the crews of those planes still intact flew on to the Eder Dam, sixty miles away. A half dozen attempts were made to breach the Eder and success only came with what had to be the final attempt, the very last bomb. The victorious aircrews watched as the wall disintegrated and the released waters poured eagerly through the gaping hole. Great damage was done to the whole industrial complex of the area. Perhaps more importantly the beneficial effect on the morale of all Allied peoples was immense. The cost to 617 Squadron was high. Only 11 of the 19 aircraft returned, some destroyed near the dams by anti-aircraft fire, others shot down on their way home by German fighters. Over 50 members of the crews perished.

Wing Commander Guy Gibson pictured above the strong dam wall between the Howden and Derwent reservoirs where the Dambusters did much of their training for the raid on the German dams in May 1943.

Wing Commander Guy Gibson was awarded the VC. His fame became exceptional. From the raid a new form of tactic, the Master Bomber attack, evolved, in which one very experienced pilot controlled and marshalled the whole operation in the sky.

Guy was taken by Winston Churchill to the Quebec Conference of Allied leaders in August 1943 and travelled extensively in both Canada and the USA being fêted everywhere. By December 1943, he was worn out and spent two weeks in hospital on his return.

In many ways Guy was now too important for his life to be risked by flying duties - and so it was that, in early 1944, he found himself in Macclesfield becoming prospective parliamentary candidate. He seemed to have accepted his adoption with enormous pleasure. But after being shown off as an icon of youthful wartime bravery for the better part of a year he found himself posted to East Kirby in Lincolnshire as a staff officer in late June 1944, just when the invasion of Europe, spearheaded with the landings in Normandy, was getting under way. He hated the thought of a desk job when his contemporaries were involved in the mightiest and most promising battle the Allies had ever launched against Nazi Germany.

He tried to persuade his superiors to release him and, in July 1944, he succeeded in taking a Lancaster on a bombing raid in France, the target a flying-bomb site. In August 1944 he was posted as a staff officer to Coningsby and made several somewhat surreptitious flights in Lightning planes. By some means he even managed to get involved with a bombing mission on Deelen airfield in Holland. He was in a rather desperate state of mind, always longing to experience once again a real sense of purpose. Surprisingly, he found the resolution to write of his RAF experiences up to the time of the Dambusters' raid and called his book *Enemy Coast Ahead*. In his book he listed 26 colleagues from 83 Squadron, 10 from 29 Squadron, 57 from 106 Squadron, and 16 from 617 Squadron, all of whom were now dead or 'missing'. Reflections on them and on their service, the manner of their deaths, and on the fact that he was one of the few so far to have been spared, are hardly likely to have given him any other than sombre thoughts.

Guy must have come to look upon the prospect of being a parliamentary candidate as irrelevant, perhaps distasteful. He contacted Garfield Weston and wrote to the Macclesfield Conservative Association on 23rd August 1944 to acquaint them with his decision. He also contacted Sir Arthur Harris, head of Bomber Command, who reluctantly agreed to give him the opportunity of what he described as 'one more trip'. It was agreed that Guy would pilot a Mosquito, which had a crew of two and whose purpose was to lay markers for the bombers. His navigator was James Warwick. They were part of a force which had the task of bombing the towns of Rheydt and Munchen-Gladbach, not far from the German frontier with Holland. The ten mosquitos were to put down the coloured markers for a force of 200 Lancasters.

The attack, which took place on 19th September, was very successful and Guy had instructions to return home via France. The German army had been virtually ousted from France, especially after the US Third Army under General George Patton had made its famous dash across Central France from Avranches to Metz between August and October. But it seems that Guy was anxious to take the shorter route over Holland, large parts of which were still strongly occupied by the Germans. Not far away the landings of Allied parachutists at Arnhem in the operation code-named Market Garden had been taking place for two days. Guy and James may well have been totally unaware of Montgomery's attempt to shorten the War by capturing three bridges in Northern Holland as a springboard for the assault upon Germany itself. But both airmen must have been well aware of the risk of flying over an occupied country. As the Mosquito flew towards the town of Steenbergen, flames were seen coming from its engines. Beyond the town Guy made some frantic efforts to land on a field, but the plane exploded as it hit the ground.

What was left of the two men was buried in the Roman Catholic Cemetery in Steenbergen by sorrowing and grateful Dutch people, who took the risk of displeasing the local German Kommandant. No official acknowledgement of the fact that Guy and James were missing was made for several months, to protect both men, especially Guy, if they were to become prisoners of war.

Meanwhile the Macclesfield Conservative Party were interviewing new candidates. Air Commodore A.V. Harvey was adopted on 9 December. A week earlier, on 1 December, the announcement had been made that Guy and James had been missing since 19 September. At a meeting of the Conservative Party formalising the selection of Air Commodore A.V. Harvey, time was found to say prayers for Guy Gibson. Speaking of Guy, Garfield Weston remarked that the adoption of Air Commodore Harvey, *'one of his outstanding officers'*, was very appropriate. Garfield Weston was a successful business man, but not a serviceman, and had failed to realise that an Air Commodore was superior to a Wing Commander!

The local Macclesfield newspapers reported on 2nd February 1945 that the bodies of Guy and James had been found. Since his death many memorials have been erected in different parts of Great Britain to commemorate Guy the 'Dambuster'. One of the most moving, because it reminds people of the large group of airmen whom he led, is to be found in the desolate but beautiful area between the Derwent and Howden reservoirs, one of the stretches of water where they practised their low-level flying and a short drive from Macclesfield.

Frederick Southern and Mrs Hilda Farr (Southern)

Mrs Hilda Farr died in January 1995 at the age of eighty-five. I visited her several times before her death to hear her own story of the Second World War.

She was a small lady with sharp eyes and quick movements, a very busy person, full of zest and not inclined to waste a single moment. When I visited her for the first time she spread out on a large table a mass of documents which she had kept for over fifty years. It would not be true to say that she remembered all the details contained in those papers. She confused one with another and was not completely clear about the strict chronology of her story. But the essence of it remained with her vividly.

Mrs Farr was born in 1910. Three years later her younger sister arrived. They lived with their parents in Crompton Road and attended St Andrew's School. Their father bought a cycle repair shop in Chester Road and joined the Royal Navy in the First World War, leaving his wife to take charge of this young and precarious business.

After the War it became known that he had another woman and child in Southampton. He was a spendthrift, was not running his business successfully and finally became a bankrupt. His wife was fed up and asked him to depart, which he did, and she looked after the two girls alone until she died in 1928. Hilda and her fifteen year old sister were taken in by their mother's brother and his wife in Hurdsfield, Macclesfield.

On 31 March, Easter Saturday, 1934, Hilda married Frederick Southern who was a chauffeur and gardener at a large house in Sutton, Macclesfield, and in 1935 their daughter,

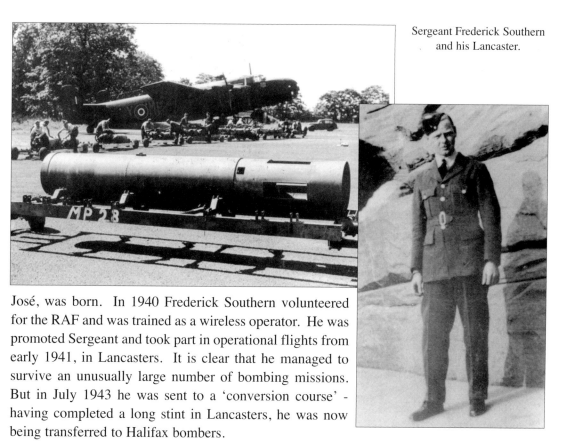

Sergeant Frederick Southern
and his Lancaster.

José, was born. In 1940 Frederick Southern volunteered for the RAF and was trained as a wireless operator. He was promoted Sergeant and took part in operational flights from early 1941, in Lancasters. It is clear that he managed to survive an unusually large number of bombing missions. But in July 1943 he was sent to a 'conversion course' - having completed a long stint in Lancasters, he was now being transferred to Halifax bombers.

He was part of a crew which hit the headlines in August 1943. Their Halifax had left its airfield in the north of England in order to attack Milan. *The Daily Herald* of 17 August 1943 (costing one penny) reported on its front page that the RAF had, for the third consecutive morning, been over Milan. The newspaper claimed that the crew of one aircraft which had been reported missing was now back home. Mrs Southern had received a telegram which had informed her that Frederick was missing. She was shocked and bewildered. But within a day or so she was informed that he was, after all, safe and well. Her relief was unbounded.

His crew had indeed taken part in the attack on Milan. But after the aircraft had crossed the Alps and before it dropped its bombs, the oxygen supply had begun to fail and leaving Milan, the Norwegian captain, fearing that he could not bring the plane back to England, gave orders to continue south from Milan. The navigator was asked to work out a course for the 700 mile journey to Tunisia, where anti-Vichy and pro-de Gaulle elements were powerful enough to warrant a welcome for an allied plane gone astray. The crew were delighted by the way the Tunisians received them, fed them and gave them clothes suitable for the climate.

The next day, fully restored (but unshaven), Frederick Southern and his RAF colleagues flew back to the U.K. They had left England in their flying kit and returned wearing khaki shorts and shirts, and loaded with bananas, grapes, lemons and melons!

Frederick arrived home in Macclesfield with a four days' pass in his pocket. Hilda and her daughter were overjoyed and rather bewildered by all that had happened. Hilda made pancakes with *'real lemon juice'*. The fruits were virtually unknown to little Josie, who took great pride in taking some to school to distribute amongst her classmates. But the four days were soon over and tears, kisses and implorations accompanied the good-byes as Fred Southern waved farewell at the railway station.

Two months later, on 23 October 1943, Hilda received a telegram to say that her husband had not returned from an operational flight against the enemy on the night of 22 October. Hilda, though greatly alarmed, found some comfort in recalling that this was not the first time Frederick had been posted missing. So she waited in hope. But a day later Squadron Leader N.J. Bennett sent a letter in which he managed to combine both extreme openness and extreme sensitivity. *'The target had been the town of Kassel'*, he wrote. This had been Sergeant Southern's 18th trip *'since coming to the squadron from his Conversion Unit last July'*. His efficiency, courage and reliability were praised. There might be more news later. Meanwhile Mrs Southern was given the sincerest sympathy of his squadron *'in these anxious days of waiting'*. Looking at this letter, and indeed the 17 others which were to follow in the next three years, one cannot but compliment the authorities on their kindness, thoughtfulness and tact.

But definite news was very slow to come. On 7 February 1944 the Air Ministry wrote that the International Red Cross Committee, quoting German information, had named four members of the crew who had been killed, but stating that there were also 2 (later 4) unidentifiable bodies, presumed to be those of the remaining members of the crew. The Soldiers', Sailors' and Airmen's Families' Association, Park Lane, Macclesfield, received the same message by a letter written on 9 February 1944. On 5 March 1944 the Air Ministry wrote to Mrs Southern that her husband was believed to have lost his life on 22 October 1943 and that all members of the aircraft's crew were buried in Brakel Cemetery in the Hoxter district, Westfalen, Prussia (*'a place about 9 miles south west of Hoxter and 21 miles south east of Detmord, Germany'*).

Finally a letter came from the Air Ministry on 18 November 1946. This letter stated that the original location of Sergeant Southern's remains as being Brakel was incorrect. It had now been discovered that the 8 airmen, comprising the crew of a British aircraft which had crashed near Buhne (a village 19 miles north west of Kassel), were buried in the cemetery of that town as 'unknown British flyers', all identification discs and papers having been removed by the Germans 'prior to burial'. The body of Sergeant Southern, together with those of his companions, had now been identified.

Eventually the Imperial War Graves Commission would place his body and the bodies of his companions in a special British War Cemetery. In a letter dated 28 January 1949 Mrs Southern was informed that her husband's body had now been moved to a British cemetery three and a half miles west of the centre of Hanover.

Hilda sustained hopes from October 1943 until March 1944, when the official letters made it plain that her husband really was dead. It took her some time to adjust to this realisation and, by late March 1944, she was tempted to give way to complete despair. However she claimed to have heard a voice which reminded her of her responsibility to young Josie. She *'came to her senses, walked around the town, breathed in the fresh air and looked to the future'*.

After the War Mrs Southern met and married a Mr Farr. He had contracted ill health in the army and he died in 1963, when his wife was 53.

Ken Moss

Ken Moss was born on 30 November 1925 and was 13 years of age when the Second World War broke out. Having taken his School Certificate in the summer of 1942 at the King's School, he was briefly employed, but the moment he reached his seventeenth birthday he joined the Royal Navy via the 'Y' Scheme, which sometimes included a short university training and a guaranteed post-war university course, and was designed to recruit volunteers almost a year before the normal age of 18.

He was sent to Lochailort in Scotland to train for the Mountbatten Combined Operations Scheme. His training, in bitterly cold weather, consisted of drilling, running, swimming in lochs, and navigational work. He then underwent an AA (Anti-Aircraft) gunnery course at Bognor Regis, after which he returned to Scotland, this time to Troon, to study navigation more thoroughly. In April 1944 he travelled to Southampton to join the crew of a LCT (Landing Craft Tanks) of which, as a Midshipman, he was Second-in-Command. He was shortly to be awarded the rank of Sub-Lieutenant. He received intense training and practice in the beach-clearing of mines and in the use of AVRE* flails on tanks.

There was no doubt in his mind and in the minds of his colleagues that all this activity was to equip them for their participation in the invasion of Europe in the summer of 1944; D-Day. Ken suffered the tense atmosphere of the days leading up to 4 June 1944, but at the last minute he was told that he would not be sailing on that day after all. He felt deflated. His sleep that night was fitful. He looked around at all the boats in the harbour at Southampton, sensing that harbours and ports all over the south coast of England would be packed with craft. Eventually he sailed from Southampton - four months short of his 19th birthday - with the first flotillas of craft to the invasion beaches on the night of 5 June 1944. His LCT, one of a flotilla of 12 (102 LCT Flotilla) went slowly in the dark in convoy with hundreds of other ships of all sizes. Conditions were extremely rough.

On his LCT were several tanks, together with the Royal Engineers who manned them and whose essential job was to clear the beach at Arromanches where the British artificial 'Mulberry Harbour' was going to be set up. Eisenhower also had a Mulberry harbour at Vierville-sur-Mer in the American sector to the west of Arromanches, which was very important in the early days of the invasion, but was destroyed by a gale two weeks later.

Ken and his crew-mates saw land ahead as dawn broke on Tuesday 6 June, but there were so many boats and so much noise - explosions, the whistling of shells, the boom of naval guns, excited shouts all around, that trying to keep calm and focused on their duties was far from easy. There were so many flashing lights, bursts of flame, and smoke obscuring the sky that they felt bewildered. As they approached the shore they were slightly surprised and a little relieved that they did not seem to have been picked out as yet by any guns. Ken and his companions were well aware of the task they had before them. The great problem was to be able to land at all, for the Germans had made a good (if, in places, patchy) job of their beach defences, not least the numerous bottle mines, half submerged, which had been attached to stakes embedded in the sand.

Their LCT was approaching the beach at top speed and so far as the crew could make out, it seemed to be covered with stakes. Fortunately Ken's captain was a New Zealander of Yugoslav stock named Lipanovic, a former yachtsman who was totally at home in any craft.

*Armoured Vehicles Royal Engineers

Ken noted in breathless admiration the skill with which Lipanovic set about weaving his way frantically - yet calmly - between the stakes. He landed his Royal Engineers successfully and watched them start the process of clearing the beach. Already steps were being taken to establish the artificial harbour. Huge caissons were being towed across the channel to form the outer harbour, which would give all harbour operations maximum protection. Bulky contraptions called 'gooseberries' were being lowered into position nearer to the shore. These were low breakwaters, which consisted of small old merchant vessels sunk in the shape of half moons stem to stern, to give protection to craft of no great size.

Now it was a question of ferrying a variety of material from harbour to shore. Sometimes it was tanks, sometimes ammunition, sometimes personnel, sometimes general supplies. In the early days and weeks Sub-Lieutenant Moss and his companions were continually aware of the fire from the Germans, and the thunderous roars of their own naval guns behind them. The sea remained unsettled, but although this was Arromanches, the hub of the British landing and supply beaches, the hectic nature of their responsibilities and the lack of obvious immediate danger rendered their time there busy and tiring, rather than frightening. It is true that they fished some dead bodies out of the water; and, up river from Courseulles, they discovered a German one-man submarine and its dead occupant; but the real action had now moved on.

One incident remains firmly fixed in Ken's mind. One afternoon during those early days at Arromanches Ken's LCT had to be beached when a length of thick

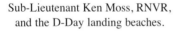

Sub-Lieutenant Ken Moss, RNVR,
and the D-Day landing beaches.

steel rope became entangled with the prop of the middle of its three screws. Ken, with the help of two stokers, was given the responsibility of freeing the prop. It was an extremely difficult and hazardous task which broke a considerable number of the hacksaw blades available at the time. Ken eyed the tide as it lapped towards the LCT and his work party. The three men sawed away, banging and pulling on the obstinate metal flex, cursing in frustration and occasionally uttering advice and warnings to each other. From time to time they had to pause for breath, and rest - sweat poured off their bodies. The tide rose higher and began to cover their feet. They struggled on knowing that they had to finish it before the tide. Soon they realised that the water was around their waist, but the long summer evening light allowed them to continue - much of the steel flex had already been cut away and safely laid on the deck for disposal. Only a short remnant remained coiled around the prop - the small ship would soon be floating. Panting and trembling, the three men gave a grunt of triumph as the last bit of wire came away; then with a shock they noted that the water was around their necks and they quickly struggled aboard and lay down in total exhaustion.

A few days later Ken was told that the two stokers had reported sick, with an illness which seemed to result from both physical and emotional stress. Ken went to see them and discovered that neither of them could swim! By one of those quirks of fate both men had failed to undergo the swimming test which was an essential element in naval administrative routine, before sailors were let loose upon the sea. Ken realised that they must have been in complete panic but were too disciplined to let him know.

But not all Ken's experiences in the Royal Navy were so grim. An anonymous but grateful French lady gave his tough, mainly Glaswegian crew a 5 kilo jug of honey - he joked that the seamen under his command had never seen a bee, let alone honey. He remembers with particular pleasure the day on which he heard his name being called out from a Merchant Navy vessel which towered above them as they worked. Looking up he recognised his old school friend Magnus (Maggie) Elliott Grant, who had left school to become an apprentice on the Manchester Ship Canal and was now in the Merchant Navy. Maggie invited Ken and his colleagues on board and introduced them to his captain, who gave orders for them to be wined and dined and - most welcome of all - to use the showers and baths on board!

In late August 1944 Ken's LCT returned to the UK and was directed to Rosyth for a refit. In 1945 he was sent to South India where a new flotilla of LCTs was being formed, ready to continue the war against Japan. One of the men he met there was Philip Mellor, another friend from Macclesfield, who was the engineer officer on a LCT from the same flotilla. Ken was struck by the thoroughness and cleanliness with which Philip looked after his beloved engine room, and had cause yet again to reflect gratefully and admiringly on companions from his home town. But at the very moment when the flotilla was totally prepared, the news of the surrender of Japan, following the dropping of the two atomic bombs on Hiroshima and Nagasaki on 6 and 9 August 1945, came through, changing their plans.

Altogether Ken served 12 months in India. He would like to have stayed in the navy but unfortunately he acquired a skin disease and TB. He has since spent his career as an agronomist, an adviser on crops and their environment, and, in retirement, in an unpaid capacity, has applied his skills to sports turf management.

A Macclesfield Bevin Boy

Ernest Bevin, later Foreign Secretary in the Labour Government of 1945-1951, was Minister of Labour and National Service in Churchill's wartime Coalition Government from May 1940 to July 1945. He was successful in mobilising Britain's manpower for the war effort but not without considerable determination and exertion, especially in the production of coal.

The War exacerbated the problems of the mining industry: many young miners joined the forces; full employment opened up other areas of work for those miners who were not happy digging for coal; and full employment meant increased demand from factories for electricity and fuel. The need for coal increased; the supply of miners decreased. By 1942 the National Government was forced to take over the running of the mines.

In 1943 it was clear to Bevin that there had been a continual slide in the production of coal from 1940. Absenteeism had risen from 7% in 1939 to 12% in 1943. There were strikes in spite of a wartime ban on them! It seemed that there might well be a shortage of coal in 1944-1945, impeding not only military operations but also a now foreseeable post-war resumption of industry, both in Britain and in Europe. On 20 July 1943 Bevin, addressing the Miners' Annual Conference at Blackpool, declared: *'It is quite obvious that I will have to resort to some desperate remedies during the coming year. I shall have to direct young men to you.'*

On 29 July 1943 Bevin repeated these warnings to the House of Commons. His scheme for dealing with the problem was ready in November and began to operate in December 1943. Every month a certain digit would be drawn out of a hat and any young man who had, according to law, registered for National Service would be sent to work in the mines instead of joining the forces if the last digit of his registration number corresponded to the one drawn by chance. The scheme was unpopular but it did boost coal production.

A total of 21,800 young men were allocated to the pits before the European War ended in May 1945, when the scheme was abandoned (although those who had been sent to the mines had to stay on to finish their service). They were called Bevin Boys and most of them served three years before being released, receiving the same demobilisation dates as their contemporaries in the Army.

Three close friends of mine - Granville Jackson, Reg Burgess and Mark Offenbach - did their National Service in the coal-mines. After training Granville worked in Lancashire and Staffordshire and Reg in Stoke-on-Trent. Mark sent an account of his experiences to the King's School magazine in 1946 and what I write now is based on that account.

Mark was sent first of all to Horden Colliery, near West Hartlepool, for a month's training. This coal pit was situated on the North-Eastern coast of England and actually went under the sea for several miles. Horden Colliery was very modern and gave Mark and his companions a very favourable impression of general conditions in the coalfields of the country. He was struck immediately by the camaraderie of all those who found themselves, rather to their chagrin, eliminated from the possibility of a more colourful and perhaps prestigious time in the armed forces. One young chap came up to him and, holding out his hand, said in a very friendly way, *'Hello, what's your name then?'* *'Offenbach'*, replied Mark, gratefully shaking his hand. *'Nice to meet you'* said the other, *'My name is Beethoven'*.

On the first day they were issued with overalls, boots, belt, safety hat, lamp number and class number. There was PT every morning, taken by an army PTI (Physical Training

Instructor), much enjoyed by the boys and intended to build up their strength and fitness for the months ahead. On three afternoons a week they were taken down the pit in order to become acclimatised to the conditions and atmosphere down there. On the other afternoons they attended lectures.

Their instructors were experienced miners who were not, of course, trained teachers but in the early stages their pupils were interested enough to pay proper attention. The task of the instructors became more difficult when the novelty of coalmining had worn off their charges, who were soon disillusioned by many things, not least the remuneration they received. They were given a weekly wage of £3, but their individual 'digs'cost 25 shillings a week. Their daily meal at the pit canteen cost 6 shillings a week. They paid tax and insurance and their bus fare in many cases was 3 shillings a week. They had to provide their own working clothes although they were loaned a pair of overalls during their training and their first pair of boots and safety hats were free. Mark's second pair cost him 25 shillings.

On their first visit to the mines the cage which took them down seemed to them enormous. It had three floors or decks, each of which held 12 men. The first deck, when filled, was lowered to allow the second floor to be likewise filled, which, in its turn, was lowered to enable the third floor to be filled. Each cage was lower than the height of a normal adult so that all the men had to squat rather than stand. The Bevin boys were doubtful whether the steel rope by which the cage was lowered was strong enough to hold so many bodies and the equipment which accompanied them, but their instructors hastened to reassure them. A silence developed as the descent began but the instructors went out of their way to chat normally so that they could pretend not to be aware of the misgivings which they knew the boys were feeling.

The training seam, some 900 feet deep, was reached and the cage was emptied one deck at a time. The area around the pit bottom (or shaft) was extensive with generous height and width and ventilation, and well lit with electric lamps. They followed a main roadway which was rough and covered with a mixture of coal dust and stone dust. They were told that since coal dust was extremely explosive, it was essential to add stone dust to it for safety reasons. The boys were soon half choking with the dust and beginning to realise that conditions down the mines could be unpleasant. But they were not given time to dwell on these thoughts as their instructors speedily led them on. They noted that side roads went off at different points, leading to other parts of the coal seam. After about half a mile the ceiling

Bevin Boys receiving their training

girders began to get lower and lower, causing problems for the taller youngsters. Now they all had to judge where exactly to direct the beam of their lamp. If they directed it down they might well bump their head; if they raised it up, they were likely to trip over something on the floor. It took them some weeks to find the right way of negotiating these roadways.

Eventually they reached the coal face which was no more than three feet high and ran for 90 yards at right angles to the roadway. They crawled, paused for breath and, stretching out their body, rubbed their knees. Then they resumed their crawling, trying hard not to think of what was above them or beyond them, reminding themselves that in an hour or so they would be taking in lovely long breaths of fresh air back on the surface of the earth. At the end of the face there was another roadway leading off at right angles. Along the whole of the face was an apparently endless conveyor belt, set low down near the floor. This belt carried the coal to another belt in the distant roadway and finally into waiting tubs.

Mark adopted what he was told was the miners' squatting position and felt elated and comfortable. A coal mine was not a bad place after all. Then he realised that no work was going on at that moment. Later he was to discover what working at a coal face involved - dust in the eye, nose and throat; ears deafened by the noise of hammering, drilling and of falling coal; and overpowering heat which resulted in the nose being assaulted by the constant stench of sweating flesh. In that first month of training they learned how to hook on tubs, look after ponies, drive engines and work signals. It was not so bad a time and all the trainees were a little relieved, indeed quite pleased by their beginning in this unusual life-style. They were then distributed to various mines in the area.

Mark went to a pit six miles south of Durham. His accommodation was in a miners' hostel, a series of Nissen huts which were cosier and more cheerfully decorated on the inside than they looked from the outside. There were lounges, a radiogram, a library, a darning service, an ironing board, and a games room. The food, however, was not very good, even by wartime standards. Each dormitory had twelve young miners but, unfortunately, there was no means of avoiding a mixture of different shifts. This meant that there were few opportunities of sleeping without being disturbed by colleagues returning from a different shift. Mark's wages were now £3-10s a week, out of which £1-5s was deducted for board.

Underground the conditions were far less pleasant than at Horden. The area at the bottom of the shaft was very small; the main haulage road was one and a half miles long and Mark, who was over 6 ft tall, could only find half a dozen places along it where he could stand to his full height. Bits of the roof hung down and there were twisted girders and warped planks everywhere. Mark's normal shift was from 6.20 am to 1.50 pm, with 25 minutes break to consume the lunch he took with him, together with water from the water bottle which he, like all the others, always carried down the mine. The less said about toilet arrangements, the better. The hostel was two miles from the pit and, since no transport existed in the early morning, Mark had to walk to work. On Saturdays the first shift started at 4 am, which meant that, theoretically he had to get up at 2 am. However on Friday evenings the normal practice was to sit up talking, smoking and playing cards until it was time to make a move. There were no pit showers but the hostel had baths. The Bevin Boys, like the miners, went to work in their pit clothes and, if it rained, they arrived wet and sometimes remained wet for several hours before drying out through exertion and the heat underground.

Mark was eventually transferred to Lancashire, to a reasonably modern colliery and made few complaints. Looking back the memory of comradeship not only amongst his fellow Bevin boys but also amongst the miners in general stayed with him. He also admitted to a sense of both pride and adventure. Nevertheless he was pleased to complete his three years as a miner and to embark upon a university course. He had certainly fulfilled his National Service obligations.

Sydney Henshaw Gleave

In the 1920s, 1930s and 1940s virtually every person in Macclesfield had heard of Syd Gleave. He was an outstanding local hero. My friend Paul Maybury, who wrote an excellent booklet on Syd's life in 1981, has given me permission to use the material which he gathered together for that booklet, *Syd Gleave and his Specials: The Story of a T.T. Rider.*

Syd Henshaw Gleave was born in Macclesfield on 31 January 1905. He inherited the considerable mechanical gifts of his father (who nevertheless spent his career looking after a dairy) and became an apprentice in a motorcycle business owned by the Simister family, first in Hurdsfield and later in Jordangate..

Starting in 1926 he competed in many TT races in the Isle of Man and also in many other races both in Great Britain and Europe. The TT races normally coincided with the Macclesfield 'Barnaby Week' holiday and this enabled many Macclesfield people to follow his exploits. Locally at least, he became famous. He began to make his own motorcycle, the S.G.S - the Syd Gleave Special. With premises at the side of his father's dairy in Davenport Street, he set up a showroom and started the Gleave Engineering Company. Between October 1927 and May 1931, 60 S.G.S. machines were sold as well as one S.G.S. sports sidecar.

Syd won the Lightweight Class of the Ulster Grand Prix with his own S.G.S. in 1930. Two years later, riding a New Imperial, he came second in the Ulster 250 Race. In 1933, riding a 'Mechanical Marvel' (produced by the Excelsior Company of Birmingham) and reaching 106 mph on certain sections of the TT course, he won at an average speed of 71.59 mph, a speed which was only improved on some three years later. A telegram of congratulation from the Mayor of Macclesfield, Councillor E. Lomas, was delivered to him at the Metropole Hotel, Douglas, the Isle of Man. He was welcomed home to Macclesfield by a large and delighted crowd.

He then competed in races in Holland, Germany, Belgium, France, Italy and Spain. In 1935 he was badly injured (with 40 fractures) in the Isle of Man but recovered well. His appetite for dangerous pursuits seems not to have been affected, however. Indeed, by that time he had already shown great interest in flying and in 1932 had obtained his private pilot's licence. In 1936 he was placed 6th in the London to the Isle of Man Air Race.

In 1938 he joined the Civil Air Guard, pledging himself with other

private airmen to give his services in a national emergency in return for having his flying subsidised. On 8th July 1939 he won a wager of £100 by playing a round of golf in 5 countries in one day. Leaving Manchester he flew in turn to Scotland, Ulster, the Isle of Man, Wales and then returned to England. It took him 17 hours to complete this feat, which was fully documented in *the Macclesfield Courier and Herald* of 13th July 1939 and was illustrated by photographs of Syd *'relaxing'* in all the countries concerned.

After a spell of amateur flying with the Lancashire Aero Club he volunteered for the Fleet Air Arm in 1939 and, having been commissioned, he was seconded to the Air Transport Auxiliary as a senior pilot.

In August 1940 during the Battle of Britain when the Spitfire fighter plane became famous, a fund was launched to build more and more of these magnificent planes. Syd's contribution was to stimulate enthusiasm for the fund by giving an aerobatic display in a Spitfire over the town. In 1941, during the War Weapons Week Appeal (17th-24th May 1941), he flew the Mayor of Macclesfield, Alderman F. Baron, over the town, distributing leaflets to boost the Appeal. In March 1942 he started testing with Avros at Woodford, Cheshire (only a short distance from Macclesfield), principally on Lancaster bombers, which were being produced at a rate of 35 a week and this became his principal occupation.

Syd was to spend over 3000 hours testing these bombers in the next two years. On Monday 11th September 1944 Syd took up a new Lancaster bomber PB579, together with his flight engineer, 41 year old Harry Barnes who came from Wilmslow. When he landed he reported that he had had trouble with the controls. Work was done on the ailerons in Hangar Number 5, allowing Syd and Harry to resume the test flight later the same day. The plane flew normally for half an hour but about 4.30 pm people around Birtles, only three miles to the west of Macclesfield, became aware of strange noises from its engine and, horrified, saw it plunge into the ground.

Some five days later an inquest was held at which an aircraft inspector from Woodford could give no explanation for the crash. Syd had been identified by pieces of clothing, and Harry only by a tie and a penknife. Two parachutes remained unused. The funeral took place in the Macclesfield Cemetery on the same day as the inquest, Saturday 16th September 1944. About three hundred mourners were present. The vicar of St Paul's Church, the Rev F. S. Thetford expressed the hope that the work of Syd and Harry might result in fewer accidents to airmen in the future.

Paul Maybury suggests that the cause of the crash might have been damage to the elevators of the tailplane. It was normal practice for test pilots to power-dive a plane. But Syd was unable to bring the Lancaster out of the dive and it seems that fabric from the leading edge of the wing of the aircraft broke loose and jammed in the tail elevators, rendering them unworkable. Avro engineers looked at the design yet again and decided to cover the elevators with metal. Hence the mighty Lancaster bomber, which, like the Spitfire, has been an icon of wartime endeavour and success for many generations of British people, became safer for the men who would be flying it in future. The deaths of Syd and Harry were not in vain.

On 22nd September 1944 the magazine *The Aeroplane* contained an obituary of Syd. The writer of the article claimed that Syd had the cool brain, 'hands', and sensitive feeling for an engine that mark the exceptional racing motor-cyclist. Such qualities were, he wrote, ideal qualifications for the test pilot. Few would disagree with that judgement.

EPILOGUE
with some cuttings from the Macclesfield Express of 1942

On the memorial tablets in the Park Green Cenotaph Gardens there are 195 names of 192 Macclesfield men and 3 women who died in the British armed forces in the Second World War. Since it is usual for every small village to have its own war memorial it is likely that the full number of casualties from the town and surrounding countryside is around 250.

Of course not all who were killed died in action. In April 1941 Private J.W. Heard was returning to his camp in Gloucestershire during an air raid and was knocked down and killed by a vehicle. Three weeks later Sergeant Andrew Farquarson was killed on his army motorcycle in Scotland. Driver Colin Shaw was directing lorries at a park entrance when he lost his life in July 1942. In the same month John Hampton, who had just completed his training at a flying school, contracted an illness of short duration and died. Two others - Dorothy Jean Lawton, aged 20, and Leading Photographer Joseph Simpson, aged 24 - were in a group being taken back to camp at Warrington from a local dance in a naval truck which crashed, killing them and four other service men and women, in June 1943.

Otherwise the majority of Macclesfield deaths punctuated the successive events of the Second World War, and all, in different ways, were thought-provoking. Leading Seaman Arthur Norman Oldfield, 28, was drowned (as were most of the total crew of 1260) when the aircraft carrier HMS Courageous was sunk by a U-boat on 17th September 1939. Leading Aircraft Fitter A.W. Cresswell lost count of the hours he spent in the water before being rescued. Petty Officer F. Connor was one of the 786 sailors lost when the battleship HMS Royal Oak was sunk on 14th October 1939, at Scapa Flow, by U-47.

By 28th December 1939 5 Macclesfield men had been lost in action. The personal disasters continued without reprieve. In May and November 1941 Mr and Mrs J.W. Parr were informed of the death of two sons. Mrs Morrison of Vincent Street learned of the death of her two sons James and William within a single month. In March 1943 she was informed that a third son, Graham, had been killed. These three deaths came from five serving brothers. The Kershaw family from Kerridge had lost their second son Pilot Officer John Kershaw in the air battles of July 1940. In March 1941 their youngest son Anthony, also a Pilot Officer, was also killed in action at the age of 21. He was due to begin his university career at Oxford in October 1939 and his early death annulled his exceptional all-round ability. There was a third son in the Royal Navy, Sub-Lieutenant Peter Kershaw, who thankfully survived the War.

The entry of Japan into the War, on 7th December 1941, was followed three days later by the sinking of the battleships HMS Prince of Wales and Repulse, victims of suicide pilots. In the former was Wireman William Kinghorn who was rescued from the water but who was to then face severe ill-health as a result of his experiences.

So far people had expected news of deaths in action to concern young single men. But now they had to become accustomed to looking after bereft families in their midst. Private James Rogers had been wounded twice in his escape from Dunkirk. Now, in April 1942, he lost his life in the Libyan campaign. The townsfolk were reminded that this was an especially cruel disaster for the family, because on 12th August 1938, his wife Doris, mother of a nine weeks old boy, had died in the disastrous fire at the factory of Peter Davenport's in Bridge Street. The orphaned boy was not yet four years old. Sergeant Air-Gunner James Eric Hough, aged 28, was killed on active service in May 1942. He left behind a widow and two small children. Lance-Corporal Thomas Daniel Dale, a Royal Engineer, married and with a 3 year old daughter, was killed in action in North Africa by the accidental explosion of a mine on 24 May 1943 '... *after coming through the Tunisian fighting without a scratch'*.

By 1943 news was already beginning to come through of the deaths of servicemen as prisoners of war of the Japanese. Aircraftman J.E. Higginbotham and Gunner Patrick Brannan, died this way - *'cause of death unknown'*, 3rd September 1943. AC 2 James Jackson likewise perished on 26th September 1945 after several years as a prisoner of war in Java.

The obituary columns continued to pinpoint the various stages of the War and at times its geographical course: Thomas Broomhead, assault on the Mareth Line, 22nd April 1943; Private Cliffford Hudson, 7th May 1943, North Africa; Private Levi Sutton, Sicily, 5th August 1943. Then came a long list of casualties from the 'Central Mediterranean area', followed by a longer list from Italy. Burma appeared in the casualty lists from April 1944, and there were 6 reported deaths of Macclesfield servicemen in that country between April and June 1944.

There was almost a score of deaths in the Normandy and France campaigns and, by October 1944, Belgium began to feature: Arnhem (17-28 September 1944) claimed the lives of at least two Macclesfield men, Gunner Eric Stubbs, whose glider crashed, and Flight Sergeant Stanley James Cooke, on his first flight, taking food to the beleaguered men at Arnhem.

Other Macclesfield people died as firefighters in Liverpool fires, or as servicemen and civilians in air raids. A soldier shot himself, there were several accidental drownings, and two victims of accidental explosions. It is possible to talk and write in a remote and detached way, perhaps even glibly, about casualties and suffering, especially when huge numbers are involved. When the focus is on details, on families and individuals known and loved, the facts of war are seen in a different dimension; the emotional and human rise above the statistical.

Harold Roach   J. E. Roach   W. R. Roach   J. H. Roach   Kenneth Roach

Kathleen Roach   Barbara Roach   J. Finnighan   J. Walkinshaw   William Island

10 members of the Roach family of Mayfield Avenue, Macclesfield, in service in 1942.

Serving Their Country

Fred.

James.

William.

Harold.

Wm. Grant.

Arthur.

A FAMILY AFFAIR

MR. and MRS. J. E. OLDFIELD, of 6 Water Street, have three sons, Marine James Oldfield, Pte. Harold Oldfield and A/c. Fred Oldfield, their brother-in-law, Pte. Arthur Lomas, and their daughter's fiance (Spr. William Lennard) all serving in the Forces.

Their eldest son, Marine James Oldfield, has been serving for nearly nine years and has been in many countries including the East Indies, America and Egypt. He was educated at the Central School and before joining up worked for Farrer's, of Elizabeth Street.

Pte. Harold Oldfield, the second son, is the only son who is married, and his wife resides at 67 Bridge Street. He attended Athey Street School and prior to joining the East Lancs nearly two years ago, was employed by Holland's, of Castle Street.

The youngest son, A/c. Fred Old-field, has been serving in the Royal Air Force for nearly twelve months. He received his education at Athey Street School and was employed at the Oxford Road Mills of B.W.A. Ltd. before joining up.

Pte. Arthur Lomas, the only son of Mr. and Mrs. H. Lomas, of 155 Park Lane, is serving as a cook in the R.A.O.C. He attended St. George's School and was employed by Messrs. G. H. Heath and Co. before joining up. He is married, his wife residing at 52 Vincent Street.

The prospective member of the family is Sapper William Lennard, youngest son of Mr. and Mrs. L. Lennard, of the Railway View, Byrons Lane. He is engaged to Miss Florence Oldfield, daughter of Mr. and Mrs. Oldfield, of Water Street. He was employed by Hall's prior to which he went to St. George's School. He has been serving in the R.E.s for about fourteen months.

With the Cheshires In Bombay

Hoping To "Do Their Stuff"

SOME OF THE LOCAL LADS

Back Row (left to right) : Pte. W. Swindells, L Cpl. Allen, Pte. N. H. S. Parker, Pte. F. Barnes, L Cpl. Hodkinson, Pte. J. Finnegan. Centre : Sergt. N. Barratt, Sergt. A Reid, C.Q.M.S. Whaley, L Cpl. P. Swindells. Front Row: Pte. W. Mason, Pte. F. Hind, Pte. McManus.

"I WOULD like to say, on behalf of the boys, that all are well and hoping to 'do their stuff' when the time comes." Thus writes Sergt. Alec Reid, in an interesting letter to a member of the "Courier" staff, on their activities abroad. Sergeant Reid, who is well-known locally, has many years' service to his credit, and prior to the outbreak of hostilities served with the local Territorials. Mobilised at the outbreak of war, he served in France, and took part in the evacuation from Dunkirk. Educated at Christ Church School, he was afterwards employed in the office at the "Courier." He later served his apprenticeship as a joiner, but his last position before joining up was that of Steward at the Old Boys' Club. He writes:—

Well, as is probably known by now, we have left old England's shores again for "furrin" parts, and whatever destiny has in store for us. Most of us had a similar experience in 1940, but the distance was by no means so great, and our return was one which was as unexpected as it was unfortunate, so we are all hoping that this time our particular star will shine to the benefit of all concerned, and that the chasing will be done by us for a change. We had an interesting but uneventful trip by sea, looked after by the "Nurses of the Army," those lads in blue who are always on the job, thank God ! I said uneventful, but probably one event will live long in the memory of those who were privileged to enjoy our four days' stay in a certain port en-route.

The treatment we received from the inhabitants was nothing short of marvellous: nothing was too much trouble—entertainments, car rides, and invitations to dinner and tea were the order of the day, numbers no object and, believe me, the boys thoroughly enjoyed themselves, and I am very pleased to be able to state that the behaviour of all was reported by the local authorities as being exemplary.

TERRIFIC HEAT

It was a nice break, but, like all good things, came to an end. After another splendid trip by sea we at length arrived at our destination port, but did not stay long enough to look round: we are now well up country, and is it hot ? phew, if the Barnaby holiday folk had a week of this at Blackpool they would want a month to get over it; it is as hot at 9 o'clock in the morning as any part of the hottest day in an English summer, and all parades are done early morning and sports in the evening, with siesta in the afternoon.

As I write in the shade of my hut perspiration is running off my chin. Among the many discomforts are the flies, ants and dust; the latter is especially a nuisance, it covers everything, and nothing will keep it out of the huts, clothing or food. Scorpions, centipedes and mosquitoes are the more dangerous pests, and precautions against the latter are extremely necessary to prevent malaria, the scourge of the Tropics.

"Old sweats" who have served out here will need no reminding about that menace with wings, the Kite Hawk, known to the troops as another kind of hawk. This bird circles over the cook-house, and if you neglect to cover up your food it swoops down like a dive-bomber and snatches it off your plate. I used to take this old soldier's tale with the proverbial grain of salt, until one of these ——hawks took my dinner—salt and all, and taught me a lesson.

In spite of these pests and conditions, the lads are more or less settled down and making the best of it. It is a big change from anything they have been used to, but it takes a lot to upset them, and they are taking to it like a duck to water, bolo-ing the char and fruit and dhobie wallahs like old-timers.

One thing about this country, there is no shortage of tea, sugar, oranges and fags, and onions are more or less our staple food, with eggs and tomatoes for a change !

Dangerously Injured

Local Man In Bombay

MR. and Mrs. John Stevenson, of 22, Princess Street, have received official notification this week that their son, Pte. Herbert Stevenson, Cheshire Regt., who recently landed in Bombay, is dangerously ill owing to spinal injuries received in a motor accident. They have heard nothing further.

Pte. Stevenson, who is 32, was born in Macclesfield and attended Daybrook Street School.

Formerly employed by Messrs. W. and A. E. Sherratt, Thorpe Street Dyeworks, he was a member of the Territorials, called up at the outbreak of war. He was in the Dunkirk evacuation.

J. T. Buckley

H. Taylor

J. G. Allen

F. McAll

K. H. Wilshaw

A. Kirk

Three Brothers-in-Law

Mr. and Mrs. T. Stevenson, of 5 Newgate, have their eldest son (Fred McAll) and their two sons-in-law (Herman Taylor and Arthur Kirk) serving in the Forces.

Pte. Fred McAll, who joined up at the outbreak of war, is serving with the Sherwood Foresters. He attended St. Paul's and Athey Street Schools and was employed by a firm at Lincoln before joining up.

Pte. Herman Taylor is the only son of Mr. and Mrs. G. Taylor, of the local Farmers' Trading Society, Castle Street.

Pte. Arthur Kirk, the second son of Mr. and Mrs. J. Kirk, of Cornbrook Road, attended Athey Street School and was employed by Messrs. Ashton and Holmes, Sutton Sidings, before joining up.

Privates Taylor and Kirk are both serving in the Pioneer Corps, and joined up within a month of each other.

Local Sportsman

A LOCAL young man, who has won many cups and prizes at table-tennis, cricket and other sports is now serving as a Corporal in the R.A.O.C. He is Kenneth H. Wilshaw, youngest son of Mrs. J. Wilshaw, of 2 South Street. He was educated t St. George's School, and before joining up was employed as a clerk at the M.E.P.S. Office, Park Green. For about ten years he was a member of St. George's Choir. Cpl. Wilshaw volunteered only a few days before war broke out in 1939, served in France, and was in the epic evacuation from Dunkirk.

R.A.F. Volunteer

Aircraftman John G. Allen, younger son of Mr. and Mrs. W. H. Allen, of 7 Roe Street, volunteered for service in the R.A.F. seven months ago, before which he was employed as an apprentice mechanic at the Park Garage Ltd., Rodney Street. He received his education at the Central School. He is 19 years of age.

O.S. J. T. Buckley

Serving in the Royal Navy is Ord. Seaman John Thomas Buckley, eldest son of Mrs. J. F. and the late Mr. J. Buckley, of 9 Garden Street. Educated at St. Alban's School, he joined the Navy in May, 1941

J. A. Vickerstaff

S. Jackson

A. J. Wilson

F. Tomlinson

N. Palfreyman

F. Edge

Brothers-in-Law.

TWO brothers-in-law, both serving in the Royal Artillery and both stationed abroad, one in the Middle East and one in the Far East, are Gnr. Stanley Jackson, of 34 Parkgate Road, Moss Estate, and Gnr. Alfred James Wilson, who is a native of Stoke-on-Trent.

Gnr. Jackson is a native of Macclesfield, and was employed as a painter before joining up, which was about twelve months ago. He is married, and his main hobby is gardening.

Gunner Wilson worked for Mr. Russell, butcher, of Macclesfield, before joining up. He has been serving for six years, at present being stationed at Singapore. He is married, his wife residing at Farnham, Surrey.

TWO brothers-in-law, who before joining up were employed as clerks at Hovis Ltd., are now serving in the R.A.F. and the Cheshire Regiment respectively. They are L.A/c. James Alfred Vickerstaff, the eldest son of Mr. and Mrs. Vickerstaff, of Buxton Road, and Pte. Frank Tomlinson, youngest son of the late Mr. and Mrs. Tomlinson, of 9 William Street.

The former was educated at the King's School, and he joined the R.A.F. at the outbreak of the war. The latter was educated at the Central School, and he joined up about 18 months ago.

They are both keen footballers, both having played for Hovis, and the latter for the Central School.

L.A/c. Vickerstaff is married, his wife residing at 5 Vernon Street.

A/c. N. Palfreyman

A FORMER TEACHER at St. George's Sunday School now serving with the Royal Air Force is A/c. Norman R. Palfreyman, eldest son of Mr. and Mrs. G. Palfreyman, of 61 Chapel Street.

He was educated at St. George's School, and before joining up was employed by the local M.E.P.S. He has been serving for over five months.

In Submarine Service

SERVING as a telegraphic operator in the Submarine Service is the youngest son of Mr. and Mrs. J. Edge, of 40, Cornbrook Road. He is Frank Edge, a former employee of Barracks Fabrics Printing Co. Ltd., before which he went to Athey Street School. He joined the Navy as a boy, and was posted to the Submarine Service at the age of 18. He is at present serving abroad.

W. Lake.

J. Lake.

M. L. Davies.

E. F. Davies.

M. Lomas.

B. Capper.

Four Relatives

An old soldier of the last war, Mr. E. Lake, of 1 Briarwood Ave., and his wife have the pleasure of seeing two of their sons, one of their daughters and her husband helping to win this war.

Pte. W. Lake

Their eldest son, Pte. Walter Lake, is now a prisoner of war in Germany. He attended Daybrook St. School. and was formerly employed by Messrs. Neckwear Ltd.

Nearly seven years ago he volunteered for service, and was posted to the Cheshire Regiment, and went abroad four years ago. His parents received official news from the War Office on January 14th saying he was a prisoner of war in the Middle East.

Gnr. J. Lake

The second son, Gnr. Joseph Lake, has been serving with the Royal Artillery for about ten months.

He received his education at Christ Church School, and was employed by Messrs. M. Belmont, Ltd., before joining up.

Pte. M. L. Davies

Mr. and Mrs. Lake's eldest daughter, Pte. Mary Lilian Davies, also attended Christ Church School and worked at the Adelphi Mill, Bollington, before joining the A.T.S. nearly six months ago.

Pte. E. F. Davies

Her husband is Pte. Edward Frederick Davies. Although not a native of this town, he worked in Macclesfield before joining the Forces. His home address is 1, Briarwood Avenue.

A/cw. M. Lomas

The second daughter of Mr. and Mrs. H. Lomas, of White Gate Farm, Gawsworth, is serving with the W.A.A.F. She is A/cw. Maud Lomas, and has been serving since September of last year. She was educated at Gawsworth School, and was employed by Leodian, Pool St. Mills, before joining up.

Didn't Like Australia

Because he didn't like the farm life of Australia, Bernard Capper, only son of Mr. and Mrs. Capper, of Western Ave., returned to England nearly two years ago, and after being employed by McClure and Whitfield, Mill St., for a short time, joined the Royal Artillery. He is now an Acting Sergeant.

He attended St. Paul's School, and was first employed by Mr. S. W. Morley, jeweller, of Mill St. Later he worked at Simister's garage, after which he went to Australia. He remained there for nearly eighteen months, but not liking farm work, came back to Macclesfield. Last June he joined H.M. Forces. A capable mechanic and electrician, he celebrated his coming-of-age last week.

147

G. Evans

D. Dobson

N. Southall

N. Warren

C. Adamson

B. Perkin

Father and Son-in-law

FATHER and son-in-law serving in the Pioneer Corps and Royal Artillery, respectively, are Sergt. Norman Warren, second son of the late Mr. and Mrs. Warren, of Stockport, and Gnr. Cyril Adamson, eldest son of Mr. and Mrs. A. Adamson, of 61, South Park Road.

Gunner Adamson was educated at Athey Street School, and before joining up was employed at the London Road dyeworks of Messrs. J. Arnold Ltd. He has been serving for eighteen months.

Sergt. Warren was educated at Stockport and was employed at the Langley Mills of Messrs. B.W.A. Ltd. before joining up. He has been serving for two years and four months, part of that time being spent in France.

Gunner D. Dobson

Formerly serving in a N.A.A.F.I. canteen and now a gunner in the A.T.S. is Miss Dorothy Dobson of 77, Mill Street. She was educated at the High School, and has been serving since July, 1941.

L.A/c. N. Southall

A native of Leamington Spa, whose home address with his wife is at 77 South Park Road is L.A/c. Norman Southall, second son of Mr. B. Southall, of Leamington, and the late Mrs Southall.

A/c. G. Evans

When he was young, Grahame Evans, only son of Mrs. and the late Mr. J. W. Evans of 1, Langford Street had a craze for building model aeroplanes. One of the most important results of this was, that eleven months ago, he joined the R.A.F. and is now serving as A/c 1.

He attended Christ Church School and before he entered the R.A.F. was employed by Messrs J. E. Barker and Son, Decorators, Cumberland Street. A/c. Evans is married, his home address being 15 Springfield Road, Broken Cross. He was formerly connected with Macclesfield Model Flying Club, and was also a keen cyclist.

Pilot Officer Brian Perkin.

Brian Perkin, eldest son of Flight Sergeant and Mrs. Perkin, of 19 Flint Street, is to be heartily congratulated on rising, in just under nine months' time, from the rank of A/c. 1 to Pilot Officer.

Educated at the Central School he was later employed by the M.E.P.S., and joined up in May of last year. He arrived in Canada last August, where he served at Swift Current, Saskatchewan, and later at Medicine Hat.

Reported Missing

SIG. P. CARNEY

AFTER coming through the battle of Singapore safely, Patrick Carney, of the Royal Navy, son of Mr. and Mrs. W. Carney, of Prestbury Road, sent a heartening telegram to his parents saying 'Safe, well, happy. Hope you same.'

Then, last week their happiness was shattered by another telegram this time from the Admiralty which said: "Deeply regret to inform you that your son, Patrick Carney, Signalman, has been reported missing on war service."

The last letter received by his parents was in the first week of March, and they last saw him months ago, when he was on leave.

SIG. F. SHUFFLEBOTHAM

MR and Mrs. Shufflebotham, 35 Churchside, have received notification that their son, Sig. Frank Shufflebotham, is missing following the capitulation of Singapore. Before joining up he was employed by McClure and Whitfield's as an electrician.

CASUALTY

THE DEATH in action in Libya of a local man, Pte. James Rogers, recalls a tragic event in the town in August, 1938, when his wife, Mrs. Doris Rogers, was burned to death in the fire at Davenport Mill, Bridge St. They have one son, Ian, who will be four on June 9th. His guardian is Mrs. Slack, 37 Beech Lane, Macclesfield, and it is she who has this week received notification from the War Office of Pte. Rogers' death. He was a machine-gunner.

Local Airman Honoured

HIS MAJESTY THE KING on Tuesday presented the Distinguished Flying Medal to Flight Sergeant Philip Kirk, elder son of Mrs. Kirk, of Barley Croft, Ivy Road, and the late Mr. A. Kirk.

Flight-Sergt. Kirk joined the R.A.F. in 1936 and went out to France at the outbreak of war. June, 1940, he was reported missing after an operational flight, but a few days afterwards was stated to be safe and sound.

V. W. Lovatt R. Lovatt E. Darlington

S. Albinson E. Nelson L Hough

Missing On Submarine Service

MRS. PIKE, of 62, Maple Av. has received a telegram informing her that her husband, Acting Leading Seaman George Edward Pike, of the Royal Navy Submarine Service, is missing. A native of London, he was employed as an engineer before joining up at the commencement of the war.

The telegram read as follows:- "It is with deep regret that we have to inform you that your husband, George Edward Pike has been reported missing, believed killed, while on active service."

Until recently, A.L.S. Pike was on board H.M. Submarine Thunderbolt, formerly the Thetis, which submerged in Liverpool Bay just before the outbreak of war, with the loss of 99 lives. When salvaged the ship was re-fitted and re-named.

Before her marriage, Mrs. Pike was Miss Shatwell, of Byrons Lane.

ENTERTAINED IN SOUTH AFRICA

A/c. Leonard Hough, who is serving as an air mechanic with the R.A.F., left England for an unknown destination overseas just before Christmas, and last week his parents, Mr. and Mrs. J. B. Hough, of 28 Jodrell Street, received an air mail letter from him saying he had landed in the Middle East. On the voyage out one of the ports of call was Capetown, South Africa, and there he was entertained by a man who emigrated from England to Africa many years ago.

Leonard Hough was educated at St. Paul's and Mill Street Schools, and before joining up was employed in the engineers' department of Messrs. Josiah Smale and Son. He volunteered for the R.A.F. on the 21st of February and left England just before Christmas. He is twenty-one years of age.

FORMER COLLEAGUES

Both formerly employed by the Cheshire Building Society, Castle Street, and both educated at the Central School, Cpl. Eric Nelson, only son of Mr. and Mrs. F. Nelson, of 84 Vincent Street, and L/Ac. Stanley Albinson, are now serving with the Coldstream Guards and the R.A.F. respectively. Eric has been serving two years, is married, and his wife resides at 134, High Street. Stanley is also married, his wife residing at 32, Cranford Ave. He was prominently connected with Church Street West Meth. Church and the Scouts. He has been serving for about 18 months, and is now with the R.A.F. in Egypt.

TWO BROTHERS

Mr. and Mrs. J. S. Lovatt, of 9, Lyme Avenue, have their two sons serving in the Army. The elder, Raymond, is a staff-sergeant in the Royal Engineers. Twenty-five years of age he has been in khaki since the outbreak of war and served in France until the evacuation. As announced in the "Courier" last week, he has recently been presented with a certificate for good service. A registered architect he was employed by the C.W.S. architectural department, Manchester, until he joined up, previously having been articled to Mr. F. C. Sheldon, F.S.I., King Edward Street. Educated at the Central School he later attended Manchester College of Technology. He is married, his home address being 23, Lyme Avenue, and his wife is best known locally as Miss Edith Atkin, the talented soloist.

His younger brother, Vernon William is 20 years of age. He has been serving as a signaller in the Royal Corps of Signals practically twelve months, previous to which he was employed in his father's building business in James Street. He received his education at Mill Street and St. Paul's Schools.

WOMAN R.A. GUNNER

Gunner in the Royal Artillery is the rank of Miss Edith Darlington, only daughter of Mr. and Mrs. T. Darlington of 28, Nicholson Ave. Educated at the Central School, she was employed by Mr. Lawson, of the Standard Manufacturing Co. before joining up, just three months ago.

KILLED IN TANK ACTION

Trooper T. Shufflebotham

AFTER having the tank he was driving wrecked on two occasions, and being wounded in the leg in recent tank battles, Trooper T. Shufflebotham, R.T.C. 2, Gunco Lane, has been reported killed in action following the fall of Tobruk.

The letter conveying the information to his father from the War Office was received on July 16th, and it stated that Tr. Shufflebotham had been reported killed on June 26, 1942, whilst serving with His Majesty's forces in the Middle East.

He volunteered for service in H.M. Forces at the beginning of June, 1940, served in England until October, 1941, and then went to the Middle East. He had been in numerous tank conflicts (being a driver), and, as already mentioned, he was wounded in the leg. This was two months ago, but he soon recovered, rejoined his unit and then again went into battle, fighting until he was killed in the vicinity of Tobruk. The last letter which his father received from him stated that he was "in the pink," resting by the sea and expecting to go into action again soon. Trooper Shufflebotham received his education at St. George's School.

His chief sport was football; he assisted in winning the Crew Cup and also played in the Macclesfield Town Boys' team for two seasons, being captain.

E. Holmes

C. C. Arnold

P. Carney

H. J. Adamson

H. Mitchell

Private C. C. Arnold

To date no news has been received of a former warehouseman now serving as a private in the R.A.S.C. He is Charles Clifford Arnold, son of Mr. S. Arnold of 22, Princess Street, West Bollington. Educated at St. Oswald's School, he was employed by Messrs. Thos. Oliver and Sons (Bollington) before joining up.

Connected with St. Oswald's Church he left this country in January for an unknown destination, and has not been heard of since. He his married, his wife residing at 27, Grimshaw Lane.

Gunner E. Holmes

Now serving as a gunner in the Royal Artillery is Edward Holmes, son of Mr. and Mrs. James Holmes, of 39, Kingsway, Bollington Cross, a veteran H.G. He was one of the first to joined the Bollington Home Guards and served with them until he enlisted in the Army. Formerly employed by the Bollington Printing Co. he was educated at St. Oswald's School. In January he was married at St. Oswald's Church to Miss Marion Williams, eldest daughter of Mr. and Mrs. F. Williams of 74, Bollington Road. His home address is now 74, Bollington Road.

Private H. J. Adamson

The eldest son of Mr. and Mrs. Adamson, of 46, Cornbrook Road, has been serving in the Royal Artillery for six months. He is Pte. Harold John Adamson formerly employed by Scragg and Sons. Prior to this he worked for J. Swindells, Ltd. He attended Athey Street Council School.

Patrick Carney

Patrick Carney joined the Navy in 1938 at the age of seventeen, and has had many interesting experiences in the Seven Seas. He is the eldest son of Mr. and Mrs. W. Carney, of 1, Prestbury Road. As a boy he attended St. Alban's School, and before he went to sea was employed by Messrs. W. Frost and Sons, Ltd. During the first year of the war he spent twelve months in Canada, and he has also been on a destroyer in the Mediterranean for nine months. His last leave took place fifteen months ago, but his mother is not worried over her lad's safety, his last letter to date arriving only last week. Perhaps his most thrilling experience was when he helped in the evacuation of the British Army from Greece, rowing to the shore under heavy gunfire.

Sig. H. Mitchell.

Exactly two years on Wednesday Harold Mitchell, eldest son of Mr. and Mrs. W. M. Mitchell, of School House, High Street, joined the Royal Corps of Signals. He attended St. George's and the Central Schools, and was employed by the M.E.P.S. before joining up. At the end of last month he married Miss M. Glathorn, of Pitt Street.

Missing in Middle East

PRIVATE H. HARTLEY

NEWS has been received by Mrs. H. Hartley, of 90, Chester Rd., that her husband, Pte. Harry Hartley, has been posted as missing as from June 4th in the Middle East. Pte. Hartley has been serving with the East Yorkshire Regt. for three years, during which time he has seen service at Dunkirk, and he has been in the Middle East for the last sixteen

months. He is the second son of Mr. and Mrs. J. Hartley, 44, High Street. He also has a daughter. Pte. Hartley was educated at Athey Street Council School and was formerly employed by B.W.A. (Langley) and later by Messrs. Frosts (Park Green Mills). He was formerly a staff sergeant in the first Macclesfield Boys Brigade (Hurdsfield).

Gunner Harold Whalley (Private Hartley's brother-in-law) is serving with the R.A.F.

GUNNER W. LANDER

MRS. Lander, 7, Poole Street, has received official intimation that her husband, Gunner William Lander, who had been serving with a light anti-aircraft battery, R.A., in the Middle East. has been reported missing as from June 20th.

Gunner Lander joined H. M. Forces on the 13th March, 1941, was stationed in England for a short time and then embarked on

September 3rd, 1941. In the last letter his wife received from him on the 13th June he stated that he was well and happy and that up to then he had not met any Macclesfield boys. Gnr. Lander was employed as a labourer by Wimpey's Ltd., contractors.

PTE. S. BRERETON

Mrs. Brereton, 109 Bank St., has learned that her only son, Pte. Stanley Brereton, Cheshire Regiment, has been reported missing as from June 25th, 1942. The communication also stated that her son might have been temporarily cut off from his regiment, or be a prisoner of war.

RIFLEMAN K. R. BOUSTEAD

Rifleman Kenneth R. Boustead, eldest son of Mr. and Mrs. J. Boustead, "Meadow Bank," Buxton Rd., has been reported missing in the Middle East as from May 27th.

FUSILIER HARRY HATTON

News was received on Thursday morning by Mrs. Connie Hatton, of 74 Vincent St., that her husband, Fusilier Harry Hatton, of the Royal Northumberland Fusiliers, is missing in Egypt. Mrs. Hatton is the daughter of Mr. and Mrs. A. McKinnell, of the Drill Hall, Bridge Street,

K. Gaskell

H. Gaskell

G. K. Haye

W. Haye.

H. Haye

J. Haye.

FOUR SONS

Four sons of Mr. and Mrs. Haye, of 28 Pool Street, are serving with the Forces, two in the Royal Artillery and two in the R.A.F.

The second son, Harold, has been serving as a driver in the Royal Artillery for ten months. He was educated at Athey Street School, and before joining up was employed by the Cheshire County Council. Married, his wife lives at 33 Cedar Grove, Moss Estate.

Also a former scholar of Athey Street School is the fourth son, Jack. Before he joined the Royal Artillery as a gunner two years ago he was employed at the Langley Mills of Messrs. B.W.A. Ltd. A keen footballer, his wife resides at 4 Bedford Road.

William, another former B.W.A. employee, attended Christ Church School. The fifth son, he has been serving as an Aircraftman in the Royal Air Force for ten months.

The youngest son, George Kenneth, attended Daybrook St. School. Formerly employed by Messrs. Wright and Sons, he has been serving with the R.A.F. for 14 months.

BROTHERS SERVING

DVR. Harry Gaskell, R.A.S.C. (31) is the husband of Mrs. Gaskell, of 14, Fairfield Avenue, West Bollington, and the elder son of Mr. and Mrs. John Gaskell, of 31, Lord Street. Recently he was reported missing abroad. From leaving school he was employed by Messrs. Henry and Leigh Slater Ltd. He joined the Forces 12 months ago.

His younger brother, Dvr. Kenneth Gaskell, 1237, of 31, Lord St., has been serving in the Forces three years. He experienced the Dunkirk evacuation. At present he is in England. He was educated along with his brother at the C. of E. School and later became an employee of Messrs. Hammond and Sons, Ltd., Bakestondale.

In Far East

Sergt. Joule

Sergt. Ray

TWO LOCAL MEN who were formerly in Malaya, and who are now presumed to be in Singapore, are Sergeant Leslie Joule, second son of Mr. and Mrs. F. Joule, lately of Berristall, Rainow, and now residing at 40 Newhall Street, and Sergeant Sydney Ray, of Wilmar, Moran Crescent.

Both these two men have sent Christmas and New Year greetings to their families by cable. Sergt. Joule says that he is fit and well, and Sergeant Ray asked his relatives not to worry, and that he is well and safe.

Sergeant Joule was educated at Rainow School, and was employed by the Britannic Assurance Co., of Castle Street, before joining up in the R.A.O.C. He is married, his wife residing at 23 Roe Street.

Sergeant Ray has been in the Royal Corps of Signals for about eight years. He was in Shanghai for three years, but left for Malaya when it was evacuated.

Soldier Missing

MR. and Mrs. T. Ainsworth, of 10 Hurdsfield Road, received official notification on Wednesday that their son, Bdr. Kenneth Ainsworth, has been reported missing. He was serving in Hong Kong at the time of the Japanese occupation

I. Bloor

M. Bloor

M. Hibbert

T. C. Hoggarth

A. Hunt

E. Brocklehurst

Miss M. Hibbert

Serving as a gunner in the A.T.S. is Miss Margaret Hibbert, youngest daughter of Mrs. Hibbert, of 28, Water St and the late Mr Hibbert.

Educated at Mill Street School, she was employed by Messrs. Neckwear Ltd. before joining up seven months ago. She is a keen swimmer and cyclist, and was formerly connected with Trinity Church.

L.-Cpl. T. C. Hoggarth

A Lance-Corporal in the Yorks and Lancs., T. C. Hoggarth, son of Mr. and Mrs. L. Hoggarth, of Dry Knowle, Wildboarclough, is 25.

He was educated at Macclesfield Forest School, and prior to being called up two years ago was employed by the County Council.

Gunner A. Hunt

Arthur Hunt, of 8 Cornbrook Rd., is serving as a Gunner in the Royal Artillery. He was employed by the Barracks Fabrics Printing Company prior to joining up, and is a keen footballer.

Sergt. E. Brocklehurst

Now stationed in this country after serving for over 12 months in the Middle East is Sergt. Edward Brocklehurst, son of Mr. and Mrs. J. W. Brocklehurst, of Prestbury.

Educated at Prestbury and the King's School, he joined the R.A.F. two years ago. While in the Middle East he was front gunner on a Wellington bomber, and was many times in action.

In Land Army and A.T.S.

Two sisters serving with the Women's Land Army and A.T.S. respectively are Margaret W. Bloor and Pte. Irene Bloor, the daughters of Mr. and Mrs. G. F. Bloor, of 3 Windsor Square, Moss Estate.

They were both educated at St. Alban's School, and before joining up Irene was employed by Messrs. Belmont Limited.

Local Sailor's Remarkable Experiences

A LOCAL WIFE received a very substantial Easter "egg" in the shape of the unexpected return of her husband whom she had not expected to see again until the end of hostilities because of his capture by the Germans. She is Mrs. Evers, of 73, South Park Road, whose husband, Stoker Petty Officer Samuel Edwin Evens, was captured in the first battle of Narvik. He was one of the brave party who took an "odds against" chance to man the Norwegian ships on their recent 700-mile dash for freedom, defying German mines, warplanes and warships to reach Britain.

K. Hanaghan

J. Hanaghan

S. Hartshorn

N. Hanaghan

F. Moore

B. Hartshorn

FATHER AND SON

Now serving abroad is A/c. Sidney Hartshorn, of 28 Duke Street. He has been serving with the R.A.F. since the outbreak of war. He attended Athey Street School, and before joining up was employed by Oberland Silk Ltd., Sutton Mills.

Eight months ago Sidney's father, Bert Hartshorn, decided he would join in the fight for freedom, and he is now serving as a Private in the Pioneer Corps.

He was employed by Macclesfield Corporation before joining up, and is a member of the Macclesfield F.C. Supporters' Club Committee.

FOUR RELATIVES

Mrs. F. Moore, of 9 Hatton St., has her husband and three brothers serving with the Forces. Three of her husband's brothers are also serving.

Mrs. Moore's husband, L/Cpl. Frederick Moore, is an accomplished musician, and also a keen swimmer and footballer. He is the second son of Mr. and Mrs. H. Moore, of 69 Mayfield Avenue.

Educated at Daybrook St. School, he joined the Forces when war was declared. He served in France, and went through the Dunkirk evacuation.

Kenneth Hanaghan, Mrs. Moore's eldest brother, is son of Mr. and Mrs. J. Hanaghan, of 9 Hatton St. He has been serving for two years, before which he was employed by Messrs. W. A. Smith and Son, and for a period of about six months was in the Borough Police War Reserve.

The second son, John Hanaghan, was employed at the Langley mills of Messrs. B.W.A. Ltd. before joining up. Like his brother-in-law, he joined up at the outbreak of hostilities and served in France. While he was there his parents received an official War Office telegram stating that he was missing. Jack was not missing long, and when the Boche over-ran the Continent he left for this country via Boulogne.

The "baby" of the family, Norman Hanaghan, joined up last September, formerly being employed by Messrs. Backhouse and Coppock Limited.

All the brothers were educated at St. Alban's School.

Air Gunner Killed

MRS. HOUGH, of 29 Arbourhay Street, has received a telegram from the Air Ministry stating that her husband, Sergeant Air-Gunner James Eric Hough, eldest son of Mrs. Hough, of 9 Brown Street, and the late Mr. Hough, has been killed while on R.A.F. service.

The telegram, which Mrs. Hough received on Whit Monday, stated: " We regret to inform you that your husband, James Eric Hough, lost his life this morning in an aircraft accident. Please accept profound sympathy."

Sergeant Hough was formerly employed by Messrs. Burgons, Ltd., of Mill Street. He entered the Service more than two years ago.

He leaves two children—both boys—aged one and two years.

The funeral is at the Borough Cemetery to-day (Friday).

MISSING AT SEA

A.-B. F. Trueman

ONLY 21 years of age, a young Rainow sailor, A/B. Frank Trueman, son of Mrs. J. Trueman, of Brookhouse Farm, and the late Mr. Trueman, has been reported missing.

The letter which conveyed this news stated: " It is with deep regret that we have to inform you that your son, A/B. Frank Trueman, has been reported missing, presumed killed, while on active service."

The letter went on to state that there was no hope that A/B. Trueman is still alive, and on behalf of the officers and men of the Royal Navy it expressed the high traditions which he helped to maintain. It concluded: " Sincere sympathy with you in your sad bereavement."

L.-Stoker F. Rogers

A NATIVE of Leek, Leading Stoker Frederick Rogers has been reported missing after his ship had been sunk near Singapore. This news was received from the Admiralty by his wife, who resides at 68 High Street, Bollington.

His parents are Mr. and Mrs. Rogers, of Mill Street, Leek, and he has been serving with the Royal Navy for about eight years.

His wife is a daughter of Mr. and Mrs. Snape, of 68 High Street, Bollington.

H. Egan   W. Egan   M. Bann

C. Jackson   H. Jackson   L. Griffiths

Cpl. M. Bann

Mr. and Mrs. S. Bann, of 121, Bond Street, have their youngest son, Cpl. Maurice Edward Bann serving in the R.A.F. Educated at Athey Street and the Central Schools, he was employed by the M.E.P.S. grocery department before joining up. He has been serving for about eighteen months. His brother Eric was killed while on R.A.F. service last year.

Brothers Served in France

Two brothers who both went to Henbury School, both worked for Hovis Ltd. and both served together in France, are now stationed in this country. They are L.-Cpl. William Egan, eldest son of Mr. and Mrs. J. Egan, of Horse-shoe Cottage, Henbury, and Dvr. Harold Egan, the youngest son, of the R.A.S.C. During the retreat from France, William left via St. Nazaire, and Harold by Dunkirk.

L./Ac. Griffiths

For nearly two years L.A/c. Les Griffiths has been serving with the R.A.F. He is the only son of Mr. and Mrs. J. Griffiths, of 180 Newton Street.

Educated at St. George's School he was, prior to joining up, employed by Messrs. Hovis Ltd.

Above and Below

The two sons of Mr. and Mrs. Jackson, of 177 Newton Street, are both serving with the Royal Navy. Although in the same Service, their jobs are entirely different.

Charles is a member of the Fleet Air Arm, and Harold is one of the crew of a submarine.

The eldest son, Charles, was educated at Athey Street School. A keen footballer, he formerly played with Macclesfield Wednesday F.C.

With three years' service to his credit, Harold, the second son, was transferred to the submarine service last October, prior to which he was in Africa for two years.

F. W. Randall

H. A. Morgan

H. Worthington

M. Roberts

A. Sharp

H. Rigby

Local Soldier's Remarkable Experiences

HARDLY a day passes without reference in the National Press to atrocities committed by the Japanese after capturing lands belonging to the Allied Powers. Some of these are so horrible that many people do not believe the tales they hear, but those people should have a chat with a young Macclesfield soldier now back in England from the Far and Middle East. He is 23-years-old James William Morris, second son of Mr. and Mrs. J. W. Morris, of 4 Beech Grove, off Byrons Lane, who joined up when 14½, and arrived back in England recently.

On Tuesday a "Courier" reporter had the opportunity of interviewing this tall, sun-burnt soldier at his home.

All the facts and photographs he has in his possession are perfect records of the eight years he has spent abroad. If they were put together they would make one of the most interesting and exciting travel tales ever published.

The part of his travels that will always remain in his memory was during the Chinese-Japanese war. Trouble with the Japs started when he was in Shanghai, on the northern boundary of the International Settlement. While there assassinations of high officials were frequent occurrences. From Shanghai he went to Tientsin, where the "yellow devils" burst a dam, and the surrounding district was flooded to a depth of 16 feet, causing many civilian casualties. Corporal Morris and his colleagues never saw any bread for six months, and they had to patrol in small, flat-bottomed boats, pulling Chinese dead out of the water.

The Japs next electrified all the barbed wire round the Settlement, and it was in this horrible way that many of his friends met their death.

Dead Chinese men, women and children were utilised by the Japs for bayonet practice. Corporal Morris showed the "Courier" representative photographs of Japanese officials supervising torture operations. Horrible deformed and grotesque figures lay on the ground. On one picture a youngster was about to be beheaded, and on another adults were lined up against a wall facing a firing party. In another picture a field was littered with bodies; some had been there so long that they had rotted, and only the skeletons remained. Murders and rape were committed openly.

Pte. H. Rigby

Serving with The King's Regiment is Pte. Harry Rigby, of Brown Street, second son of Mr. and Mrs. H. Rigby, of Brookfield Lane.

Before joining up four months ago he was employed by Barracks Fabrics Printing Co.

Gnr. H. Worthington

Gunner Harry Worthington, R.A., of 20 Clarence Road, is the youngest son of Mr. and Mrs. Harry Worthington, 23 Palmerston Street. He has been with the Forces about two years, and is still serving in England. He was educated at the C. of E. School. Later he was employed as a set-wheeler at Oak Bank Printing Works. Gnr. Worthington is a member of the Bollington Bowling Society.

Sergt. A. Sharp, R.A.F.

Now stationed in this country after having had many thrilling and dangerous experiences in the Middle East for the last three years, is Sergt. Arthur Sharp, youngest son of Mr. and Mrs. A. Sharp, of 8 Fieldbank Road.

Twenty-two years of age, he has served in Libya, Abyssinia, Greece, Iraq, and Syria. He joined the R.A.F. five years ago, prior to which he was employed by Messrs W. H. Smith and Sons at their branch in the Market Place.

Pte (Mrs.) Mary Roberts

Pte. (Mrs.) Mary Roberts, eldest daughter of Mr. and Mrs. L. Palfrey, of Sunnyside, Robin Lane, Lyme Green, has been serving with the A.T.S. for about six months. Educated at Bosley School she was employed by Messrs. H. W. Hewetson Ltd., before joining up.

Evacuation Veteran

Cpl. F. W. Randall, elder son of Mr. and Mrs. F. C. Randall, of Melton, Clifford Road, is now an evacuation veteran. When France fell he had to leave Abbeville; then when the Malayan aerodrome of Kuala Lumpur was overrun by the Japs he managed to make his escape. He took part in the general evacuation of Malaya, and later escaped to Australia.

Cpl. Randall's wife resides in Liverpool. He joined the R.A.F. a year before the outbreak of the war.

A.B. H. A. Morgan

At present afloat on one of H.M. destroyers is A.B. Herbert Arthur Morgan, son of Mr. and Mrs. G. Morgan, of 12 Lyme Green, Sutton. Before joining up over two years ago he was employed by Messrs. W. Frost and Sons Ltd. Twenty-four years of age, he is married, his wife residing in Black Road.

L. Joule

F. Hulme

S. Ray

J. Shelley

S. Ardern

H. Swindells

Former Assurance Agent

A man well-known both in Macclesfield and Bollington as an agent for the Britannic Assurance Co., of Castle Street, is now presumed to be in Singapore. He is Sergt. Leslie Joule, of the R.A.O.C., second son of Mr. and Mrs. F. Joule, of 40 New Hall Street.

He is a native of Rainow, and he received his education at Rainow School. He is married, his home address being 23 Roe Street.

Gunner S. Ardern

GUNNER Stanley Ardern, of 38, Lansdowne Street, has been serving in the Royal Artillery for six years. He is 32 years of age, married, and before being called up was employed at McCoy and Sons, Brunswick St. Educated at Athey Street School, he was in his younger days a prominent local footballer, and for some time was the secretary of the Unemployed F.C. His father, Mr. Fred Ardern, resides at 29 Beech Lane.

Pte. F. Hulme

Mr. and Mrs. H. Hulme, of 102, Pierce Street, have their only son, Pte. Fred Hulme, serving with the Corps of Military Police.

He attended Christ Church School, and was employed by Messrs. New Day, of Mill Street, before joining up about 16 months ago. He was married last week to Miss Jenny Palfrey, of Lyme Green.

R.A.F. Instructor

At present serving with the R.A.F. as an instructor is Sergeant-Pilot Jack Shelley, the 21-years-old son of Mr. and Mrs. F. Shelley, of 41, Nicholson Avenue.

When war broke out he joined the Middlesex Regiment, and went through France and Dunkirk. Later he was transferred to the R.A.F. as a cadet. He is an old boy of the King's School, and before joining up was on the staff of the Education Office. He is at present in Canada.

Prisoner of War.

Reported missing in June of last year after evacuation from Greece, and now a prisoner of war, is Spr. Herbert Swindells, son of Mrs. W. Slack, of Crooked Yard Farm, Macclesfield Forest.

He attended Langley School, and was afterwards employed at the Langley Mills of Messrs. B.W.A. Limited.

In Far East War Zone

Another local man who, it is believed, escaped from the Malay mainland to Singapore, is Sydney Ray, of Wilmar, Moran Crescent, serving as a Sergeant in the Royal Corps of Signals.

He has been serving with this Corps for about eight years, was stationed at Shanghai for three years, and when it was evacuated left for Malaya.

In Father's Footsteps
SIX SONS SERVING

THE SIX SONS of Mr. and Mrs. A. Ash, of 5, Cedar Grove, Moss Estate, are following the fine example set by their father, who has completed thirty-two years' service in the Army, by carrying on where he left off in 1918. One of them has been reported missing during fighting in the Middle East.

They are:—Pte. Harry Ash, of the Durham Light Infantry; Pte. Saml. Ash, also of the Durham Light Infantry; Trooper Arthur Ash, of the Armoured Corps of the Lancashire Fusiliers; Gunner Joseph Ash, of the Royal Artillery, and Pte. Lionel Ash, of the Royal Ulster Rifles.

They all attended St. Paul's School. Before joining up, Harry, Arthur and Lionel were employed by the Barracks Fabrics Printing Co. Ltd., and John at the Langley Mills of Messrs. B.W.A. Ltd.

Harry

Arthur

Joseph

Lionel

Their younger brother, fifteen years-old Ernest Ash, is a member of the Home Guard Cadet Corps.

Samuel

The second son, Pte. S. Ash, was reported missing on July 28th after serving in the Middle East since January. He was formerly employed by Messrs. W. Frost and Sons Ltd., and was a member of the Territorials for four years. On the outbreak of hostilities he went to France with the Durham Light Infantry, and was evacuated from there via Dunkirk.

Mr. S. Ash, senr., their father, served on three fronts during the last war, and has had 32 years' service in different branches of the Army, eight of which were spent in India.

E. Morris

G. Morris

L. Morris

J. W. Morris

S. Brown

E. Savage

SAVED FROM "JACKALL"

EARLY this week the Admiralty announced that three of our destroyers had been sunk in the Mediterranean following dive-bombing attacks off Crete. They were "Lively," "Kipling," and "Jackall."

On board the latter was a 24-years-old local seaman, Herbert Arthur Morgan, son of Mr. and Mrs. Geo. Morgan, of 12, Lyme Green.

On Wednesday morning his parents received a telegram from their son, which, although not giving away any details, helped to relieve the tension. It stated: "Safe and well on H.M.S. Canopus."

FOUR BROTHERS

A soldier of the last war, Mr. J. W. Morris, of 4 Beech Grove, off Byrons Lane, and his wife have their four sons serving in the present conflict.

Mr. Morris was a member of the 29th Division, which made the historic landing at Gallipoli in 1915. He has travelled in most countries which, during the last few years, have been covered by his second son, Cpl. James Wm. Morris.

This young soldier—he is only 23 years of age—joined up when he was 14½, and at the age of 15 sailed for India. He arrived back in Macclesfield recently with a tale of his remarkable experiences all over the world. This was fully reported in last week's "Courier."

The eldest son, L.A.c. Ernest Morris, has been serving for two years. He attended St. Peter's School, and was employed by Barracks Fabrics Printing Co. before joining the R.A.F. He is the only married son, his wife residing at 9 Arbourhay Street.

Serving as a cook in the Royal Navy is the third son, Laurence Morris. Like his elder brother, before joining up he was employed by Barracks Fabrics Printing Co.

Geoffrey Morris, the youngest son, was employed by Mr. J. Forrest, butcher, of Chestergate, before joining up.

As the family originate from Middlesbrough, both Laurence and himself were educated there.

WORLD TRAVELLER IN FORCES

In peace time Samuel Brown, son of Mr. and Mrs. Brown, of Bollington Cross, was very fond of travelling, particularly by air.

Like other young men, it was not long before he joined the Forces, and was accepted by the R.A.S.C. as a driver.

The craze for travelling still remains, for at the present time he is serving with the Middle East Forces.

Dvr. Brown was educated at Bollington Cross School, and from there he went to the Clarence Mill, Bollington, as a silk dresser. Apart from travelling, his chief hobby was model ship-making.

CHOIRBOY NOW SEAMAN

For a number of years a prominent member of St. George's Church choir, Ord. Signalman Ernest Savage only son of Mr. and Mrs. E. Savage, of 298 Peter Street, is now serving on a minesweeper with the Royal Navy.

He was educated at St. George's School, and before joining up was employed by the Co-operative Wholesale Society in Manchester. His father is Education Secretary of the M.E.P.S.

Five Days Before Son's Birth

MRS. J. FORRISTER, of 32 Vincent Street, last week received a letter from the War Office stating that her husband, Corporal James Forrister, of the 8th Hussar Regt., had been killed in action in the Middle East on June 26th. She had just returned from hospital after having given birth to a son.

Five days before he was killed he sent a telegram to his wife asking for news, and saying that he was very worried. The photograph we reproduce here was only received by Mrs. Forrister last week. Their son was born five days after the death of his father, and on July 6th a cable was dispatched telling him of the event.

A native of Stoke-on-Trent, Corpl. Forrister joined the Army when he was 15 years of age. He had served for seven years in India and two in Egypt, and for eighteen months was attached to a parachute unit.

His younger brother, Sergt. Victor Forrister, was reported missing after the Crete evacuation.

Wounded Soldier

DIED IN HIS BROTHER'S ARMS

IN a letter received by his parents this week, Mr. and Mrs. G. Mc-Kie, of 94 Mill Lane, Corporal Cyril McKie, of the Cheshire Regiment, now serving in the Middle East, conveyed the sad news that his brother, Corporal Jack McKie, of the Green Howards, whose wife resides at 12 Hollins Road, had died in his arms and had been buried out there. Cyril added that he was present at his brother's funeral.

Only last week Jack's wife received a cheerful letter from her husband saying that he and his brother, although in different regiments, had met.

In the short note received this week Cyril says that he and his brother were talking together in a trench along with another man, when a shell exploded, killing the third man outright and wounding Jack, who died a short time later in in his brother's arms.

Corporal Jack McKie leaves a wife and two young children, aged five years and eight months old respectively. He was educated at St. Peter's and Athey Street schools, and before joining the Army, about two years ago, was employed by Jack Moss and Co., builders. He went out East five months ago.

He has two brothers serving, Cyril, whose home address is 122 Bridge Street, and Sam, who is a Signaller with the Cheshire Regt. Two of his brothers-in-law are also in the Forces, Pte. Leonard Goodier, R.A.M.C., and Dvr. Walter Twist, who is serving abroad.

Local Family's Proud Record

UNTIL a short time ago, five members of a local family were serving their country in H.M. Forces. Last week (as reported in the "Courier"), one of these men was stated to have died in his brother's arms somewhere in the

Jack McKie   **Cyril McKie**

Middle East, leaving two brothers and two brothers-in-law to carry on the fight and avenge his death.

The member of this family who died for his country is Corporal Jack McKie (28), of the Green Howards, of 12 Hollins Road, son of Mr. and Mrs. G. G. McKie, of Mill Lane, and the four other serv-

Sam McKie   **Walter Twist**

ing relatives are Sig. Sam McKie (33), 4th Cheshire Regt., of 5 Havana Lane, Congleton, and Corporal Cyril McKie (31), 6th Cheshires of 122 Bridge Street, who reported Jack's death in the Middle East and Dvr. Walter Twist, R.A.S.C., of 27 Park Street (also serving in the Western Desert), and Pte. Leonard Goodier, R.A.S.C., of 8 John Street, Salford, Manchester.

The three brothers were all educated at Athey Street School. Sam afterwards working at Brocklehurst — Whiston Amalgamated (Langley Printworks), Cyril being employed by Messrs. Adshead and Geeson, Ltd. Jack was a member of the staff of Jack Marsden and Co., Builders. The latter was a Physical Training Instructor in the Army before going out East five months ago. Driver Twist and Private Goodier were both employed in Manchester.

Leonard Goodier

A memorial service for Corporal Jack McKie was conducted by the Vicar (Rev. T. Lever), at St. Peter's Church on Sunday.

Men In Far East

RELATIVES ANXIOUS

IN addition to the local men in Singapore whom we mentioned last week, two more local families are anxiously awaiting news of their relatives in the Far East.

Company Sergeant Major G. and Mrs. Dobson, of 28 Rutland Road, have been anxious for some weeks because they have heard no news of their eldest son, A/c. Cecil Dobson, since he left England for the Far East in June of last year. He has been serving with the R.A.F. for a year, and his parents hope that possibly some other local man has met him since he left the shores of this country. If anyone can give them news they hope the informants will contact them immediately.

Last heard of in Singapore Driver William Anderton, only son of Mr. and Mrs. W. Anderton, of Frith Terrace, Moss Estate, who went abroad five months ago, and they, together with his wife, who lives at 32 Belgrave Road, Congleton, are awaiting news of him. He has a three months' old son. Educated at Athey Street School, he was employed by Williamson, mineral water manufacturers, Brunwick Street, and then, before joining up over nine months ago, by the G.P.O. cable department.

"SAFE" CABLEGRAM

Last Thursday afternoon Mr. and Mrs. C. Mottershead, 19 Lord Street, received a welcome cablegram from their eldest son Air Fitter Arthur Mottershead, who is serving with the Fleet Air Arm.

It states :— "Safe and well; address following." Air Fitter Mottershead left England in April 1941, and he has been stationed in Singapore. It is presumed he has escaped.

His parents last heard of him about a week before Christmas, when they received a cable saying he was quite well. Educated at Athey Street School, he was later employed at Scraggs, engineers, until he joined up almost two years ago.

MISSING

BELIEVED KILLED
PILOT-OFFICER NADEN.

Pilot Officer John Wilfred Naden, younger son of Mr. and Mrs. J. H. Naden, "The Byrons," Byrons Lane, who was reported missing a short while ago, is now reported "missing, presumed killed." A communication from the Air Ministry reads: "In view of information from the International Red Cross Society, your son is believed

to have lost his life as the result of air operations. The telegram, quoting German information, states that the other four members of the crew of the aircraft were captured, and that your son is dead. It contains no information regarding place of his burial, nor any other details. Although there is, unfortunately, little reason to doubt the accuracy of this report, it will be necessary to regard the casualty as "missing, presumed killed," until confirmed by further evidence, or until, in the absence of such evidence, it becomes necessary owing to lapse of time, to presume.

TORPEDOED, BUT SAFE
GUNNER J. MOORE, R.N.

R.N. Gunner Joseph Moore, son of Mr. Moore, 19 Coppice Rise, is safe, following the torpedoing of his ship. His father has received a card from him stating that he was safe, and a communication from the Admiralty states that Gunner Moore was picked up and landed after the ship had been torpedoed.

His 17-years-old brother, Thomas, was a member of the crew of the "Exeter," and was reported missing about six months ago.

LCE.-CPL. R. NEWTON

News was received on Thursday by Mrs. Newton, of 8 Moss Square, that her husband, Lance-Corporal

Raymond Newton is a prisoner of war in Italy. A card was received from the missing man stating that he was quite well and proceeding to an Italian prisoner of war camp. A former employee of the 'Courier,' Lance-Corporal Newton was captured in the Middle East, being reported missing in the big Libyan battle.

SERGT. E. R. BRISTOWE

Sergt. W.O./A.G. Ernest Reginald Bristowe, who was reported missing following a bombing raid on Martuba Aerodrome

on June 7th, is now reported to be a prisoner of war in Italy. His mother, Mrs. Dean, of 95 Peel Street, received a postcard from him on Thursday last stating he was well, and was being moved to a prison camp, from where he would send his new address.

Sgt. Bristowe attended St. George's School, and between leaving there and joining the R.A.F. he studied at the Art School in the evenings. He was employed as a designer by Messrs. A. W. Hewetson Ltd., and was, for a number of years, Secretary of St. George's Children's Church.

PTE. W. J. HANCOCK

Mrs. B. Hancock, of 62 Commercial Road, learned on Monday that her only son, Pte. Wm. James Hancock, of the Durham Light Infantry, is a prisoner of war in Italian hands. This glad news was conveyed to her by postcard from the Vatican.

By the same post came a letter from a Mrs. Gladys Hough, of Chipperfield, Herts,

who heard a broadcast from Vatican City on Saturday morning. Apparently, Mrs. Gough is rendering useful service by informing relatives when their sons are reported prisoners from Vatican City. She asked that a stamp be sent so that she could inform any other anxious relatives.

Mrs. Hancock immediately obtained from her friends 25 postage stamps and forwarded them on to Chipperfield, to enable this good work to be carried on.

DEATH FROM WOUNDS
L/CPL. ARTHUR KIRK.

L/Cpl. Arthur Kirk, Royal Corps of Signals, 26-years-old son of Mr. and Mrs. Arthur Kirk, 44 Bridge St., has died from wounds in the Middle East. The news was received on Tuesday. His cousin, Flt.-Sergeant Philip Kirk, of Ivy Road, was recently awarded the D.F.M., and his brother, A/B. Harry Kirk, R.N., was recently wounded.

Soldier Killed

MIDDLE EAST CASUALTY

"REGRET to report Gunner J. Bennett killed in action. Letter follows.—Middle East."

The above telegram was the first news received by Mr. and Mrs. S. Bennett, of 74 Chester Road, that their eldest son, Gnr. Jack Bennett, had been killed while serving with the Middle East Forces.

The news was confirmed on Sat. when his parents received a letter from the Records Office, which stated that he was killed on the 14th December last.

Gunner Bennettt was formerly a Reservist, and he volunteered for service in May, 1939. He sailed from England in July of the same year. He attended Christ Church School, and his last place of employment before joining up was on the extensions at Parkside Hospital. He was a regular attender at the Parish Church Men's Bible Class. Gunner Bennett took part in the Abyssinian campaign.

His brother, Geoffrey, is in Egypt, having been there since April of 1940. In August of this year he will have completed four years of Army life.

Sailor Shipwrecked

OVER on 14 days' leave after a thrilling experience off the West Coast of Scotland is Seaman Frank Ellis, youngest son of Mrs. A. Sutton, of 74 Arbourhay Street.

In Italian Hands

LCE.-CPL. J. GIDMAN

AFTER many weeks of anxiety without news, Mrs. J. Gidman, of 1 Clowes Street, has received a card from her husband, L/Cpl. John Gidman, that he is a prisoner of war in Italian hands.

The last communication she received from him before this latest message was on June 19, in the form of a cablegram. Since then she

has had an airgraph in July from one of her husband's pals, stating that he had been missing from June 28th. He had been serving in the Green Howard for two and a half years, eighteen months of which had been spent in the Middle East. Prior to joining up he was employed as a shirt cutter by Messrs. T. Clapham Ltd., Athey Street Mill. He is 26 years of age. In the message to his wife, L/Cpl. Gidman says he is fit and well.

Serving Their Country

W. Storer

F. Whittaker

N. Cooke

T. D. Dale

W. D. Dale

Two Brothers

THE two sons of Mrs. Dale, formerly of the Bulls Head Hotel, Broken Cross, and the late Mr. Dale, are both serving with the fighting forces.

Driver William D. Dale, the elder son, has been serving in the R.A.S.C. for twelve months. His wife is at present carrying on his newsagent's business at Broken Cross.

The younger son is Sapper Thos. D. Dale, of the Royal Engineers. He has been serving for three years, and during the retreat from France was evacuated from Dunkirk. His wife resides at 27 Bond St.

Both brothers received their education at Broken Cross School.

Cpl. F. Whittaker

SERVING in the Hertfordshire Regiment is Corporal Frank Whittaker, a native of Mow Cop. His sister is married to Driver Stanley Hooley, of Rodney Street, Macclesfield. At present they are both serving in Ireand.

Private W. Storer

FORMERLY connected with St. Andrew's Church, Sunday School, Scouts, and also a junior sidesman, Pte. William Storer, only son of Mr. and Mrs. C. H. Storer, of 224 Crompton Road, is now serving with the King's Own Regiment.

He attended Christ Church School, and was later employed by Mr. Norman Brocklehurst, Chestergate. He was also an A.S.M. in the 20th St. Andrew's Scouts.

Young Yeomanry Bridegroom

THE second Fife and Forfar Yeomanry has a young Macclesfield man, Trooper Norman Cooke, stationed in its ranks. He married Miss Dorothy Vera Whalley, of Snow Hill Cottage, Snow Hill, just over a week ago.

Trooper Cooke, is the second son of Mr. and Mrs. John Cooke, of 90, Great King Street. A Central School Old Boy, he was employed by the local M.E.P.S. before joining up.